RETHINKING
THE KOREAN WAR

RETHINKING

THE KOREAN WAR

A New Diplomatic and Strategic History

WILLIAM STUECK

PRINCETON UNIVERSITY PRESS • PRINCETON AND OXFORD

Copyright © 2002 by Princeton University Press
Published by Princeton University Press, 41 William Street, Princeton, New Jersey 08540
In the United Kingdom: Princeton University Press, 3 Market Place,
Woodstock, Oxfordshire OX20 1SY

Second printing, and first paperback printing, 2004
Paperback ISBN 0-691-11847-7

The Library of Congress has cataloged the cloth edition of this book as follows

Stueck, William Whitney, 1945–
Rethinking the Korean war : a new diplomatic and strategic history / William Stueck.
p.   cm.
Includes bibliographical references and index.
ISBN 0-691-08853-5 (alk. paper)
1. Korean War, 1950–1953—Causes.   2. Korean War, 1950–1953—Diplomatic
history.   3. World politics—1945–1955.   4. United States—Foreign
relations—1945–1953.   I. Title.

DS918 .A555 2002
951.904'21—dc21   2001059167

British Library Cataloging-in-Publication Data is available

This book has been composed in ITC Berkeley

Text design by Carmina Alvarez

Printed on acid-free paper. ∞

www.pupress.princeton.edu

Printed in the United States of America

3   5   7   9   10   8   6   4

For Pat

Contents

Illustrations

MAPS

PHOTOGRAPHS

Unless otherwise stated, all photographs are courtesy of the National Archives II,
College Park, Maryland.

Acknowledgments

I WAS TOLD AS A GRADUATE STUDENT THAT HISTORIANS WRITE A book to forget about a topic. Since 1995 I have become more inclined to the notion that, in the academic and foreign policy communities, a massive conspiracy exists to prevent scholars from ever escaping a subject on which they have published. Surely I would never have written this book had it not been for the numerous invitations I have received—and accepted—to deliver papers on the Korean War. All but three of the eight chapters herein began as conference papers, and because I have few regrets about seeing this project through to fruition, I want to thank those people, conspirators or not, for their invitations. They include Professors Bonnie Oh and David I. Steinberg of Georgetown University, Professor Lew Young-Ik of Yonsei University, Professor H. W. Brands of Texas A&M University, and Professor Chaejin Lee of Claremont McKenna College. I also wish to thank Brigitta van Rheinberg of Princeton University Press, whose enthusiastic response to my proposal of the project gave me the last needed boost to see it through and whose critical reading of the first draft of the manuscript contributed substantially to its improvement; Chen Jian and Paul Pierpaoli, who wrote referee's reports that were both positive and enormously helpful in their criticism (including Chen's suggestion of the book's title); Jim Cobb, whose encouragement and leadership of the History Department at the University of Georgia have helped me recapture the sense of purpose and excitement of being there that I possessed at the beginning over twenty years ago; and Susan Ecklund, who did a masterful job of copyediting. Finally, I want to thank Pat, my precious partner through life, whose love and devotion are never-ending sources of my growth and happiness.

RETHINKING
THE KOREAN WAR

INTRODUCTION

POLITICAL SCIENTIST JOHN MUELLER HAS CHARACTERIZED THE
Korean War as "quite possibly the most important event since World
War II."[1] I have labeled it "a substitute for World War III."[2] What we
mean is that in its timing, its course, and its outcome, it had a stabi-
lizing effect on the Cold War. It did not end that conflict; indeed, it
intensified and militarized it as never before. For Koreans it was a
total war, with some 10 percent of the population either killed,
wounded, or missing. In property, South Korea lost the equivalent of
its gross national product for the year 1949. North Korea lost eighty-
seven hundred industrial plants, its counterpart twice that number.
North and South each saw six hundred thousand of its homes destroyed.[3] Yet the fighting did not expand beyond Korea. The costs and
risks of the war, combined with the success of the United States and
the Soviet Union in preventing the other from enabling its proxy government in Korea to unify the peninsula, discouraged future efforts on
each side to venture beyond its zone of influence by military means.
The rearmament in the United States and Western Europe provoked
by the war created a rough and sustainable balance of military power

_Cold
war_

in the key theater of superpower competition. If the United States and the Soviet Union, and their allies, were better armed than before, there was less chance that either of the principals would employ their forces in a manner leading to direct confrontation.

This book is an interpretive account of the major diplomatic, political, and strategic issues of the Korean War. Rather than providing a lengthy narrative of the international dimensions of the conflict as I did in my 1995 volume, my approach here is issue-oriented and synthetic.[4] My aim is to provide an overview, of interest to specialists and general readers alike, that takes into account the vast body of new documentation that has surfaced in recent decades.

When I began studying this event in 1968, the standard synthetic treatment of the event was David Rees's *Korea: The Limited War*, which was based almost entirely on published sources.[5] Then, during the 1970s a wide array of official records and private papers became available in the United States. From the Soviet side, there emerged the memoirs of Nikita Khrushchev, although their legitimacy and/or accuracy was questioned in some circles.[6] During the next decade, this wealth of new material began to be exploited in scholarly monographs and new narrative syntheses.[7]

There also appeared a major new revisionist account, the first volume in Bruce Cumings's magisterial *Origins of the Korean War*. Cumings exploited Korean-language sources as never before and challenged other treatments for their downplaying of internal Korean factors in the coming of the war and their emphasis on Soviet and North Korean aggressiveness.[8] Since the appearance during the war of journalist I. F. Stone's *Hidden History of the Korean War*, a revisionist literature had existed in the United States; but the firm grounding of *Origins* in archival and Korean sources gave the genre a new legitimacy.[9] Cumings's follow-ups, a brief coauthored volume designed for a popular audience in 1988 and then his massive second volume of *Origins* two years later, ensured that the revisionist perspective on the conflict as essentially a "civil war" would continue to receive a wide hearing.[10]

Nonetheless, by the time Cumings's second volume appeared, revisionism was on the verge of facing major new challenges. As early as

1989, Dutch scholar Erik van Ree questioned Cumings's view of the Soviet role in North Korea from 1945 to 1947. Drawing upon heretofore untapped memoirs of Soviet officials in Korea, van Ree concluded that the Soviet Union had played a far more dominant role in its occupation zone above the thirty-eighth parallel than Cumings portrayed.[11] Yet van Ree's work received little attention in the United States, and, in any event, it covered a period well before North Korea's attack on South Korea of June 25, 1950. It was not until 1993 that a study appeared that analyzed the periods both leading up to and following that seminal event *and* drew on new archival sources and memoirs from the former Soviet Union and China. Written by a Russian, an American, and a Chinese national, *Uncertain Partners: Stalin, Mao, and the Korean War* argued, contrary to the revisionists, that the Soviet Union and China were intimately involved in the process by which North Korea decided to launch and execute its military offensive.[12] This volume was merely the first in a series of studies based on new documentation from the Communist side that challenged aspects of the revisionist account of the war's origins.[13]

Still, the day had long since passed when the civil aspect of the Korean War's origins could be largely ignored.[14] A major task before scholars today is to weigh the internal and external factors in the coming of the war. This is the primary focus of part I of the account that follows.

Why was Korea divided in 1945 into Soviet and American occupation zones? Why did the two powers fail to reach agreement on unification and, in 1948, decide to establish independent governments in the areas under their control? What was the impact of the irascible Syngman Rhee and the declaration of the Truman Doctrine on U.S. policy toward Korea? Why did the United States withdraw the last of its combat troops from Korea in 1949 and then fail to secure its creation, the Republic of Korea (ROK), from outside attack? Why did the United States rush army units back to the peninsula in response to the North Korean invasion in June 1950? Why did the North Koreans decide to launch that invasion, what roles did the Soviet Union and China play in the process, and why did they play the roles they did?

The overriding theme of this part is that the origins of the war must be understood in the context of events both inside and outside of Korea. Korea became a war of broad international dimensions after June 1950 because, since the defeat of Japan in 1945, the peninsula had been a setting for intense great power competition. That competition grew out of the transformation of the structure of power in northeast Asia with the defeat of Japan and the sharp divergence in ideology between the two nations, the Soviet Union and the United States, that took its place. Although these two powers occupied Korea and divided it at the thirty-eighth parallel without direct input from native peoples, perceptions in Washington of conditions on the peninsula were critical in that decision. Under the tight control of Japan for nearly two generations, Korea lacked indigenous political institutions or a population experienced in self-government; and independence forces in exile were deeply divided. Surely, planners in Washington believed, the country needed a period of tutelage before resuming its status as a sovereign nation. Division occurred because neither of the potential occupiers believed it possessed the capacity, given other priorities, to seize the entire country before the other arrived.

The occupiers went to Korea with the objectives, first, to remove the Japanese and, second, at minimum, to contain the influence of the other. The first objective proved relatively easy to achieve for both the Soviet Union and the United States, but over time the latter encountered greater difficulty than the former in exercising containment. A neighbor of Korea, the Soviet Union possessed a direct security stake on the peninsula, whereas the United States, located thousands of miles away, did not. The Americans lacked a tradition of direct military involvement on the Asian mainland. As commitments in other more crucial areas continued in the aftermath of World War II, Washington looked to reduce its presence on the peninsula. That reduction speeded creation of an independent government below the thirty-eighth parallel, the ROK, but it also led to the withdrawal of American troops. This withdrawal, in turn, combined with the victory of the Communists in the civil war in China, left the area vulnerable to attack by the Soviet creation above the dividing line, the Democratic People's Republic of Korea (DPRK).

Koreans were hardly passive bystanders in the process by which their nation became the first major military conflict of the Cold War. Deep divisions existed among Koreans prior to the actions of the United States and the Soviet Union in 1945, both among exiles and among those who remained at home. These cleavages contributed significantly to the course of events in the years immediately following, even helping to produce some one hundred thousand casualties on the peninsula prior to North Korea's momentous action of June 25, 1950. Furthermore, no Korean accepted the idea of the country's division over the long term, and the leaders of the independent governments that emerged in 1948 were far more determined than their great power sponsors to restore unity at an early date. Together, the internal divisions and the intense desire for reunification played key roles in the course of events between 1945 and 1950. It is the interaction of these internal forces with external ones that explains the coming of the war.

Part II deals with the strategies and diplomacy of the major parties in the war from June 25, 1950, to the signing of an armistice on July 27, 1953. Although the fighting contained an important civil dimension, although Koreans themselves suffered far more than any of the other participants, and although the Korean governments lobbied persistently for their points of view—and not without effect—the great powers ultimately made the key decisions on the parameters of the war. Initially, for example, the United States defined the objective of its intervention as restoration of the situation prior to the North Korean attack, and it did so without consulting the ROK government and against the fervent desire of ROK leaders. Upon reversing the military situation on the peninsula in September 1950, the United States took military action in pursuit of unification of the peninsula under the ROK, but *not* primarily because of ROK pressure. Why did Washington choose this course? Why, in response to the move across the thirty-eighth parallel of troops fighting under the banner of the United Nations, did China decide to intervene? The Korean party, this time the DPRK, played an active, even influential, role, but the final decision came only after intensive exchanges between Chinese and Soviet leaders. Finally, in the face of the initial Chinese intervention, why did Washington refuse to order a halt to the UN military offensive? Here again, this decision accorded with ROK wishes, but these remained secondary in U.S. calculations. Chapter 4 addresses these questions.

By late November 1950, China was fully engaged in Korea against UN forces. For a time it appeared that China might even drive the enemy into the sea, thus enabling the DPRK to achieve its original objective of uniting the peninsula under its rule. Why, in the face of the Chinese onslaught, did the United States refuse to expand the war beyond Korea? Why, eventually, did Beijing decide to negotiate for an end to the fighting short of total victory? These questions provide the focus for chapter 5.

Despite the decision by July 1951 of leaders of the great powers on both sides to accept a military-political stalemate in Korea, the war took over two more years to end. Why, then, did it take so long for them to agree on an armistice? Chapter 6 grapples with this question.

Part II emphasizes the important yet secondary nature of Korea to the larger conflict between the United States and the Soviet Union, the influence of allied interaction on both sides of the conflict, and the depth of the situational, cultural, and ideological divides between the contestants. Korea became a battleground between the United States and China because of its symbolic value to the former and its symbolic and strategic value to the new government, the People's Republic of China (PRC), of the latter. In the end, Korea was important enough to generate a lengthy, bitter, and destructive war but not so important as to produce the ultimate tragedy of another global bloodletting.

While revisionism is not nearly so well developed on the course of the war as on origins, its thrust is to emphasize divisions among the allies on both sides, the excessive belligerence and ideological rigidity of the United States in contrast to the flexible and defensive postures of the Soviets and Chinese, and the proactive nature of the Korean actors.[15] As in part I, my analysis integrates some of the insights of the revisionists. In drawing upon new documentation from the Soviet and Chinese sides, however, I adopt a framework closer to traditional than to revisionist accounts. Although divisions existed on both sides, the fundamental unity on key issues is often at least as important in explaining short-term events. Although the United States possessed an ideological agenda and at times overreacted to stimuli, it just as often showed flexibility and responded prudently to difficult and complex conditions. The Communists, on the other hand, also possessed an ideological agenda and frequently adopted courses that both threatened the other side's fundamental interests and produced results contrary to their own. The ROK and DPRK generally played active roles in the development of policies within their respective alliances, but ultimately their great power sponsors defined the broad outlines of the conflict.

The final part addresses issues that, while relating to the origins and course of the war, transcend that event topically, chronologically, or both. Chapter 7 deals with the impact of the war on the American relationship with Korea. Historians, even those focusing on Korean-American relations, have failed to deal systematically with this issue, and my goal here is to fill that gap. Dividing the relationship into military, political, and economic affairs, I argue that, while the fighting greatly increased the U.S. presence on and commitment to the peninsula, it often reduced Washington's influence on the ROK. In moving toward the present, I suggest that the war left a mixed legacy—of material and emotional bonds on the one hand and of impatience and resentment on the other. This mixture has tilted increasingly toward the negative side over the last generation as the balance of power on the peninsula has shifted in favor of the ROK, thus calling into question the continued need for an American presence. The location of Korea has not changed, however, and this fact ensures the country's ongoing vulnerability and importance to regional stability. These realities, combined with the bonds produced by many years of intimate contact, leave hope that timely adjustments will continue to prove sufficient in maintaining a positive bilateral relationship.

Both the practice of democracy in the United States and the evolution of that system of governance in the ROK have influenced that relationship. Chapter 8 examines the Korean War as a test of *American* democracy, of its ability to compete with its authoritarian enemies abroad, as well as of its sustainability at home in the face of that competition. Many observers in the West, at the time and later on, doubted the competitiveness of the American political system over the long term in confronting a challenge abroad of indefinite duration and led by systems of seemingly iron discipline. Indeed, David Rees concluded in his classic treatment of the war that, although in keeping the Western "coalition intact," repulsing "the Communist aggression," and bolstering North Atlantic Treaty Organization defenses the United States produced its greatest political victory since World War II, it also missed a possible opportunity "to unite Korea and to inflict a decisive defeat on China" while the relative military and industrial strength of the West was far superior to what it would be in the future. Whether or not history would judge as correct Truman's decision to fight a limited war in Korea was far from clear to Rees.[16] Rees wrote while the outcome of the struggle between socialist authoritarianism and capitalist democracy remained uncertain. With the uncertainty gone, we can now say with some confidence that Truman made the wise decision. The democratic system in the United States did not always produce advantageous results—either before, during, or after the Korean War, in relation to either the nation's interests abroad or its ideals at home. Yet on balance that system performed better than its Soviet or Chinese counterparts. With new studies emerging on American political culture during the Cold War and with new and complex challenges confronting the United States both at home and abroad, the time is ripe for a fresh examination of democracy's performance during the Korean War era.[17]

The Korean War was a multifaceted event, the mastery of which challenges the capacity of the most diligent of historians. I make no pretense herein to cover the major battlefield events of the contest or to provide details of the civil conflict that occurred on the peninsula from 1946 to 1953. Although the general outlines of the latter, especially prior to June 1950, are integrated into the analysis, my emphasis is on the broader strategic, diplomatic, and political issues that preoccupied the three great powers most concerned about Korea—the United States, the Soviet Union, and China—and on the ways in which Korean political leaders influenced their more powerful allies. If much remains to be learned about the war, and if much that is known is omitted from this account, my hope is that this limited effort at synthesis will further understanding and debate through a focused discussion of many of the key issues raised by a truly momentous event.

PART I

ORIGINS

CHAPTER 1

The Coming of the Cold War to Korea

BRIGADIER GENERAL GEORGE LINCOLN SPENT THE NIGHT OF AUGUST 10–11, 1945, in his office at the Army Operations Division in Washington. During the past week his country had dropped atomic bombs on the Japanese cities of Hiroshima and Nagasaki. In between those attacks, the Soviet Union had declared war on Japan and commenced attacks against its forces in continental northeast Asia. On August 10 the United States had received word of Japan's willingness to surrender, provided the position of its emperor was not compromised. The news produced a scramble among planners in Washington to craft an order for postwar operations to American forces in the Pacific. As the army's adviser to the State-War-Navy Coordinating Committee (SWNCC), General Lincoln was one of dozens of U.S. officials working through the night to carry out that task.[1]

Sometime after 2:00 A.M. the phone rang in Lincoln's office. The State Department's James Dunn, SWNCC's chairman, was on the line. He stated that the United States needed to move troops into Korea, which had been part of Japan's empire since early in the century. Soviet troops reportedly had already entered the peninsula in the extreme northeast, so Dunn wanted a point at which Korea could be divided between Soviet and American forces. After hanging up Lincoln gazed at a map on the wall, quickly focusing on the thirty-eighth parallel, a line dividing Korea nearly in half.

Uncertain, he called in Colonels Charles Bonesteel and Dean Rusk, instructing them to see if they could do better and giving them a half hour's time to decide. Equipped with a small *National Geographic* map titled "Asia and Adjacent Areas," they soon confirmed Lincoln's judgment. With that the general hurried off to a meeting of the Joint War Plans Committee, armed with a proposal on Korea as part of a draft of General Order Number One, the directive that would determine to whom Japanese forces surrendered.

The thirty-eighth parallel was a line on a map, nothing more. It followed no political boundaries or physical features within Korea. As a U.S. Army historian later noted, it passed through more than "75 streams and 12 rivers, intersected many high ridges at variant angles, severed 181 small cart roads, 104 country roads, 15 provincial all weather roads, 8 better-class highways, and 6 north-south rail lines."[2]

General Order Number One went through numerous drafts over the next four days. In considering Korea, planners discussed lines as far north as the fortieth parallel, which in the west extended virtually to the Yalu River, the border with Manchuria. But the original proposal survived in the draft that went to the White House on the morning of August 15, only hours after Japan's surrender. President Harry S. Truman quickly approved, and the proposal was sent on to Moscow for the consideration of Soviet premier Joseph Stalin. His response came immediately, and although he did request an occupation zone in northern Japan—which was denied—he assented to the proposed line in Korea.[3]

Thus the thirty-eighth parallel became the demarcation line between the Soviet and American occupation forces in Korea, which were to accept the surrender of the Japanese there and return them to their homeland. Soviet troops rapidly spread out across their zone. The Americans did not begin landing in Korea until September 8.[4] Each of the occupiers set up a military government in its zone.

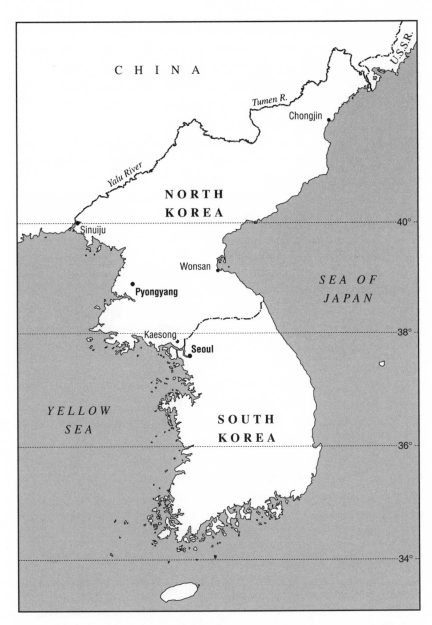

MAP 1. The thirty-eighth parallel was the boundary between the Soviet and American occupation zones. The armistice line of July 27, 1953, was south of the thirty-eighth parallel in the extreme west, but otherwise north of it.

It was December before an initiative was taken to end the division. Then, at a foreign ministers' meeting in Moscow, the United States proposed the immediate establishment of a unified administration in Korea under the occupation commanders. This accomplished, the United States and the Soviet Union, joined with China and the United Kingdom, would create a four-power trusteeship with an executive council and a high commissioner at the top. The council would organize a "popularly elected Korean legislature." In five to ten years Korea would become independent.[5]

The Soviets countered with a proposal of their own. It provided, first, for an early conference between representatives of the two commands to discuss "urgent problems affecting both northern and southern Korea" and coordination "in administrative-economic matters" between the two zones. Second, the Joint Commission, also made up of representatives of the two commands, was to be established "to make proposals for the formation of a provisional Korean government" and, after such a government emerged, for "a four-power trusteeship for a period of up to five years." All commission recommendations required approval by Moscow and Washington.[6] This plan merely provided for negotiations at the level of the occupation commands. The U.S. delegation, anxious to reach quick agreements and squelch perceptions at home of deteriorating Soviet-American relations, accepted the proposal virtually unchanged. *accepts soviet proposal easily*

The preliminary conference between the occupation commands began in Seoul on January 16, 1946. The Americans wanted a broad and early administrative integration of the two zones, but the Soviets desired discussions only on economic exchanges and transportation. The primary Soviet interest was in negotiating for rice from the South. Since the Americans faced a shortage of this commodity in their zone, they were uncooperative in this area. Three weeks of talks resulted in only narrow agreements, several of which were never implemented. In the end, little was accomplished other than periodic exchanges of mail and meetings of military liaison personnel.[7]

The Joint Commission did not convene until mid-March. It soon became stalemated over consultation with Korean groups for establishment of a provisional government. The Americans wanted a broad range of groups consulted, whereas the Soviets insisted on excluding groups that demanded immediate independence and thus opposed trusteeship. On May 8, after weeks of sometimes acrimonious exchanges, the commission adjourned at the United States' request without plans for future meetings.[8]

Although the commission would reconvene a year later, the issues that arose in the first session proved irresolvable, a predictable result given the ongoing polarization of both Korean politics and Soviet-American relations. In reality the die was cast on Korea's division when the Joint Commission first adjourned, arguably well before that. The first major step toward the fighting that broke out on June 25, 1950, was in place. The Cold War had come to Korea.

Why was this so? Why did the United States and the Soviet Union divide Korea at the thirty-eighth parallel in August 1945? Why did they fail to eliminate that boundary in the months that followed? Why did Koreans fail to unite to prevent this result? An understanding of the origins of the Korean War begins with answers to these questions.

I

The thirty-eighth parallel decision of August 1945 alone heavily weighted the scales toward Korea's long-term division. American aspirations for a position in Korea following Japan's defeat clearly derived from a desire to contain Soviet influence. For their part, the Soviets had inherited an interest in the peninsula from their Russian predecessors, who in the late nineteenth century had expanded their country's boundaries to the western Pacific and, early in the new century, had fought a war with Japan for influence in Korea and Manchuria. Japan had prevailed and, for two generations, had held a powerful position in continental northeast Asia. Naturally, the Soviets wanted to change that situation to their advantage, and establishing a foothold in Korea represented an important means to that end. Once ensconced in their halves of Korea, the Soviets and the Americans, authoritarian socialist in the first case, liberal democratic in the second, were bound to find it difficult to reach common ground in establishing a unified indigenous government.

The total defeat of Japan, of course, was what brought Korea back

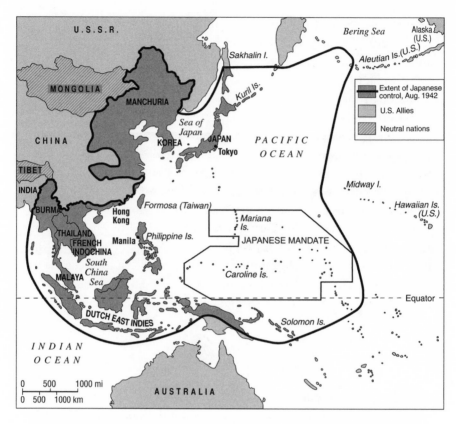

MAP 2. Japanese-held territory in the western Pacific and East Asia, August 1942.

into the international arena. Japan was to be deprived of its overseas empire, built since the 1890s, and it was to be occupied and temporarily denied its status as an independent power. This meant that the peninsula would no longer be under the Japanese yoke and, most likely, that the restoration of Korea's nationhood would be far from smooth.

Anticipation of these developments led to concern about a power vacuum in northeast Asia. The Soviet Union would want to ensure that the vacuum was not filled by hostile forces—and the best way to guarantee achievement of that objective was to itself fill as much of the vacuum as possible. On the other hand, the United States, the primary instrument of Japan's defeat, did not consider itself a major

[handwritten annotation in left margin: Prevent other power from moving in by moving in themselves]

U.S.

power on the Asian mainland. It hoped that China, once rid of Japan in Manchuria and coastal areas farther south, would emerge as a great power to help create a new balance in the region. As World War II progressed, however, a free China split between Nationalists in the south and Communists in the north showed limited capacity to contribute to the struggle against Japan. Increasingly, China appeared as likely to emerge weak and divided at war's end, a prospect that produced growing apprehensions in Washington that the Soviet Union would reign uncontested in continental northeast Asia. A U.S. State Department paper of the fall of 1943 concluded:

> Korea may appear to offer a tempting opportunity [for Soviet premier Joseph Stalin] . . . to strengthen enormously the economic resources of the Soviet Far East, to acquire ice-free ports, and to occupy a dominating strategic position in relation both to China and to Japan. . . . A Soviet occupation of Korea would create an entirely new strategic situation in the Far East, and its repercussions within China and Japan might be far reaching.[9]

Actually, concern about Russian expansion was not new. At the turn of the century, with Russia having acquired huge blocks of territory in the region over the previous two generations and now on the verge of completing the trans-Siberian railroad, such American strategists as Alfred Thayer Mahan and Theodore Roosevelt expressed apprehension about Russian expansion on the Eurasian landmass. In industry, though, Russia remained the most backward of the great powers. In the hands of a clumsy, autocratic government, it was unlikely to catch up anytime soon. Thus Roosevelt opined, "Undoubtedly the future is hers, unless she mars it from within. But it is the future not the present." For the moment, he thought, a rising Japan provided "a check on Russia," a goal that would be furthered by the former's acquisition of Korea.[10] Japan's success in doing just that, combined with its expansion into Manchuria, largely eliminated concerns about growing Russian influence in the region.

What was new in 1943 was the impending elimination of Japan from its position on continental Asia and the prospect of an already powerful Soviet Union taking its place uncontested. The prospect was all the more real given the desire of American leaders to secure Soviet assistance, once Germany was defeated, in the struggle against Japan. Wartime needs threatened to compromise postwar aims.

To the authors of the State Department paper just quoted, the prospect of Soviet domination was even more likely due to the apparent existence of some thirty-five thousand Koreans stationed in the Soviet Far East who were "thoroughly indoctrinated with Soviet ideology and methods of government." To be sure, exiled Korean nationalists were congregated as well in China and the United States, and many of them were strongly anti-Communist. Yet they were a weak and divided lot, incapable of raising a significant armed force to contribute to the fight against Japan; they also appeared to lack substantial support from Koreans in their homeland. In a word, projected conditions, both international and indigenous, seemed to give the Soviet Union a distinct advantage in Korea—unless the United States itself played a direct role. That the same could be said of the resource-rich, industrially developing region of nearby Manchuria added to American concerns.

American leaders did not for the moment adopt a competitive attitude toward the Soviets regarding Korea. Indeed, insofar as President Franklin D. Roosevelt gave thought to the peninsula, it was largely in an attempt to avoid postwar competition there. His favored method was a multipower trusteeship, including the United States, the Soviet Union, and China. The great powers with interests on the peninsula would share in an arrangement that would at once prepare Koreans to govern themselves and enable the trustees to amicably work out their differences.[11]

In the spring of 1943, State Department planners looking to the postwar era prepared a series of papers outlining the rationale for the trusteeship approach.[12] Their analysis grew out of a reading of Korea's history since the late nineteenth century. Although the peninsula had enjoyed several centuries of relative stability prior to that time, by the late 1800s "internal weakness" deriving from the corruption, inefficiency, and lack of "virility" of governing elites had produced serious "internal weakness." Since Korea had "become important as a gateway to the fast-developing Asian mainland," this condition led to the rise of an intense rivalry there among China, Japan, and Russia. The eventual result was Korea's subjugation by Japan.

By the 1940s Koreans had lived for more than a generation "as a subjugated people with little practical experience in self-government." True, more than half of the public officials in Korea in 1939 were Korean; however, such officials were always under strict Japanese supervision and had "no opportunity for choice as to policies to be pursued." Furthermore, "the whole educational system" sought to make "Koreans loyal Japanese subjects, with the help of obliterating all vestiges of Korean opposition and culture." Exiled groups *had* formed various organizations to agitate for independence, including the Korean Provisional Government (KPG) now stationed at Chungking, the wartime capital of the Chinese Nationalists; but none of them had had "the responsibility of governing at home." The KPG had failed to unite all exile groups even in Chungking, where the Korean National Revolutionary Party, made up of generally younger, more progressive exiles, contested its authority. In the United States Dr. Syngman Rhee, who claimed to speak for the KPG despite a contentious relationship with it over many years, refused to cooperate with Kilsoo Haan, who assumed the mantle of representative of the Korean National Revolutionary Party.[13] The image of the KPG was dimmed further by recent reports that its president, Kim Koo, had "accepted arrangements from the Chinese government which restricted the Korean revolutionary movement in return for a monthly subsidy."[14] As for Haan, although he claimed to be an anti-Japanese spy and presented numerous reports to various agencies of the American government characterizing conditions among Koreans in the Soviet Maritime Provinces, Manchuria, Korea, Japan, and Hawaii, American intelligence agencies doubted his loyalty to anything other than his own aggrandizement, pecuniary and otherwise.[15] It remained unclear whether he or any other of the exiles was in a position to return to Korea after Japan's defeat and establish a viable indigenous government.[16]

Koreans hardly seemed prepared economically for immediate independence. Since Japanese operated the vast bulk of industrial enterprises, Koreans lacked "an adequate supply of trained and skilled personnel" to take them over. An independent government would probably quickly confiscate Japanese property and remove Japanese personnel, which would lead not only to poor management of the businesses concerned but also to a disinclination on the part of Japan to keep open its market to Korean goods. Under such conditions, "economic instability would be such as to threaten the very existence of the new government." The internal weakness leading to foreign intervention, war, and subjugation that had occurred at the turn of the century might repeat itself.

The course that stood out as in the best interest of Koreans and the world community alike was "recognition of the right [of Korea] to be free and independent and of independence after a period of self-government under international trusteeship." Oversight of Korea's movement toward independence by the nations with the greatest stakes in the country would at once encourage orderly development, both politically and economically, and ensure protection of the fundamental interests of the major outside powers.

This approach led the United States to reject a proposal by Nationalist China to recognize the KPG. Such recognition would do nothing to further the war effort against Japan while creating suspicions in Moscow as to U.S. postwar intentions regarding Korea. At Cairo in late 1943, Roosevelt persuaded the British and the Chinese Nationalists that Korea would "in due course . . . become free and independent," but he received no commitment on trusteeship. Shortly thereafter, at Teheran, he broached the subject with Stalin, who he thought agreed to a period of tutelage for Korea. Then at Yalta in February 1945, Roosevelt proposed a trusteeship, to include the United States, the Soviet Union, China, and perhaps Great Britain. Stalin did not demur, but he expressed a desire to make any trusteeship period as short as possible. He seemed pleased when Roosevelt said that troops would not be stationed on the peninsula.[17]

It was natural for Roosevelt to initiate discussion on the issue: the Soviet Union was not yet in the war against Japan and even had a neutrality treaty with that country. In addition, Stalin was more intent on nailing down with Roosevelt an advantageous position in Man-

churia before the Chinese Nationalists staked their claim. Stalin probably wanted to avoid detailed discussions and concrete commitments
on Korea, since his ability to exert direct influence in the area was
bound to improve once Germany was defeated and he augmented
Soviet forces in northeast Asia. In a few months the Soviets might be
in a strong position to get a good deal more than one place in a four-
power trusteeship on the peninsula.[18]

During the visit of Harry Hopkins to Moscow in late May, Stalin
expressed general support for a four-power trusteeship in Korea. Hopkins had been appointed by Harry S. Truman, who succeeded to the
U.S. presidency upon Roosevelt's death on April 12, to lead a special
mission to talk with Stalin about recent difficulties in Soviet-American
relations and to help prepare for a summit conference in July. As
a former intimate of Roosevelt and a well-known sympathizer of
friendly relations with the Soviet Union, Hopkins was considered the
ideal person to deal with Stalin at a time when bilateral relations
threatened to deteriorate over a series of postwar issues.

Among other things, the State Department hoped that Hopkins
would negotiate specific agreements on the nature of the Korean trusteeship, ones that would provide for, as one historian has written,
"equal representation in the civil administration" and emphasis "on
training *local* Koreans for self-government."[19] The latter objective reflected, first, the continuing concern that Stalin would favor those
Korean exiles who had spent the war years in the Soviet Union and,
second, a willingness to bypass Korean exiles in the United States and
southern China in developing indigenous political institutions on the
peninsula. But Hopkins was in poor health, and Stalin was disinclined
to engage in detailed conversations on Korea. In any event, issues
involving Poland and the United Nations seemed more pressing.[20]

At the Potsdam summit in July, neither American nor Soviet negotiators showed particular interest in discussing Korea. Soviet foreign
minister V. M. Molotov did mention that country at one point, but in
the context of Soviet efforts to secure a place in trusteeships for Italy's
African colonies. The move probably represented a bargaining ploy
rather than an effort to reach detailed agreements on the peninsula.[21]
For their part, American military planners talking about theater opera-

tions with their Soviet counterparts mentioned only air and naval operations in and around Korea. These were to be part of their invasion of Kyushu, the southernmost of Japan's main islands, which would not commence until late October.[22] Yet, privately, top American leaders, having received reports of the successful test of an atomic device in the New Mexico desert, believed that Japan might be forced to surrender before the Soviets entered the war, which would give the United States the opportunity to occupy all of Korea.[23]

Despite the Hopkins mission, Soviet-American relations remained touchy during the summer. On Asia the most prickly issue related to China, as the Soviet Union pressed the Nationalist government there for concessions in Manchuria that exceeded those granted by the United States and Great Britain at Yalta.[24] Each party was now more likely than ever to seek every possible advantage in its relations with the other. With the Soviet Union approaching readiness to enter the war against Japan, and the United States seemingly lacking plans for operations in Korea, Stalin probably thought continued delay on reaching agreements regarding the peninsula would redound to his advantage.[25] The Americans, in turn, were willing to wager that the atomic bomb would soon turn the advantage *their* way.

In the end, time gave neither side a decisive advantage in Korea. The main thrust of Soviet operations against Japan beginning on August 9 was into Manchuria. Nonetheless, on August 10 a new order was phoned to the commander of the Twenty-fifth Soviet Army. It included an early move into Korea to capture the ports of Ch'ongjin and Wonsan.[26] By the time Japan surrendered five days later, Soviet troops were at the gates of the former city, some fifty miles down the east coast on the Sea of Japan.

Why, then, with American troops still several hundred miles from Korea in Okinawa, did Stalin accept Truman's proposal of the thirty-eighth parallel? Context suggests two factors, one primary, the other secondary. First, the situation in northeast Asia generally and in Korea specifically probably did not appear altogether favorable to Stalin. The Americans had mobilized huge forces in the area in preparation for an invasion of Japan, and they had just leveled two Japanese cities with atomic bombs. The Soviets had moved major forces to the region as well, but their overall strength in air, ground, and naval power could not match that of the Americans, especially given the latter's greater capacity for resupply. Furthermore, Stalin undoubtedly suspected—if he did not actually know through espionage—that Truman was now considering early landings in Korea and Manchuria.[27] Stalin also feared that the Americans might cut a deal with the Japanese to continue to resist the Soviet advance in Manchuria and Korea after they surrendered to the United States.[28] With the Japanese possessing nine army divisions on the peninsula, they certainly had the capacity to resist the Soviets, who had only two divisions and were operating over rugged, unfamiliar terrain. In the meantime, U.S. troops might rush into the southern part of the country, and into Manchuria's Liaotung Peninsula as well.[29] It is no coincidence that, two days before accepting the thirty-eighth parallel, Stalin signed a treaty with the Nationalist government of China adhering to the Yalta accords.[30]

If the military conditions and fears of American intentions alone were enough to persuade Stalin to cut an immediate deal with Truman on Korea, a supplementary consideration may have been the hope that the United States would grant the Soviet Union a share in the occupation of Japan. In his message of August 16 accepting the U.S. proposal regarding Korea, Stalin requested that in the northern part of Hokkaido, the northernmost of Japan's main islands, the Japanese be ordered to surrender to Soviet troops.[31]

Why did Truman ultimately back off from any attempt to seize all—or at least more—of Korea and a foothold in Manchuria? Here, too, the answer appears to be twofold. First, American planners in Washington and in the field overestimated the Soviet head start in both areas. Lincoln, Bonesteel, and Rusk had chosen the thirty-eighth parallel because it was north of Seoul and would thus place the Korean capital in the U.S. zone. They were surprised when Stalin accepted it. Second, General Douglas MacArthur, the American commander in the western Pacific, was determined *not* to divert forces from the occupation of Japan, where resistance to American operations might develop despite the government's surrender.[32]

By the time of the agreement on the thirty-eighth parallel, a competitive relationship existed between the Soviet Union and the United

States over the peninsula. Washington had recently considered an attempt to occupy all or most of the country, and the eventual proposal of the thirty-eighth parallel represented an effort to contain Soviet influence there. As for Soviet thinking, in addition to the circumstantial evidence already covered here, one document has surfaced written in late June by two members of the Second Far Eastern Department of the Soviet Foreign Ministry. The paper summarized the background of Korea as a focal point for conflict in northeast Asia and emphasized that "Japan must be forever excluded from Korea," that an independent Korea must have "friendly and close relations" with the USSR, that the United States and China might post a threat by attempting to preserve Japan's economic position in Korea, and that, if a trusteeship was to be established on the peninsula, "the Soviet Union must . . . participate in it prominently."[33] The vague nature of agreements on Korea's future at the time of occupation provided a firm foundation for future stalemate.

It is difficult to see a point prior to August 1945 in which an alternative foundation was likely to have emerged. Detailed agreement on neutrality for an independent Korea would have been the solution best suited to balancing the needs of the three great powers involved and the aspirations of the Koreans themselves. Yet Korea was never a high-priority item for either the Soviets or the Americans; and never was the relationship between them sufficiently trusting that either was willing to go out of its way to reach accord on an issue not essential to the war effort. Even in countries more central to that effort, such as those in Eastern and central Europe, detailed agreements failed to emerge until the balance of military power on the ground became clear, and sometimes not even then. Austria, the one place in which neutralization occurred, did not possess a national provisional government recognized by all the occupying powers until mid-October 1945, by which time they all had been in place for several months.[34] Neutralization was not agreed upon for ten years. In Korea, unless Japan was to be left on the peninsula to manage Korea's transition to independence, or unless Koreans, without viable leaders and with a recent history of difficulty in cooperating with each other, were to be left completely to their own devices, the peninsula had to be occupied by outside forces at the end of the war.

The Americans deserve credit for advancing an idea reflecting a degree of sensitivity toward the interests of the Soviets while envisioning eventual independence. Yet such sensitivity was at least as much a result of a sense of weakness and limited interest as of visionary benevolence. Although the United States at one point flirted with a more assertive policy toward Korea, the likelihood remains that Stalin was never willing to negotiate detailed agreements on a trusteeship prior to the end of the war.

The behavior of Koreans contributed to a sense that the eventual victors must occupy the country temporarily and that no obligation existed to grant its people immediate independence. Americans in contact with Koreans in the United States and China were appalled by their factionalism and disappointed at their inability to mobilize significant forces to fight Japan.[35] They were also well aware that the Japanese had mobilized the peninsula to assist *their side* in the struggle. Although the Soviets were in touch with thousands of Koreans in exile who had resisted—or were still resisting—the Japanese from bases in Manchuria, they knew that these patriots faced constant pressure from antiguerrilla forces often made up in part by Koreans.[36] Moreover, unlike in Austria, where the Soviets in the spring of 1945 moved quickly upon occupying their zone to establish a provisional government, Korean Communists were scattered and had a history of factionalism and independence from the Comintern and Soviet party line.[37] Certainly Moscow regarded a period of occupation of at least part of the country as fundamental for the achievement of its aims.

II

Once the Soviets were in Korea, they had no intention of risking creation of an unfriendly government over the entire country.[38] Already they had made disparaging remarks about the KPG in China and the right-wing independence leader Syngman Rhee in the United States.

While the Soviet occupiers soon displayed a willingness in the North to work with "people's committees" set up by the Koreans themselves, they refused to acknowledge the Korean People's Republic (KPR), established in Seoul on the eve of the American arrival, which was leftist in orientation. Perhaps if the Soviets had occupied the capital city, as they did in Austria, they would have worked with the KPR. But without control in Seoul, they probably regarded Communist participation in creating the KPR as an undesirable act of independence, especially given its offer of the top leadership position to the absent Rhee.

The Soviets preoccupied themselves with establishing dominance in the North rather than setting the stage for national unity.[39] They sharply restricted economic activity between the zones. In October, over the objections of Communists who had spent the war years in Korea, they sponsored the establishment of a northern branch of the party. Two months later they referred to it as simply the North Korean Communist Party. Kim Il-sung, an early advocate of creating the organization, became its chairman.[40]

The Soviets did not rule out unification, however. Although Stalin's views remain uncertain, several documents are available from the Soviet Foreign Ministry for the period from September to December 1945. Three papers from September reveal that the Soviets had no definite program for resolving the Korean issue but viewed the U.S. trusteeship proposal as potentially strengthening their position in northeast Asia. Specific concerns focused on control over three ports below the thirty-eighth parallel: Inchon in the west, Pusan in the south, and Cheju Island off the southwestern coast. After up to two years of joint occupation of Korea, Soviet control of these strategic points between the Soviet naval bases in Vladivostok and Port Arthur might be gained through negotiations for a four-power trusteeship. In return for American acceptance of these Soviet positions, Moscow might support Washington's desire for trusteeship over the western Pacific islands, the Bonins, Volkano, the Marianas, the Carolines, and the Marshalls.[41] By the time the Moscow meeting of foreign ministers approached in December 1945, the Soviets focused on establishment of a provisional government for all Korea. Yet they were dubious, given U.S. occupation policies in the South, that such a government could be established that would protect key Soviet interests.

Like the Soviets, General John R. Hodge, the U.S. occupation commander, did nothing to encourage the coalition-building efforts of moderate leftist Yo Un-hyong within the KPR. Before arriving, Hodge, a hard-nosed corps commander with little tact, even less knowledge of Korea, and profoundly conservative instincts, had received several messages from Japanese officials in Korea and from the War Department in Washington. They warned that Soviet troops might continue moving southward once they reached the thirty-eighth parallel. The Japanese also complained of Soviet treatment of surrendering Japanese soldiers, officials, and civilians and of efforts to place some Koreans in positions of administrative authority.[42] When he arrived in Seoul, Hodge found few Soviet soldiers in the South, and, with the exception of those on the isolated Ongjin Peninsula in the extreme west, these quickly departed. Yet his interaction with Japanese officials already had made him suspicious of leftist activity among Koreans. He also suspected that they were in collusion with members of the Soviet consulate in Seoul, which, because the Soviet Union did not declare war on Japan until August 8, had stayed open throughout the war. The Americans possessed insufficient numbers to administer the entire country themselves, but Hodge refused to acknowledge the people's committees. Rather, he decided to work with the Japanese and with local conservatives, who as landowners and businessmen had collaborated with their colonial masters and had recently organized the Korean Democratic Party (KDP) to counter the KPR.[43]

Hodge's decision to temporarily retain Japanese officials in top administrative positions was soon altered in the face of widespread Korean protests and instructions from home. Nonetheless, he continued to consult the Japanese and to keep the basic administrative apparatus, including the hated Japanese police force in which many Korean collaborators served. His approach was evolutionary, which was consistent with the wartime view in Washington of Koreans' inability, in the short term, to govern themselves: he kept the existing government organizations largely intact and manned with some Japanese

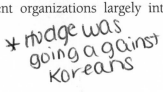

✻ Hodge was
going against
Koreans

FIG. 1. Welcome to American troops at Inchon, September 1945.

FIG. 2. Lowering the Japanese flag in Seoul, September 1945.

FIG. 3. The primary negotiators of the agreement on Korea in Moscow, December 1945, from left to right: British foreign minister Ernest Bevin; Soviet foreign minister V. M. Molotov; U.S. secretary of state James F. Byrnes.

FIG. 4. Opening session of meetings between the Soviet and American occupation commands in Korea at Seoul in January 1946. Seated at left at the front of the table is Lieutenant General John R. Hodge, the head of the U.S. occupation in the south. To his left is Colonel General Terentii F. Shytkov, the head of the Soviet occupation in the north.

personnel until new institutions could be developed and sufficient Korean personnel trained to fully replace the colonials. He also worked to get back into the country prominent exiles such as Rhee and KPG officials who could provide conservative leadership without facing the stigma of collaboration. Rhee arrived in mid-October, KPG officials a month later.

Rhee quickly emerged as a formidable political operator. He made an initial gesture for unity between Left and Right by creating the Central Council for the Rapid Realization of Korean Independence, but he also lambasted the Soviet Union and its policies in the North. Although Yo and Pak Hon-yong, the leader of the Communists in the South, attended the first council meeting, they soon abandoned it because Rhee refused to work with the KPR, clearly favoring the KDP. His refusal to accept membership in that collaboration-laden party did not hide his rabid anti-Communism. And the return of KPG president Kim Koo merely added to the anti-Communist chorus in the South.[44]

Hodge's tolerance of considerable leftist activity in the South did not eliminate concern in Moscow. On the eve of the Moscow meeting, one Soviet official wrote that

> the question [of creating a united government] is extremely complex, because of the multiplicity of political parties and groups, the lack of unity among them and the solicitations of the USA. . . . The character of the future government . . . will be one of the decisive moments in the determination . . . of whether Korea will in the future be turned into a breeding ground of new anxiety for us . . . or into one of the strong points of our security in the Far East.[45]

Despite Soviet concerns about the U.S. position, another analyst concluded that "it would be politically inexpedient for the Soviet Union to oppose the creation of a single Korean government."[46]

Stalin was in no hurry to unite Korea. The American position in the South aside, conditions in the North, though well under Soviet control, were far from tidy. Soviet soldiers raped thousands of native women and engaged in widespread pillage, thus alienating many Koreans. As in most Eastern and central European countries, the Soviets mounted a united front policy. This entailed placing Korean Communists, especially ones who had spent the war in the Soviet Union, in important positions in a government bureaucracy, but also cooperation with non-Communist groups. The Soviets even cultivated the conservative Christian leader Cho Man-sik, allowing him a prominent place in public events organized and endorsed by occupation authorities. Cho often protested Soviet grain procurement policies, and he had plenty of support among Koreans. In November 1945, demonstrations and riots broke out in Sinuiju that had to be suppressed by Soviet soldiers and police.[47] Hodge's policies in the South had generated considerable turmoil as well, both because of his use of Japanese and because his conservative policies toward land and labor left intact many of the social and economic injustices of the colonial period. Yet surely Stalin believed that work remained to be done in the North before moving toward a provisional government. Fortunately for him, Washington accepted without dispute the Soviet counter to the U.S. proposal, which Moscow saw as a ploy to allow Americans to penetrate the economy above the thirty-eighth parallel.[48]

In all likelihood, Stalin's aims were similar to those in occupied Germany, as characterized recently by two leading Soviet scholars: "He wanted to establish Soviet hegemony in the USSR's zone of occupation. Then he hoped to undermine British influence in West Germany, which would not be difficult, provided that American troops withdrew from Europe. As an endgame, he had in mind a unified, 'friendly' Germany, leaning toward the USSR."[49] Another Soviet specialist notes that, like many dictators "faced with seemingly flaccid and indecisive democracies," Stalin believed that the Americans lacked the key quality of "will" and thus were likely with time to retreat from a large-scale military presence abroad.[50] By mid-November 1945 the United States had reduced personnel in its armed forces by nearly a third from wartime highs, and the clamor from Congress and the public for a continued headlong demobilization showed no sign of abating.[51]

The agreement at Moscow in December to negotiate with the Americans in the Joint Commission served Soviet interests nicely, since it included the possibility of a unified provisional government and a trusteeship without making either one inevitable. Thus the Soviets at once averted an immediate clash with the Americans and avoided giving up anything. Since many on the right wing in the South already had declared their opposition to trusteeship, the agreement might create difficulties for the Americans with their natural allies while giving the Soviets an excuse for trying to exclude them from the process of creating a provisional government.[52]

III

The reaction in Korea to the Moscow agreements provided the context within which the final polarization between the Soviets and the Americans and Korean political groups occurred. When word of the Moscow agreement reached Korea in late December, expressions of outrage sprang up immediately among many political groups in the South, Left and Right alike. On January 7, 1946, however, a shift occurred: the Communist Party and other leftist groups joined with the KDP and the moderate rightist Korean Nationalist Party to support the agreement. Unfortunately for the prospects of national unity, that coalition quickly split apart, as the KDP reversed itself and joined Rhee and Kim Koo in opposition to trusteeship.[53] Hodge, who had warned Washington against pursuing trusteeship because of widespread indigenous opposition, probably encouraged this change.[54]

In response to the campaign against trusteeship, the Soviets, who in all likelihood had engineered the change in the position of the Communists in the South, launched a sharp attack on the Right. An article on January 12 in the leading Soviet journal, *Izvestia*, argued, among other things, that the Korean people lacked "sufficient experience to solve the political and economic difficulties on the way to the creation of a democratic state."[55] Soon Stalin protested the none-too-subtle resistance of the American occupation to the Moscow agreement.[56] Even before that, a polarization had begun in the North, where Cho Mansik, the top non-Communist figure in the Soviet zone, adamantly rejected trusteeship. Soviet authorities quickly arrested him, thus ending their united front policy above the thirty-eighth parallel. In February they approved establishment of a central People's Committee in the North, in effect a provisional government, with the thirty-three-year-old Kim Il-sung as its chairman and Communists firmly in control. The youthful Kim had made his name as a guerrilla fighter in Manchuria during the 1930s and had spent most of World War II in the Soviet Union.[57] He had no base in the South, and his position largely rested on the support of Soviet occupation authorities. His emergence as the top Korean leader in the North reflected the determination of the Soviets to stay in control there as a priority over unifying the peninsula. The radical turn in political and economic policies, which included the redistribution of land to the peasants, also reflected these concerns, as did the purge of domestic Communists—that is, those who had spent most of the period of Japanese rule in Korea and were not always disciplined in following the Moscow line.[58]

Almost simultaneously, the Representative Democratic Council was installed under the American occupation in the South. This advisory body was so dominated by the antitrusteeship Right that the leftists appointed to it refused to serve.[59] Unlike the Soviets in the North, the Americans still tolerated a good deal of dissent in the South, but their continued favoritism of the Right in the face of its opposition to trusteeship demonstrated that unification was not their top priority either.

The storm over trusteeship combined with events abroad to dim prospects for successful negotiations in the Joint Commission. The Right now had an issue over which it could challenge the nationalist credentials of the Left and broaden a popular base heretofore limited by its economic interests and the collaborationist record of some of its members. The Soviets, in turn, could legitimately cry foul over the U.S. occupation's failure to press South Korean political groups to fall into line behind the Moscow accords. Soviet suspicions were genuine, but Moscow's sudden championing of trusteeship also was suspect, especially given that its implementation would add Nationalist China and Great Britain as factors in the Korean equation. The trusteeship controversy probably only confirmed Stalin in his view that, for the present, a divided peninsula served Soviet interests better than a united one, and it gave him an excuse to launch an open attack on the Korean Right.[60]

As for Hodge, January events produced considerable embarrassment once the Soviets revealed to the Korean public that trusteeship had been an American, not a Soviet, idea. Yet with the Right so clearly committed against trusteeship and the Left now following the Soviet lead in supporting it—and with Soviet-American relations rapidly deteriorating outside Korea—Hodge temporarily secured greater support from Washington than ever before in his favoritism of conservative groups.[61]

The Joint Commission called for in the Moscow agreement did not meet until March 20, 1946, in Seoul. By that time, Soviet actions in Eastern Europe, Turkey, Iran, and Manchuria had drawn sharp comments and tough diplomatic follow-ups from Western leaders, and these had produced spirited ripostes from Stalin and the Soviet press. In his opening speech to the Joint Commission, Terentii F. Shytkov, the head of the Soviet delegation, stated that "the Soviet Union has a keen interest in Korea being a true democratic and independent country, friendly to the Soviet Union, so that in the future it will not become a base for an attack on the Soviet Union."[62] This was largely a paraphrase of a statement by Stalin published on March 14 in the leading Soviet newspaper, *Pravda*, which included a broader defense of his policy on the entire Soviet periphery.[63]

Talks in the Joint Commission produced nothing but stalemate, and the hardening of zonal division proceeded apace. When, on May 8, Shtykov informed Hodge that he and his delegation were leaving Seoul, he emphasized again that the Soviets wanted a "loyal" government in Korea. The rightists who rejected trusteeship, he asserted, had "slandered the Soviet Union and smeared it with mud." If they formed a government, they would organize "hostile actions on the part of the Korean people against the Soviet Union."[64] Hodge responded with a demand that the Soviets permit the United States to establish a consulate in Pyongyang, the northern capital. The Soviets had had a consulate in Seoul all along, and in recent months the Americans had become persuaded that they were using it to coordinate leftist activities below the thirty-eighth parallel. Either the Soviets must now reciprocate by permitting an American consulate in the North, or they must close down their operation in Seoul. The Soviets chose the latter option, and they delayed the reconvening of the Joint Commission until the following spring.[65]

DIVISION AND COLD WAR CAME TO KOREA FIRST AND FOREMOST because of the inability of outside powers, the United States and the Soviet Union, to devise a unification plan that would protect the interests of both. From the start the two powers regarded internal political configurations as highly unpredictable, so they were disinclined to encourage creation of an indigenous government that crossed zonal boundaries. The best opportunity for the emergence of such a government came in September 1945 with the rise of the KPR, a group that possessed strong linkages with the people's committees at the local level. Had the Americans supported the KPR, thus encouraging the KDP to play coalition rather than class politics, Koreans might have taken the lead in developing a vision of a united, independent country unthreatening to the great powers. Yet the best opportunity in this case does not represent a good opportunity, since such an outcome would have required extraordinary patience and trust on all sides, ingredients that were far from common at the time.

Such qualities certainly were absent in General Hodge, so any plausible if imaginary scenario for peace and unity would have to replace him with General Joseph Stilwell as U.S. occupation commander. This was *not* a remote possibility, since the former American commander in the China theater was in August commander of the U.S. Tenth Army, the unit initially scheduled to occupy Korea. Unfortunately, Stilwell's old adversary, Nationalist Chinese leader Chiang Kai-shek, vetoed the idea of his having a command on the Asian mainland.[66] Stilwell had spent years in East Asia, was far more sensitive than Hodge to the economic conditions that bred discontent there, and was flexible in dealing with Communists.[67] On the other hand, he was not a tactful man—"Vinegar Joe," he was called in the press. Whether he or any other American could have navigated the rapids of Korean and interoccupation politics in a manner that would have averted long-term division remains uncertain. What can be said is that Stilwell would not have possessed the predisposition of Hodge against the KPR and in favor of the KDP.

Nor can we imagine him lobbying Washington, as did Hodge, for the return of Rhee and leaders of the KPG. Rhee's presence in particular plunged a dagger into the heart of prospects for unification; he was uncompromising in his opposition to any deal with the Communists or the Soviet Union—and he was a sufficiently adept manipulator of political trends in the South to command a hearing. None of the KPG leaders were in his league, and the conservative president Kim Koo was at least balanced by the more moderate Kim Kyu-sik. We know that the State Department personnel who had dealt with Rhee and the KPG were not anxious for them to return to Korea.[68] Had Stilwell been of the same mind, a powerful conservative coalition congregated around Rhee and the KDP might not have developed.

The question remains of how the Soviets would have reacted to more moderate developments in the South. We know that in the North, as in Eastern and central Europe, the Soviets initially did not exclude non-Communist forces from political activity. In addition, prior to 1945 the Soviets had not had an altogether positive relationship with the domestic wing of Korean Communists. With the Americans controlling Seoul and nearly two-thirds of the Korean population residing in the South, it is questionable that the Soviets would have risked undermining their buffer by permitting the KPR to penetrate the North. The best that can be said is that the indigenous climate for negotiations between the occupations in late 1945 and early 1946 might have been more conducive to moderation than it actually was.

But this assumes that the deterioration of Soviet-American relations in general from the fall of 1945 onward would not have overwhelmed any spirit of compromise that might have remained in Korea. The assumption requires us to envision Koreans cooperating consistently with each other for a common outcome rather than playing the inherent ideological differences of the occupiers for personal advantage—a dubious prospect, given the preexisting divisions in Korean society and political groups, even excluding Rhee and the KPG. It also requires imagining both the United States and the Soviet Union risking loss of their positions in Korea at a time when the overall lines of conflict between them were hardening.

This brief excursion into counterfactual analysis highlights the structural barriers to Korean unity that came into place once the occupation forces had arrived on the peninsula. The simple fact—unpleasant as it may be—is that division was the price Koreans paid after World War II for their failure to liberate themselves from the Japanese. As a shrimp among whales—and a weakly integrated shrimp at that—Korea was not in a position to control its own future.

To articulate this painful truth is not to concede that the war that ravaged the peninsula from 1950 to 1953 was inevitable after August 1945 or even May 1946. If the foundation for war had been firmly laid, much of the structure to accompany it had yet to be built. Most important, despite the stalemate, neither the Soviets nor the Americans wanted a direct military clash over Korea, so as long as both maintained troops there, all-out war remained unlikely.

Privately, there were already some on the American side who wanted out of Korea. As early as October 1945, the War Department showed interest in U.S. withdrawal as part of the general plan for demobilization.[69] In December a frustrated Hodge suggested to Washington that "serious consideration" be given to proposing to the Soviets a joint withdrawal so as to "leave Korea to its own devices and an inevitable internal upheaval for its self-purification."[70] Five months later, with the Joint Commission adjourned, William Langdon, the State Department adviser to the occupation, pleaded with his superiors at home for an initiative in Moscow to seek a mutual withdrawal by early 1947, an idea that had plenty of support in the Pentagon.[71]

Yet President Truman and most in the State Department remained a long way from giving up on Korea. Convinced that the U.S. retreat from international responsibility during the 1920s and 1930s had produced World War II, they were determined that their nation play a global role as political and economic stabilizer. A State Department paper of early June 1946 applied this conception to Korea. Soviet domination of the peninsula "would further endanger Chinese control of Manchuria and would thus lessen the prospect [for] . . . a strong and stable China, without which there [could] . . . be no permanent political stability in the Far East."[72] Two weeks later, U.S. reparations commissioner Edwin Pauley, who had recently visited Manchuria and Korea to study the reparations issue, reported to President Truman that the peninsula was "an ideological battleground." As the only country in which U.S. and Soviet occupation forces faced each other without the presence of others, Korea provided a unique testing ground "of whether a democratic competitive system can be adopted to meet the challenge of defeated feudalism, or whether some other system, i.e., Communism will become stronger."[73] Truman agreed.[74]

In the weeks following the adjournment of the Joint Commission, the Americans devised a strategy on Korea that they hoped would lead the Soviets to a settlement. The U.S. occupation would gradually turn over the functions of government to Koreans, both through employing them in civil administration and through creation of an interim legislative assembly. Simultaneously, an effort would be made to build a centrist coalition around moderate rightist Kim Kyu-sic and moderate leftist Yo Un-hyong. The military government had lowered rents for tenant farmers the previous fall but had postponed land redistribution because opinion surveys indicated that most Koreans desired to await creation of a provisional government so they could implement such a program themselves.[75] Once the interim legislative assembly came into operation, the Americans hoped, it would institute reforms that would quell growing discontent in the countryside. Together, these measures would stabilize conditions in the South and undermine the intensely anti-Soviet Rhee, thus setting the stage for a resumption of Joint Commission negotiations on unification.[76]

For the moment, then, stalemate reigned in Korea, as both occupying powers hung tough while striving to bolster their positions in their respective zones. While there was evidence that the Americans were impatient, the question remained as to whether or not they would eventually give ground and, if so, how much. In the answer to that question we will find the margin between a tense peace and international war.

CHAPTER 2

Syngman Rhee, the Truman Doctrine,

and American Policy toward Korea,

1947–1948

right-wing independence

SYNGMAN RHEE WAS FRUSTRATED. HE WAS SEVENTY-ONE YEARS old in December 1946, with a career that extended all the way back to the last years of the Yi dynasty, when he had participated in the reformist Independence Club and even had been sent to the United States by the Korean monarch to seek American help against a rapacious Japan.[1] That mission failed, and the experience represented the first of many over the next forty years that taught him that Korea could depend on no foreign nation to protect or advance the cause of its independence. Now, with Korea liberated from Japan, his country remained divided between the American and Soviet occupiers, who so far had refused to grant independence.

On the positive side, the Joint Commission remained adjourned, so there was no immediate possibility of a U.S. accommodation with the hated Soviets. Also, the U.S. military governor had turned over all departments under him to Korean administrators of rightist proclivities, and elections for the South Korean Interim Legislative Assembly had resulted in a smashing victory for the far Right.

Yet the United States continued to explore the possibility of reconvening the Joint Commission, and the elections occurred in the midst of widespread labor and peasant unrest, which reinforced the American belief in the necessity of reformist policies in such areas as land and rice distribution. Koreans themselves should carry out such policies, the United States thought. To give them a fair hearing in the new legislative assembly, which convened in mid-December, Hodge chose moderates or leftists for two-thirds of the appointive seats to the body.[2] This action represented an extension of the policy set during the previous summer to seek establishment of a coalition of moderate political forces led by Yo Un-hyong and Kim Kyu-sic. In Rhee's mind, the U.S. course would both undermine his own influence and increase that of the Communists, whom he tended to identify as all people unwilling to follow his lead.

Frustrated over a U.S. policy clearly in conflict with his and, in his mind, his country's interests, Rhee departed for Washington in early December 1946. His intent was to lobby against trusteeship and in favor of immediate recognition by the United Nations and the United States of an independent Korean government based on the civil administration established in September by the American military regime. To keep the fires burning in Korea, Rhee left behind plans for his supporters, including work stoppages and even violence, to agitate for his proposed course.[3]

Korean-born allies Ben C. Limb, the new chairman of the Korea Commission in Washington, and Louise Yim, the observer to the United Nations for the South Korean Democratic Representative Council, already strove to get the Korean issue before the UN General Assembly. During most of the period when Japan controlled Korea, Limb and Yim had labored for Rhee in the United States in pursuit of their country's independence. Now they continued their work on behalf of Rhee under new, more hopeful circumstances.[4]

Rhee stayed on in Washington until April 1947. During his sojourn he set himself up in a suite at the Carlton Hotel, hired a professor at Syracuse University, Robert T. Oliver, as a full-time lobbyist, and contacted a variety of people in the press and in the executive and legislative branches of government. In late January he presented a paper to the State Department entitled "A Solution to the Korean Problem," which proposed six immediate measures. The most important were establishment of an interim government in South Korea to serve until the peninsula could be reunited; empowerment of this government "to negotiate directly with Russia and the United States concerning the occupation of Korea . . . and . . . on other outstanding questions"; and the maintenance of U.S. troops in Korea until both occupation armies withdrew "simultaneously."[5]

During Rhee's visit, a seminal event occurred in American foreign policy. On March 12, 1947, President Truman delivered a momentous address to a joint session of Congress. The world confronted a grave situation, he declared, one that involved "the national security" of the United States. The most immediate crisis was in Greece, where a Communist-led revolt concentrated along its northern boundaries and supplied from Communist Yugoslavia, Bulgaria, and Albania threatened the government. Neighboring Turkey also faced difficulties, not in fighting off internal revolt but in "effecting that modernization necessary for the maintenance of its national integrity." To date Great Britain had provided financial assistance to both countries; yet now, faced with severe economic difficulties of its own, that nation must withdraw further aid. Unless the United States stepped in, "totalitarian regimes" might emerge in Greece and Turkey. This development, in turn, could produce "confusion and disorder . . . throughout the entire Middle East . . . [and] have a profound effect upon those countries in Europe whose peoples are struggling against great difficulties to maintain their freedoms and their independence while they repair the damages of war." To Truman the proper course was clear: "It must be the policy of the United States to support free peoples who are resisting attempted subjugation by armed minorities or by outside pressures."[6]

Although the president did not mention the Soviet Union, little doubt existed that the Communist giant was the primary object of his concern. "TRUMAN ACTS TO SAVE NATIONS FROM RED RULE," the *New York Times* announced in its front-page headline the next day. Washington correspondent Felix Belair Jr. wrote in the accompanying story that "there could be no mistaking his [the president's] identification of the [Soviet] Communist state as the source of much of the unrest throughout the world."[7]

Cast in globalistic rhetoric, Truman's speech raised fundamental questions about the U.S. course in countries other than Greece and Turkey. Korea was one such country. A week after Truman spoke to Congress, a *New York Times* editorial pointed out that "halfway around the world from Washington, Athens and Istanbul is a small country whose future is fully as important to the United States and to world peace as are Greece, Turkey and southeastern Europe. That country is Korea." As a result of disagreement between the United States and the Soviet Union, Korea was in a "miserable state." While the Soviets were responsible for the continuing division there, the Americans had contributed to the problem through a course of "confusion, delay and neglect." The land was "democracies' forgotten front," and it was time that it received more attention in Washington.[8] A day later, inquisitors on the House Foreign Affairs Committee asked Acting Secretary of State Dean Acheson about Korea, and he replied that the executive branch was considering a $400 to $500 million program of aid to the peninsula.[9]

Six months later the United States took the Korean issue to the UN General Assembly, proposing that the international organization supervise national elections on the peninsula as a basis for the country's independence. The Soviets opposed this course, but the U.S. plan passed the General Assembly in November in an overwhelming vote. Then the Soviets refused to permit its implementation in North Korea, which prompted the Americans to seek UN sanction for elections in the South alone. Such approval came in early 1948. In May the elections occurred under UN supervision, despite a boycott of the process by all leaders in the South except Rhee and those in the KDP and a few other rightist groups. Right-wing forces emerged victorious and proceeded to choose Rhee as the first president of the Republic of Korea (ROK), which was inaugurated on August 15, 1948.[10]

FIG. 5. A banner at Seoul's South Gate welcomes members of the UN Temporary Commission on Korea in early 1948. UN/DPI Photo

FIG. 6. South Koreans wait in line to cast ballots in UN-supervised election of May 10, 1948. UN/DPI Photo

FIG. 7. South Koreans celebrate independence and the inauguration of the
government of the Republic of Korea, Seoul, August 15, 1948.

FIG. 8. The first U.S. ambassador to the Republic of Korea, John J. Muccio, signs
over the government in South Korea to the ROK on September 12, 1948.
To Muccio's right is Minister of Foreign Affairs Chung Tak Sung; to his left,
Prime Minister Lee Bum Suk.

This sequence of events—Rhee's advocacy of establishing an independent government in the South, in part through UN action, his trip to the United States to promote that plan, the declaration of the so-called Truman Doctrine, its linkage in the press and Congress to American policy toward Korea, and the eventual U.S. introduction of the Korean issue at the United Nations as a first step toward creating an independent government in the South—raises important questions. First, what impact did the Truman Doctrine have on U.S. policy in Korea? Second, did Rhee influence that policy and, if so, how much and by what means? Third, what role did these events play in the coming of the Korean War? It is to these questions that I now turn.

I

The executive branch in Washington had been considering major initiatives on Korea for over a month prior to Truman's speech to Congress. Early in February 1947, the Truman administration had established an interdepartmental committee, which included representatives of the State and War Departments and the Bureau of the Budget, to make recommendations on Korea. General Hodge was even called home to participate in the activity.[11]

The process was largely a response to the deteriorating situation in the American zone in Korea. First, although the U.S. occupiers had suppressed labor and peasant unrest during the previous fall, the conditions that sparked it remained. Second, despite the convening of the South Korean Interim Legislative Assembly in December, the coalition policy showed little sign of working, as Rhee and Kim Koo, the strongest figures on the Right, refused to cooperate and moderates Kim Kyu-sic and Yo Un-hyong seemed unable to mobilize the resources to defeat them. Mild-mannered and scholarly, the latter Kim lacked charisma or a personal following. Yo had both but had not succeeded in organizing major youth groups or cultivating support among the police, both essentials for leadership in the increasingly violent climate of South Korean politics. Although the military government turned over more and more of civil administration to Koreans, the best it could find as the chief civil administrator was An Chai-hong, a moderate but timid man with little potential to lead a government. Under the circumstances, the Soviets showed no inclination to rush back to the Joint Commission.

During January 1947, reports on Korea to Washington became more alarmist than ever. Leftist uprisings had abated for the moment, but agitation from the Right grew by the day. At midmonth U.S. authorities prevented a major outbreak of violence, but Hodge suspected that Rhee and Kim Koo soon would provoke more turmoil.[12] The South Korean Interim Legislative Assembly provided no help, as it dragged its feet on land reform and then, on the twentieth, condemned Hodge's policies and trusteeship. Such events occurred in the midst of burgeoning economic problems. Some of these, most notably the declining availability of electricity and chemical fertilizers—for which the South was almost entirely dependent on the North—existed due to the continuing division of the country. Others derived from the influx since August 1945 of some two million people into the South from Manchuria, North Korea, and Japan. Still others, such as the lack of spare parts for railroads and difficulties in the distribution of rice, were at least in part the result of a lack of operating funds for the military government.[13] One thing seemed clear: conditions would not improve without major new initiatives by the United States.

In addition to the declining conditions in Korea, the developing political situation in the United States influenced top American officials to give the peninsula new attention. By early February Rhee had been operating in Washington for two months. Prior to October 1945, he had lived in the United States for over thirty years, mostly in the nation's capital and Honolulu, Hawaii. He was fluent in English and held a doctorate from Princeton University. During World War II he had been a persistent, if unsuccessful, advocate to the executive and legislative branches for U.S. recognition of the Korean provisional government located in Chungking, China.[14] When he returned to the United States in late 1946, therefore, he was hardly starting from scratch in making contacts in the State Department, Congress, and the press. Nor was lobbyist Oliver his only advocate. M. Preston Goodfellow, a retired army colonel who during World War II had served as deputy director of the Office of Strategic Services and was now employed by a financial firm in Washington, John S. Staggers, a successful attorney, and Ben C. Limb, mentioned earlier, all pushed Rhee's cause in Washington. Louise Yim labored in New York, partly at the United Nations, partly in cultivating such influential friends as Eleanor Roosevelt and journalists in the McCormick and Hearst newspaper chains.[15]

Sparking interest in tiny and remote Korea was no easy task, but in late January Rhee was quoted twice in the *New York Times*, once attacking Hodge for alleged "efforts to build up and foster the Korean Communist Party" and a second time calling for the resumption of negotiations between the United States and the Soviet Union for an independent Korea.[16] By early February the War Department was receiving a growing number of inquiries from Capitol Hill on conditions in Korea, and Secretary of State George C. Marshall and Secretary of War Robert P. Patterson were considering the possibility of replacing Hodge as the occupation commander in Korea.[17]

To State Department officials, however, Rhee was not a sympathetic figure. A report in that agency of May 1945 conceded that he was "perhaps the best known Korean in his country." Unfortunately, he appeared "to blame the U.S. Government for keeping Korean representatives out of international conferences," and he disregarded "all Korean attempts at unity of action and democratic forms of representation."[18] Two years later, after Rhee had returned to Korea, visited Washington, and then gone back to his homeland, General John H. Hilldring, the assistant secretary of state for occupied areas, wrote Hodge of his sense of the Korean politician before first meeting him in the American capital early in 1947: "The politicos in the State Department painted him black and warned me to keep both hands in my pockets and my gun on the table." As a career military man only recently transferred to a diplomatic position, Hilldring had kept an open mind. At State, in fact, he became by far the most sympathetic toward Rhee's proposals of any highly placed official.[19] Yet Hilldring was taken aback by his "somewhat senile and tearful interview" with the Korean patriot and afterward reflected that Rhee was "more a symbol than a person," one whose support on the peninsula probably derived "from his long record of opposition to the Japanese conquest of Korea rather than a respect for his personal views."[20]

Chief lobbyist Oliver was anything but senile, and he got on well with Hilldring.[21] A man of extraordinary energy, Oliver peppered State Department officials with letters and American journals and newspapers with articles.[22] Still, he was most unpopular in the State Department's Office of Far Eastern Affairs, which had equal input into Korea policy as Hilldring. He hardly endeared himself with members of that office when in January he informed them that he was about to contact members of Congress to persuade them that "further appropriations for continuation of Military Government in Korea would be an unwarranted expenditure of the taxpayers' money"; or that, if Rhee did not get his way, he might "give the signal for a general uprising in Korea against Military Government."[23]

Rhee and his allies in Washington drew attention to the Korean issue in a manner that made difficult a continuation of the watch-and-wait strategy of the previous year. Yet the Truman administration had its own reasons for a new initiative and, for the moment, little incentive to move in the direction of an independent South Korea.

II

The State-War-Budget committee on Korea made recommendations on February 25, less than three weeks after its creation and only days after the Truman administration learned that British aid to Greece and Turkey would end in less than two months. The committee proposed that the United States approach the Soviets before the end of the upcoming meeting of foreign ministers in Moscow about negotiations to implement the Moscow agreements of December 1945. Meanwhile, legislation should be presented to Congress to finance "a positive program for economic rehabilitation, educational and governmental improvement, and political guidance for Korea." The first year of this projected three-year program of $600 million would cost $250 million, $113 million more than the amount now allocated for Korea in the proposed War Department budget for fiscal year 1948.[24]

The proposals represented a compromise between the views of Secretary Patterson, who was unpersuaded that important American interests were at stake in Korea and preferred an early U.S. withdrawal, and John Carter Vincent, the director of the Office of Far Eastern Affairs in the State Department, who regarded American interests in Korea as substantial and advocated considerable effort to protect them. The committee emphasized the importance of coordinating action in Congress and an overture in Moscow so the latter would not appear as a sign of weakness to the Soviets. While acknowledging pressure "inspired principally by the Syngman Rhee group" for an independent South Korea, the committee regarded this approach as premature, since the division of the country would produce "starvation and economic chaos" and would represent "a direct breach of our commitments . . . to a liberated people whose treatment by the great powers is watched with concern by all small powers and dependent peoples throughout the world."[25]

A day after the committee submitted its report, the pace of activity on Greece and Turkey picked up. Truman approved a recommendation for extensive aid to both nations and then, on February 27, met with congressional leaders in the White House. The president, a Democrat, had to deal with a budget-conscious legislative branch controlled by Republicans. Although Senator Arthur Vandenberg, the chairman of the Senate Foreign Relations Committee, gave his conditional approval of aid to Greece and Turkey and believed that most of Congress would follow, Truman and his advisers were under no illusions that passing the program would be easy.[26] Selling an additional program for Korea would be harder still.

Despite support for the program in top echelons of the army, Secretary Patterson continued to doubt that Korea was worth the effort. His top assistant, Howard C. Petersen, argued that, "because of our withdrawal from China and because of the political immaturity of the Korean people, their economic situation, etc.," eventual Soviet domination of the peninsula was virtually inevitable once the United States withdrew. Since withdrawal was imperative eventually, the United States was better off doing so sooner rather than later, provided the move did not entail "too great a loss of prestige." Thus, if the Soviets proposed a joint withdrawal, which seemed likely, the United States should not "hold on tenaciously to what is essentially a weak position."[27] If joint withdrawal was consistent with Rhee's last suggestion in his proposed "solution," its anticipated result—Soviet control of all Korea—was hardly what Rhee had in mind.

Patterson did not openly oppose the Korean aid program. Instead, he sought concessions within the administration for a transfer to the State Department of responsibility for operations in Korea and for a progressive withdrawal of American troops from the peninsula. By early April the State Department had agreed that a political adviser should be appointed to negotiate with the Soviets in Korea and eventually take over a civilian administration; that rapid movement should occur toward an indigenous provisional government in South Korea, which would hold authority over domestic affairs; that, if no progress was made with the Soviets on unification, the United States should either take the issue to the United Nations or create an independent government below the thirty-eighth parallel; and that the United States should withdraw from the peninsula within three years.[28]

III

Such agreements made early implementation of a new aid program for Korea all the more important—if, that is, the United States was going to stand a fighting chance of saving the South from Soviet domination. Yet, as the spring progressed, higher priorities elsewhere joined with signals from Congress to delay the administration's presentation of its program to the legislative branch. In early July the State Department gave up entirely its hope of passing even a scaled-back program until the following year.

The concession of temporary defeat came only after the administration had put considerable effort into paving the way in Congress for a Korean aid bill. Two days before Truman's presentation of his proposal to Congress on Greek-Turkish aid, Assistant Secretary Hilldring made a speech in Detroit emphasizing the need to reinforce the American position in South Korea.[29] Three days later Acheson, who with Marshall off to Moscow took on the main burden of selling the measure on Capitol Hill, went out of his way to mention Korea as a candidate for new assistance in testimony before a closed session of the Senate Foreign Relations Committee.[30]

Acheson received plenty of reinforcement in the press. Within a week the *New York Times* editorialized on the need for such aid.[31] Less than a week after that, the same paper used as its lead headline on the front page "BID TO HELP KOREA FORECAST BECAUSE RUSSIA BARS UNITY." The follow-up story stated that Acheson's testimony before the Senate committee had "brought [this issue] into sharp focus."[32] In its Sunday "Week in Review" section on April 6, the paper reprinted a cartoon originally published in the *Rochester Times-Union* showing a bear sitting on an Asian man lying face down on ground marked "Korea" and yelling "Help!" In the distance a benevolent-looking Uncle Sam was carrying a huge sack labeled "Aid to Greece and Turkey." The caption read "Next!" The *New York Times* was far from alone. During late March and early April, numerous newspapers and radio commentators endorsed new aid for Korea. The outpouring came at precisely the time that Marshall in Moscow had proposed to the Soviets the reconvening of the Joint Commission in Korea, which had been adjourned for over ten months.[33] Clearly Acheson, with the help of much of the nation's press, was following through on the interdepartmental committee's proposal to combine an overture to the Soviets on Korea with an initiative for aid.

But this strategy lost momentum during late April and May, when growing apprehensions emerged in Congress over what threatened to become a never-ending expenditure of funds for foreign aid programs. Senator Harry F. Byrd, a powerful Democrat, spoke for many in warning that "new foreign burdens" threatened "increased taxation on an already overburdened people" and even endangered the well-being of the American economy, which was the nation's most potent weapon against Communism.[34] Such concerns became more pronounced after May 8, when Acheson made an important speech in Cleveland, Mississippi, indicating that major new funds soon would be needed to assist with the recovery from war of free nations in Europe and Asia.[35] Although an authorization for Greek-Turkish aid passed both houses in late May, a full appropriation remained in doubt; the War Department's appropriation for civilian relief, not to mention its overall budget for fiscal year 1948, also stood in danger of substantial cuts. The time did not seem opportune for the State Department to request funds for Korea.

The diplomats did not give up easily, however, continuing until July to explore methods of getting Korean aid through Congress.[36] No method materialized. On July 7 Major General Archer Lerch, the American military governor in Korea who was visiting Washington, wrote General Hodge that "a very definite revolution [was] going on in Congress against the State Department." Legislators felt that administration requests for foreign programs had been "sloppily handled." Consultation had been inadequate, proposed aid to foreign countries had been "piecemeal," and funds requested had been excessive. Legislators might not even pass appropriations to sustain the effort in Greece. Marshall, who in early June had delivered a well-publicized address at Harvard University projecting a large aid program for the recovery of Europe, now planned "to study the needs of the world as a whole, to roll it all up into one big request, and if, as appears quite likely now, Congress meets in a special session this fall, he will present the whole thing at one time."[37] For the moment, the best he could do to show U.S. concern about Korea was to include the peninsula in the itinerary of Lieutenant General Albert C. Wedemeyer, who had just been appointed to head a mission to China to study American policy there.[38]

IV

The situation regarding U.S. support for South Korea got worse before it got better. During the summer Congress cut $45 million from the administration's proposed relief funds for Korea for fiscal year 1948 and over seventy thousand officers and civilian employees from the army.[39] The latter reduction did not explicitly address Korea, but its impact was considerable, as foreign occupations inherently involved a high proportion of officers and civilians to combat soldiers.

Faced with such cuts, the army had to make difficult choices regarding its four occupations—Germany, Austria, Japan, and Korea. As usual, Korea proved to be "the end of the line." Earlier in the year Army Chief of Staff Dwight D. Eisenhower had opined that "in the long run the costs of our retreat from Korea would be far, far greater than any present or contemplated appropriation to maintain ourselves there."[40] In September, however, he signed off on the judgment of the Joint Chiefs of Staff that the United States had "little strategic interest" in maintaining troops on the peninsula. If the Soviets extended their control over the entire country, they would increase their capacity "to interfere with United States communications and operations in East China, Manchuria, the Yellow Sea, Sea of Japan and adjacent islands." Yet the United States could neutralize such a threat "by air action," which "would be more feasible and less costly than large-scale ground operations."[41]

In fact, army officials believed that Korea was of considerable importance and that American abandonment of the South would have substantial consequences, both physical and psychological, in Japan and China.[42] But they had been worn down by attacks on the occupation by Rhee, from Congress, and in the press, and by complaints from soldiers stationed there—or their families back home—about primitive conditions on the peninsula and the failure of the army to provide a reasonable standard of living.[43] Lacking a powerful constituency to hang on in Korea, the army was now anxious to "bug out."

The State Department, concerned about American credibility worldwide, remained determined to launch a salvaging operation. Since the reconvening of the Joint Commission in May 1947 had not led to an end to the stalemate with the Soviets on procedures for unification, by September State Department officials were ready to take the Korean issue to the UN General Assembly. The Soviets probably would resist the American scheme for UN-supervised elections as a method for establishing an independent, united country, even though American observers there knew the Communists would have an excellent chance of emerging victorious through such a process.[44] If the Soviets did resist, the Americans would push the international body to supervise elections and to endorse establishment of an independent regime in the South alone. With American troops on the way out and U.S. economic aid an uncertainty, prospects for such a regime were not good, but at least the course would assuage the tenacious and passionately anti-Communist Rhee, who by all accounts—and for good or ill— was the most effective political leader in the South.[45]

As already noted, in less than a year, implementation of the State Department's plan led to establishment of the ROK under Rhee leadership. Less than two months before this event, Congress passed an economic aid bill that included $150 million for Korea. A year late and $100 million less than the initial allotment projected by the interdepartmental committee in February 1947, the sum was still over $30 million greater than the mere relief funds provided for fiscal year 1948.[46] And despite ongoing pressure from the army to withdraw American troops from the peninsula—by the end of 1948 there would be fewer than eight thousand remaining—the State Department continued to insist that the United States had a commitment to South Korea from which it could not lightly retreat.

Still, conditions in the South were far from stable. To undermine sources of unrest in the countryside, the Americans during March 1948 finally had taken the initiative to redistribute formerly Japanese-held land to the peasants who worked it; but this affected just under one in four members of the farm population.[47] In April a major revolt broke out on Cheju Island off the south coast of Korea. Despite brutal repressive measures by police, constabulary, and rightist youth corps from the mainland, unrest continued into the fall. In mid-October, two thousand troops in the ROK constabulary revolted as they were about to debark for Cheju from the port city of Yosu. The revolt quickly spread to the nearby railway junction at Sunch'on. Early the next month more constabulary revolted at Taegu, the third-largest city in the South. Rhee soon declared martial law over one-fourth of South Korea, although his suppression campaign was so inept that many of the rebels escaped into the mountains to join already existing guerrilla bands.[48]

Soviet actions complicated matters for the Americans. Less than a month following establishment of the ROK in August 1948, the Soviets formed the Democratic People's Republic in the North. Led by Kim Il-sung, this regime, like its southern counterpart, claimed authority over the entire peninsula. Unlike its counterpart it was in firm control over its half of the country, and it showed no inhibition about seeking to undermine its rival through covert action below the thirty-eighth parallel.[49] Moscow, in turn, felt confident enough of the DPRK's strength to withdraw its last troops from Korea at the end of the year, thus putting pressure on the Americans to do the same.[50] With the Communists in China marching to victory against the Nationalists in neighboring Manchuria and the tide moving in the Communists' favor farther to the south as well, the prospects for an internally weak South Korea were far from promising.

I NOW RETURN TO THE FUNDAMENTAL QUESTIONS OF RHEE'S AND the Truman Doctrine's impact on U.S. policy toward Korea, as well as the impact of the preceding sequence on the coming of war to the peninsula. As Rhee visited Washington in early 1947 and the executive branch of the American government moved to formulate the doctrine, a process began of reevaluating Korea policy. This reevaluation led to the conclusion, most firmly held in the State Department but also adhered to by top military brass, that new expenditures were essential to protect the U.S. position in Korea. The State Department planned to present to Congress a program for such expenditures once Greek and Turkish aid had passed, and Rhee and his allies had little impact on the process. Their marginal influence is made all the more apparent by the fact that, in the spring, the United States initiated an approach in Moscow to reopen the Joint Commission, a move in direct conflict with Rhee's wishes.

By early in the summer of 1947, growing concerns in Congress about expenditures abroad, which were heightened by the administration's intention to request large sums for the recovery of Europe, ruined any prospect for passage of the program for Korean assistance. That fact, joined with the continuing stalemate with the Soviets on unifying Korea, the reduction of the U.S. military budget by Congress, and the ever-growing pressure in the South to grant independence, produced the American move to the United Nations in September.

Here it is essential to return to the question of Rhee's influence. As Hilldring later wrote to Oliver, once the United States took the Korean issue to the United Nations, "everything fell into place quickly."[51] That is, the United States abandoned trusteeship, with its effort to cooperate with the Soviet Union, and adopted a course that led, in less than a year, to creation of an independent South Korea. Rhee, in short, had his way.

Yet was this outcome a result, as Hilldring suggested, of "the persistent and patient labors of Rhee, Oliver and Limb that converted first one and then another official and reporter to the point of view that to deal honestly with Korea . . . was more important than to persist in the error [of trusteeship] for fear of displeasing Russia?"[52] The evidence provides little reason to conclude that Oliver's or Limb's activities in the United States influenced the outcome. Officials in the State Department, the key players in adopting the policy of moving to the United Nations and then to an independent South Korea at a time when military leaders cared little about anything but withdrawal from the peninsula, did not need Oliver's or Limb's input to detect the options available to them.

Nor did the press play a significant role in the process. Korea in 1947 was not important enough in the minds of Americans to receive sustained attention in the most prominent print media. After the brief flurry of activity for Korean aid early in the spring, the peninsula largely disappeared from view.[53] Oliver's pen, prolific as it was, could not penetrate the minds of enough citizens or officials to help shape policy.

Rhee, though, did make a mark, but because of what he did in Korea, not in the United States. Indeed, his stature in Washington was so low that, at the end of March, the State Department was able to block arrangements for him to fly home in an American military plane. Then, after he booked to Tokyo on a Northwest Airlines flight and even gained an audience with General Douglas MacArthur, the U.S. occupation commander in Japan, he took a side trip to China to meet with Generalissimo Chiang Kai-shek, only to be delayed further in his return to Korea by Hodge, who struggled to prepare South Koreans for the reconvening of the Joint Commission.[54]

Before Rhee departed from Washington, Acting Secretary of State Acheson wrote a biting assessment of him. Back in 1945, Acheson recalled, U.S. occupation leaders had given Rhee every opportunity to rally South Koreans around him; but "his sympathy toward conservative banking, landlord and merchant classes, his opposition to the terms of the Moscow Accords, his uncompromising attitude toward those who opposed him and his close association with a number of Koreans and Americans who . . . advocate the Korean cause solely for . . . personal advantage, alienated many moderate elements in Korean politics and identified him as a right wing extremist." Still, Acheson conceded, "he has . . . retained great emotional popularity in Korea."[55] In the spring and summer of 1947, Rhee's continuing "great emotional popularity" in South Korea and his ability to exploit it in his campaign against trusteeship contributed to the eventual shift in U.S. policy.

Hodge's worries about Rhee's presence back in Korea were borne out by events. In May, with the Joint Commission about to reconvene, the State Department's political adviser in Korea, William Langdon, wired home that the "Rhee, Kim Koo crowd have been trying to stage anti-trusteeship demonstrations, which we have blocked." Simultaneously, Rhee and his allies attempted "to bulldoze all rightist parties and groups into their movement so that the latter might automatically excommunicate themselves from consultation under the Commission's new rules," which excluded organizations that fomented or instigated "active opposition to . . . the fulfillment of the Moscow decision."

According to Langdon, Rhee calculated that, once the United States faced the choice of establishing an "extreme leftist if not a Communist provisional government" through the Joint Commission or abandoning that body, it would choose the latter. This, in turn, would pave the way for establishment of a rightist government in the South alone.[56]

Integrated into Rhee's antitrusteeship campaign was the theme that Hodge was not following American policy, that while Rhee had been in Washington he had received an assurance from Hilldring that the United States favored his plan for immediate creation of an independent government in the South.[57] Such claims were untrue, but they were widely circulated in South Korea and, until mid-August, without direct rebuttal from Washington, where the State Department feared it would simply draw attention to Rhee.[58]

Meanwhile, despite being held for a time under virtual house arrest by the American military government, Rhee succeeded eventually in organizing demonstrations against trusteeship. With civil administration along with the police now in the hands of Koreans, most of whom had collaborated with the Japanese, Rhee's right-wing nationalism appealed to most government workers. These people, after all, were likely to lose their jobs if the Soviets and the Americans reached agreement in the Joint Commission. In addition, Rhee retained support from well-organized nationalist youth corps and the conservative Korean Democratic Party.[59] With such backing, he prevented the Americans from squelching open dissent against trusteeship. That dissent, in turn, ensured problems in the Joint Commission, where the Soviets continued their demand to exclude key rightist groups from consultation for opposing the Moscow Accords.[60]

Rhee gained additional fuel for his campaign against Hodge when in early July Washington announced that General Wedemeyer would visit Korea on a fact-finding mission. Characterizing Wedemeyer as "one of my closest friends," Rhee spread the word that the general's visit demonstrated the truth of his claim that Hodge was not carrying out the wishes of his superiors at home.[61] In an immediate sense, Rhee lost ground when the State Department declared in mid-August that Hodge was merely carrying out U.S. policy. Shortly thereafter, the visiting Wedemeyer refused to give Rhee special treatment.[62] Yet during the previous month an assassin's bullet had felled Yo Un-hyong and with him the last faint hope for a centrist coalition.[63]

Chance events aside, Rhee was a remarkably resilient leader who possessed strength not only because he appeared to Koreans to possess an inside track in Washington but also because he was willing to stand up to the occupier when Korean interests seemed in jeopardy. By early September the Joint Commission was a dead letter, new American economic assistance was nowhere in sight, and the standing of the United States below the thirty-eighth parallel was more precarious than ever.[64] Rhee had won his gamble that the Americans would refuse to abandon the Right in the Joint Commission and thus pave the way for a leftist government throughout the country.

Even so, Rhee exerted limited influence on American policy. The leading analyst of the Soviet side argues that Moscow "was never [will-

ing] to sacrifice North Korea . . . [to anything short of] a leftist government in Seoul."[65] This being the case, the Soviets, even without the
excuse of rightist opposition to trusteeship, would have found a way
to deadlock the Joint Commission.[66] In this light, trusteeship was the
occasion rather than the cause of the Soviet-American stalemate, and
Rhee's activities were of peripheral importance. At most, had Rhee and
his allies supported U.S. efforts and worked to engender stability in
South Korean politics rather than the reverse, the shift in American
policy would have come later than it actually did, and probably not
much later at that. With economic deterioration in the U.S. zone on
the rise and interest in Korea in the Pentagon and Congress on the
wane, an initiative toward withdrawal and the creation of an independent state for half of the peninsula was inevitable within a matter of
months.

Actually, Rhee's contribution to the process was greatest not in producing the Soviet-American stalemate or in persuading the Americans
to create an independent South Korea but in polarizing politics below
the thirty-eighth parallel in a manner that eliminated prospects for a
center coalition. When an independent South Korea finally emerged
during 1948, it was in the hands of a government of the far Right
rather than a more broad-based regime to the liking of the United
States.

This analysis highlights the basic truth that the Truman Doctrine,
whatever its universalistic rhetoric, was merely part of an ongoing
process through which the United States took on and sustained new
responsibilities for world order. The move also accentuates the reality
of Korea's low standing on the list of U.S. priorities before June 25,
1950.[67] Had needs in Korea not escalated sharply virtually simultaneously with those in southeastern and Western Europe, the peninsula might have received a priority in Washington that would have
permitted the reasonable protection of commitments derived from the
decision to occupy half the country in 1945. As it was, the rapidly
deteriorating conditions in more strategic areas and the attitudes of
legislators unaccustomed to huge peacetime expenditures abroad
made Korea policy a constant patchwork. If that condition served to
nudge the United States along more rapidly toward granting indepen

dence to a South Korea under Rhee's leadership, it also helped to leave the new state in a highly vulnerable position. This outcome derived primarily from outside forces, namely the decisions of the Soviet Union and the United States.

Yet neither of the great powers could eradicate the thirst of Koreans for national unity. Both the ROK and the DPRK reserved the right to employ force in achieving unification, and both the great powers had left their clients with indigenous armies. For the moment neither army possessed the wherewithal to overwhelm the other. Whether with time this would change depended in part on South Korea's ability to contain and then resolve its internal divisions, but also on events in China, where tens of thousands of Koreans fought on the Communist side in the civil war, and on developments in Washington and Moscow. While the end of the occupations had shifted power on the peninsula somewhat in the direction of indigenous forces, these remained dependent—economically, politically, and militarily—on sponsorship from the outside. In this respect Rhee's success since 1945 in manipulating conditions in the South to prod the United States toward a policy of independence and division, combined with his indifference to social and economic change, had produced a strained relationship between the ROK and its sponsor. Joined with political and bureaucratic conditions in the United States, this relationship could make deterrence against adventurism in the North a difficult course to sustain. By the end of 1948, therefore, all-out war on the peninsula was more imaginable than at any time since 1945.

CHAPTER 3

Why the Korean War, Not the Korean Civil War?

THE KOREAN WAR BEGAN IN THE PREDAWN HOURS OF JUNE 25, 1950, a rainy Sunday along the two-hundred-mile boundary between North and South Korea. At around 4:00 A.M. North Korean units positioned just north of the thirty-eighth parallel on the isolated Ongjin Peninsula launched an artillery barrage against ROK forces to the south. A North Korean ground attack followed shortly thereafter. Moving eastward, at about 5:00 A.M. North Korean artillery started shelling Kaesong, Korea's ancient capital located two miles below the thirty-eighth parallel. A half hour after that, the major thrust of the invasion began along two roads down the Uijonbu Corridor headed toward Seoul. North Korean attacks also occurred in the center of the peninsula directed at Chunchon and on the east coast.[1]

The invasion achieved complete tactical surprise. Many South Korean officers and their American advisers in the five-hundred-man Korean Military Advisory Group were away from their units on weekend passes. Most of the four divisions and one regiment in the ROK army stationed near the thirty-eighth parallel were actually located ten to thirty miles to the south, thus leaving defensive positions on the border thinly manned. Despite the surprise, over the next three days ROK units at several points south of the parallel put up a spirited resistance to the invaders.

Yet the attackers enjoyed huge advantages over enemy forces. In assault troops North Korea outnumbered the ROK army by about 89,000 to 65,000, and perhaps 40,000 of the former were combat-hardened from participation on the Communist side in the recently concluded civil war on mainland China.[2] The North Koreans were equipped with at least 150 tanks provided by the Soviet Union; the ROK forces had neither tanks nor antitank weapons that could penetrate the Soviet armor. The North also possessed a small tactical air force of over two hundred planes, again courtesy the Soviet Union; the South had fewer than two dozen aircraft. In divisional artillery the northerners enjoyed a three-to-one advantage in numbers, and their Soviet-supplied guns had a maximum range of fourteen thousand yards, compared with the southerners' eighty-two hundred.[3]

By the early hours of June 28, Seoul—located less than thirty miles from the border—was on the verge of collapse to the North Koreans. In the prevailing chaos and panic in the city, an ROK demolition team blew up the key bridge over the Han River before critical supplies and several military units had escaped across it. The action destroyed any prospect of mounting a strong resistance on the south side of the river.

In the United States, meanwhile, the Truman administration had been laying the political and military groundwork for rescuing the ROK. Eastern daylight time was thirteen hours behind Korea time, so officials in Washington learned of North Korea's attack late on Saturday evening, the twenty-fourth. The State Department immediately recommended to President Truman that the issue be taken to the United Nations. Truman agreed, and the United States contacted UN Secretary-General Trygve Lie with an urgent request for an emergency meeting of the Security Council.[4]

That meeting convened in New York at 2:00 P.M. on Sunday afternoon. All Security Council members attended except the Soviet Union,

Summer 1950

U.S.S.R.

Vladivostok

C H I N A
(MANCHURIA)

Tumen R.

Roshin

Chongjin

Yalu R.

Chosan

Sinuiju

SEA OF
JAPAN

Hungnam

Pyongyang

Wonsan

**Start of North Korean Offensive
June 25, 1950**

NORTH
KOREA   38th parallel

Ongjin

Chunchon

SOUTH
KOREA

Seoul

Inchon

Osan

Controlled by U.N.

Communist advances

Controlled by
Communists

Taejon

Pohang

Kunsan

Taegu

**Pusan Perimeter
September 14, 1950**

YELLOW
SEA

Sunchon

Pusan

Mokpo

0   100

Miles

MAP 3. The military situation in Korea, June 25 to September 14, 1950.

which was boycotting the body, allegedly in protest of its failure to
replace the Nationalist with the Communist government of China in
that country's seat. By this time, the United Nations Commission on
Korea had wired Secretary-General Lie from Seoul, confirming American reports of a North Korean attack and concluding that it had

© Hulton Archive

FIG. 9. The United Nations Security Council discusses the Korean issue on June 30, 1950, as U.S. troops were being rushed from Japan to Korea. The Soviet Union was boycotting the UN Security Council at the time, so the Soviet seat is empty.

produced a "serious situation which is assuming [the] character of full-scale war and may endanger the maintenance of international peace and security."[5] The U.S. representative to the Security Council noted this conclusion and presented a resolution declaring a breach of the peace in Korea. It called on North Korea to cease hostilities and withdraw its forces to the thirty-eighth parallel, and it requested UN members to assist in bringing this about. Less than four hours after convening—just over a day after fighting had commenced in faraway Korea—the Security Council passed the resolution with minor revisions. Only Yugoslavia's abstention prevented unanimity.

Two days later, as the North Koreans marched into Seoul, the Security Council met again. Again the Soviet Union was unrepresented, and again the United States presented a resolution, this time asking the Security Council to recommend "that members of the United Nations furnish such assistance to the Republic of Korea as may be necessary to repel the armed attack and to restore international peace and security in the area."[6] Late on June 27 the Security Council passed the resolution with the bare minimum of seven affirmative votes.

Already the United States was aiding the Republic of Korea with arms, ammunition, and air support from Japan—and elements of the Seventh Fleet were steaming northward from the Philippines to help out as well. In the wee hours of June 30, with ROK forces continuing to retreat in the face of the North Korean onslaught, President Truman approved U.S. Far Eastern Commander Douglas MacArthur's request to deploy an American regimental combat team from Japan to the area of battle on the peninsula. Later that morning Truman accepted his field commander's call for a two-division American buildup in Korea. Within less than a week of North Korea's attack, the United States had committed itself, with UN support, to the military defense of South Korea.

The war would last more than three years. The United States would eventually deploy over three hundred thousand ground troops to the peninsula. Fifteen other foreign governments would commit combat units to the UN effort. On the North Korean side, the People's Republic of China would send more than a million soldiers, and the Soviets would covertly deploy hundreds of pilots and artillery personnel. Over half the military casualties would be suffered by non-Koreans, and a large portion of the casualties to Korean civilians would come at the hands of foreigners, especially UN airmen bombing and strafing territory above the thirty-eighth parallel.

These facts alone suggest that, for better or worse, the Korean War was not in essence a civil war, that its course cannot begin to be understood without devoting considerable attention to foreign involvement. Yet some scholars argue to the contrary. The Korean War, they insist, was fundamentally civil in nature, and they ground their case primarily in origins.[7]

Here I will set aside the question of whether or not an understanding of the conflict should derive largely from its origins or its course. Clearly, both are important. But for the sake of good sportsmanship—

or, less high-mindedly, good sport—I will contest the issue on the terms of the other side. I will argue that, even if we center on origins, the fighting that began between Koreans on June 25, 1950, and so quickly expanded to include the Americans cannot be understood without heavy reference to nations and forces beyond the peninsula; that although the fighting contained an important civil dimension, its outbreak at that time and at that place can only be explained through the interaction of Korean and non-Korean elements and through decisions made in Moscow, Beijing, and Washington, as well as in Pyongyang and Seoul. The fact is that, however nationalistic Koreans may have been—they were intensely so—their fate was so closely tied to the designs of the United States, the Soviet Union, and China that their ability to act independently was severely circumscribed.

I

To highlight the argument, it is necessary to review the years 1945 through 1948. There can be no more striking reflection of Korea's dependence on others than the decision to divide the peninsula into occupation zones in 1945. Koreans had no input in the decision because they had no recognized government or armed forces to defend their interests. They had been swallowed up in the Japanese empire early in the century and were now being freed from that status because of Japan's defeat in a war in which Koreans had contributed more to the losing than to the winning side. Prospects for the peaceful unification of Korea from August 1945 onward were between slim and nil. The first step toward June 25, 1950, had been taken by the great powers—alone.

Once the Soviets and the Americans were in Korea, indigenous peoples played anything but a passive role. By the end of 1947, over eight hundred thousand Koreans would move from the northern to the southern zone.[8] Long before that—indeed, even before the Japanese withdrawal—Koreans began to organize themselves locally into "people's committees." Just prior to the American arrival in September 1945, some Korean leaders of the moderate and extreme Left declared a People's Republic in Seoul, which purported to represent the entire nation. They were countered on the Right by landowners and other collaborators with the Japanese, who rushed to create the Korean Democratic Party. When exiled Korean leaders returned to the American zone in October and November, they quickly adopted a position in opposition to the People's Republic and, in many cases, in favor of the Korean Provisional Government, which had been established in China in 1919. When, in December 1945, the Soviets and Americans reached an agreement on Korea at Moscow that included the possibility of a five-year, multipower trusteeship over the peninsula, conservative forces in the South rose in protest. In the North, conservative leader Cho Man-sik objected as well.

Yet in both the North and the South, outsiders set the boundaries of political action. The Americans and the Soviets refused to work with the People's Republic. Americans in the South favored conservative Koreans, initially ones who had collaborated with the Japanese, then returning exiles from China and the United States; the Soviets in the North favored leftists, at first mostly ones from the Korean underground but eventually many who had spent the bulk of the last decade in exile in Manchuria and/or the Soviet Union. The Soviets tried to work with Cho Man-sik, but when he protested trusteeship in early 1946, he was arrested.

Koreans in 1945 were deeply split among themselves—between close collaborators with the Japanese and underground dissenters; between landowners and peasants; between businessmen and factory workers; between police and civilians. These divisions had festered beneath the surface before 1945, as the Japanese used the strategy of divide and conquer to ease the task of ruling Korea. The collaborationist issue aside, many of the disputes were foreshadowed in the divisions among exiled independence groups.[9] After liberation from Japan they burst into the open on the peninsula itself. Their existence eliminated any chance for a united indigenous resistance to the country's partition by outsiders. Yet the particular form the divisions took and the ultimate outcome of the resulting conflicts were deeply influenced, indeed often determined, by the foreign presence. That the exiled groups during the Japanese period had looked to outsiders for assistance—Nationalist China and the United States in the case of the Right, the Soviet Union and Communist China in the case of the Left—and that one of the outsiders on each side now occupied half of Korea greatly magnified the problem.

The trusteeship issue represented an extreme case, since it was totally created by the outsiders. Although the Soviets were able to keep the Korean Left in line on trusteeship, the Americans never persuaded the indigenous Right to support it—or even to exercise restraint in attacking it. Ultimately the United States gave in to Syngman Rhee and abandoned trusteeship, but only because, by September 1947, he represented the best hope for keeping South Korea out of Communist hands, an important U.S. objective in its own right.

By the end of 1948, two indigenous governments existed on the peninsula, one exercising authority above the thirty-eighth parallel, one below it, one leftist in orientation and aligned with the Soviet Union, the other rightist and aligned with the United States. It is impossible to imagine this result without the Soviet-American agreement of 1945.

If the situation in Korea at the end of 1948 cannot be grasped without reference to the foreign presence since 1945, it is also fair to say that the picture is incomplete without mention of the civil conflict that had waxed and waned below the thirty-eighth parallel since the fall of 1946. The unrest began in September with strikes and riots by workers in several cities and soon spread to the countryside, where landlords became frequent objects of attack. Hundreds of civilians and police died in the turmoil. The Left lost heavily in the violence, and for the next year, while unrest was widespread at the village level, it appears not to have been as well coordinated as before.[10]

The violence picked up greatly during 1948, with the biggest revolt against government authority beginning in April on Cheju Island. By the end of the year, guerrillas operated extensively on the mainland, so much so that the United States decided to postpone withdrawal of the last of its combat troops from the South. Six of South Korea's eight provinces eventually saw substantial guerrilla activity, which peaked in the fall of 1949 and subsided in the spring of 1950 as a result of strong counteraction by ROK forces. Violence in the South from late

1946 to mid-1950 brought death to some one hundred thousand Koreans.[11]

Outsiders played a prominent role in the violence. Historian Bruce Cumings notes that the Americans "organized and equipped the southern counterinsurgent forces, gave them their best intelligence materials, planned their actions, and occasionally commanded them directly."[12] Americans were particularly prominent in the winter suppression campaign of 1949–50. An American journalist exaggerated only slightly in October 1949 when he wrote that "only American money, weapons, and technical assistance enable [the ROK] to exist for more than a few hours."[13]

If the Americans were instrumental in suppressing the activity, the Soviets played an integral role in fostering it. Although the general strike in South Korea of September 1946 appears to have begun at the initiative of the Korean Communist Party below the thirty-eighth parallel, the Soviets soon took an active part, giving advice, which the southern rebels often solicited, encouragement, and considerable financial aid. The Soviets also pushed successfully for the merger of the three leftist parties in the two zones and participated in the training and infiltration of North Korean agents and guerrillas into the South.[14]

The unrest in South Korea grew in part out of local conditions, but neither its origins nor its course can be understood without devoting heavy attention to activities originating in the North or to actions heavily influenced by the Soviet and American presence on the peninsula. The local, national, and international forces blended together in a manner that would have made the actual course of events largely unrecognizable with the elimination of any of the three.

II

The same can be said of the more immediate sources of the North Korean attack of June 25, 1950. Kim Il-sung and Syngman Rhee were fiercely nationalistic and determined to reunite their country under their own rule. That both understood this quality in the other augmented the sense of urgency in each to achieve the objective. Rhee's advanced age further augmented his sense of urgency, since he could not help but regard time as of the essence if he was to achieve the distinction of leading a united, independent nation. He understood fully that this goal could be achieved only through the use of force, a method that he was perfectly willing to employ. Yet it was Kim's North, not Rhee's South, that launched the attack that set the peninsula aflame in a three-year orgy of violence far surpassing what had come before. To understand that fact we must examine events in the broader East Asian region, the Soviet Union, and the United States during the year and a half prior to the outbreak of war.

Kim first requested Stalin's permission to attack the South in a conversation in Moscow on March 7, 1949. The North Korean leader argued, according to the Soviet record, that "reactionary forces" would never accept "peaceful unification" and would simply wait "until they feel themselves strong enough to attack the North." At present, he claimed, "our armed forces are stronger, and in addition we have the support of a powerful guerrilla movement in the South." Southerners, who hated the present regime, would "certainly help us as well."[15]

Stalin demurred, pointing out that the North Korean army lacked "overwhelming superiority over the troops of the South," that U.S. soldiers remained in the South and were likely to "interfere in case of hostilities," and that an agreement existed on the thirty-eighth parallel between Washington and Moscow, giving the Americans all the more reason to intervene in response to an attack from the North. He told Kim to be patient, that his opportunity would come if South Korea attacked first, in which case everyone would support him in a counterattack.[16]

This meeting occurred during Kim's first visit to Moscow. In another meeting Kim pleaded with Stalin for "machines, equipment, and spare parts for industry, communications, transport and also for other branches of the national economy." In addition, Kim asked for transport planes and for Soviet specialists to assist in planning factory, plant, and dam construction and in "conducting geological exploratory work." Finally, he requested that Soviet teachers be sent to help train students in technical skills and the Russian language and that advanced North Korean students be permitted to study in the Soviet

Union.[17] As historian Kathryn Weathersby remarks, these requests join with other evidence to show that North Korea was "utterly dependent economically on the Soviet Union. . . . The collapse of the Japanese empire, Soviet occupation policy, and the civil war in China [had cut] North Korea . . . off from its former economic ties with southern Korea, Japan and Manchuria. Except for very limited trade with Hong Kong and two Manchurian ports, . . . the Soviet Union was the only source of supply and the only market for North Korean goods."[18] Kim was in no position to launch an invasion of the South without massive Soviet support, and he knew it.

So he continued to lobby Stalin. In mid-August, on the eve of Soviet ambassador Terentii Shytkov's departure for Moscow on vacation, North Korean leaders approached him with a new request to resolve Korea's division by force. American troops had now withdrawn from the country, and guerrilla infiltration into the South was on the rise. Military activity along the thirty-eighth parallel between DPRK and ROK forces was often intense. It had begun late the previous year, but in early May it had picked up significantly, mostly as a result of initiatives from the South. The fighting sometimes escalated into pitched battles involving thousands of men and producing hundreds of casualties, developments that were not to the liking of the Soviets.[19] Stalin even feared that the final withdrawal of U.S. soldiers in June was part of a scheme to free ROK troops to launch an all-out invasion of the North.[20] The North Koreans pointed out to Shytkov that the ROK had clearly rejected recent proposals for peaceful unification, but also that it appeared to have postponed a major offensive northward in favor of establishing a strong defensive position. Furthermore, Kim asserted that the U.S. withdrawal removed Stalin's objections based on concern about American intervention, as U.S. soldiers would no longer become immediately involved; nor would the thirty-eighth parallel agreement come into play because it had merely been intended to designate the boundary between Soviet and American occupation forces. Kim also believed that recent border skirmishes with ROK units indicated his army's clear superiority. Shytkov was dubious, but he indicated to Stalin that it was "militarily advisable" for North Korea to take over the Ongjin Peninsula.[21]

In early September the North Koreans proposed to begin an offensive operation by seizing this territory and perhaps moving eastward as far as Kaesong. Then, if "the international situation permits," the North Korean army could seize the rest of the South, an action that could take as little as two weeks and no more than two months.[22]

On September 24, after careful study by the Soviets, the Politburo in Moscow rejected the proposal on three grounds. Militarily, North Korea possessed "no superiority over the South"; politically, neither propaganda for peaceful unification of the country nor the guerrilla movement had been exploited adequately to prepare the people of the South; and diplomatically, a ground offensive would give the Americans a pretext for condemning the DPRK at the United Nations and for reintroducing troops to the peninsula. It was only if the ROK launched an offensive northward, Stalin emphasized, that Kim "must be ready and then act according to the situation."[23]

In early 1950 Stalin began to change his position. On January 19 Shytkov sent a telegram to Moscow describing a luncheon conversation he had had with Kim and others two days earlier. "In a mood of some intoxication," the ambassador reported, the North Korean leader had exclaimed that "lately I do not sleep at night" thinking about unification. He pressed for another meeting with Stalin or, short of that, one with Mao Zedong, the Chinese Communist leader, who was then in Moscow. Surely once Mao returned from Beijing, he would "have orders on all questions." Kim declared himself a Communist and "a disciplined person [for whom] . . . the order of Comrade Stalin is law," but he also asserted that Mao had promised him assistance in achieving unification once the civil war was over in China. During the previous summer the Chinese Communists had returned to the North two divisions of Koreans who had fought the Nationalists in Manchuria.[24] Obviously Kim believed that, with the Nationalist Chinese ejected from the mainland and holed up precariously on Taiwan, Hainan, and some smaller islands off the coast, it was time for Mao to go even further in fulfilling his promise.[25] The continuing inability of guerrillas in the South to overthrow the ROK added to Kim's impatience, although the weakness of his personal power base below the thirty-eighth parallel surely predisposed him from the start in favor of a prominent role for the DPRK army in unifying the country.[26] Stalin replied to Kim on January 30, stating that he was "ready to help him [Kim] in this matter" and to meet him again, emphasizing the need for "large preparation" to avoid "too great a risk."[27] In early February Stalin approved Kim's request for modern arms to equip three new North Korean army divisions.[28]

Why did Stalin change his mind? Key evidence comes from a Soviet report summarizing his conversations with Kim while the latter visited Moscow from March 30 to April 25. Stalin dwelled on the improved "international environment," the most significant contribution to which was the Communist victory in China. Now that Mao was "no longer busy with internal fighting," he could commit his "attention and energy to the assistance of Korea." If necessary, he could even send troops. The China situation was "important psychologically" as well, as it demonstrated the strength of "Asian revolutionaries" and the weakness of their adversaries and "their mentors . . . in America," who would "not dare to challenge the new Chinese authorities militarily." The Sino-Soviet Treaty of Friendship, Alliance, and Mutual Assistance, signed in February, reinforced this pattern, as did the Soviet explosion of an atomic bomb the previous August. "According to information coming from the United States," Stalin said, "the prevailing mood is not to interfere" in Korea. Apparently this was a reference to the U.S. National Security Council paper of late December 1948, NSC-48, which along with Secretary of State Dean Acheson's speech of January 12, 1950, defined the American defense perimeter in the Pacific as excluding territories on mainland Asia. The NSC paper appears to have been available to Stalin courtesy of his spies in the United States, who included Kim Philby, the British liaison officer to the American Central Intelligence Agency.[29]

Stalin continued to fear the American response to a North Korean attack. He made it clear to Kim that, if he ran into difficulty with the United States, he would have to depend on China, not the Soviet Union, to bail him out. He insisted that Kim receive Mao's advance approval for the attack. The Soviet leader also insisted on careful preparations, both military and political. In the second area the attack must follow new North Korean proposals for peaceful unification and their rejection by the ROK. The attack should commence on the Ong-jin Peninsula, as Kim had suggested, where it could most plausibly be disguised as a counter to a South Korean move. The North Koreans must defeat the enemy swiftly, as this would not give the Americans "time to put up a strong resistance and to mobilize international support." Kim assured Stalin that the war would be won in three days, that North Korea's conventional attack would be reinforced by a major guerrilla uprising in the South.[30]

If in an immediate sense the rise of the Chinese Communists and the negotiation of a Sino-Soviet treaty increased Stalin's confidence in dealing with the United States in northeast Asia, other aspects of the Sino-Soviet relationship created apprehension regarding the Soviet strategic position in the region over the long term. The treaty that Stalin had signed with Nationalist leader Chiang Kai-shek in 1945 granted the Soviets a naval base at Port Arthur and joint administration of the Chinese Eastern Railway, which connected that port to Soviet territory. Thus the Soviets gained control over a coveted warm water port in the Far East. At minimum Mao wanted to revise this "unequal" treaty, while Stalin was naturally reluctant to accommodate him. The latter finally agreed to a new treaty, but he moved forward only under pressure from Mao and in the midst of a palpable effort by the United States and Great Britain to split the two Communist giants.[31] The new agreement stated that the Soviets were to give up their control of Port Arthur and the railway at the signing of a peace treaty with Japan or, at the latest, by the end of 1952.[32] Technically, the terms were more transparent than real, as a secret protocol guaranteed the Soviets the right to transport troops and supplies through Manchuria under conditions similar to those articulated in the 1945 treaty. Yet Stalin surely understood that it was only a matter of time before the Chinese undermined Soviet privileges in Manchuria, and this meant the loss of direct control over its warm-water port. This development gave unification of Korea under a friendly regime new importance to Stalin. As early as March of the previous year, he had reached agreement with Kim Il-sung on building a railroad from the Soviet Union into the North, which if expanded south of the thirty-eighth parallel could serve to link the Soviet maritime provinces with warm-water ports at Inchon, at Pusan, and on Cheju Island.[33]

With the Sino-Soviet treaty signed in February and Kim chomping at the bit to attack southward, Stalin's tasks were to sign on Mao to the North's venture and to assist with its effective execution. On the first task the Soviet leader gave Kim the initiative. The Korean premier visited Beijing in mid-May and presented his plan to the Chinese leadership, claiming that Stalin already had approved. Mao immediately queried Stalin, who replied that he agreed with the North Korean idea "to commence unification" during the summer but "that the final decision . . . must be made jointly by Chinese and Korean comrades."[34]

Mao gave his consent, albeit reluctantly. The reluctance derived from the timing. Although Mao's forces had recently captured Hainan, Taiwan remained in Nationalist hands. The Chinese leader naturally preferred to eliminate this last enemy redoubt before Kim launched his venture. During the previous year he had hoped to attain this objective in 1950. In October and November, however, his forces had been repulsed, with substantial losses, in efforts to capture the islands of Jinmen and Dengbu, which were only a few miles off the China coast. Taiwan was one hundred miles off the coast, making the task of invasion of far greater magnitude, especially given the primitive nature of Communist naval and air forces. The task became all the more complicated during the early months of 1950 because in withdrawing from other coastal islands, Nationalist forces on Taiwan were able to nearly double their troop strength to four hundred thousand. This development forced Mao to augment the number of army divisions for the planned invasion, and this in turn increased the number of ships needed to transport and support them. The problem was further complicated by the Nationalist advantage over the Communists in both air and naval power. Although the Soviets were assisting Mao in training pilots and providing planes and naval supplies, Communist superiority in these areas could not be attained until sometime in 1951.[35] But Mao set aside his concerns, even offering to redeploy some of his troops to the Sino-Korean border and to send those forces into Korea if the Americans intervened there.[36]

In close consultation with Stalin and Soviet advisers in Pyongyang during the following weeks and with Soviet heavy weapons flowing into North Korea, Kim proceeded to prepare his attack on the South. At the last moment he received information that the ROK had learned of the impending attack. As a result, he proposed to Stalin alteration of the plan to begin operations on the Ongjin Peninsula and then wait for several days before expanding them eastward along the thirty-eighth parallel. Stalin quickly approved, and on June 25 the overall offensive commenced within two hours of the initial shelling on the west coast.

The preceding story reveals Kim as the initiator and persistent advocate of a military solution to Korea's division but also as a man who could not pull the trigger without Stalin's—and ultimately Mao's—aid and approval. Kim tried to use Mao's alleged willingness to help North Korea to pressure Stalin. It is doubtful that Stalin was influenced by this ploy, since the Soviet leader had other reasons for granting his approval and he surely understood that Mao held conquest of Taiwan as his top priority. Rather, it appears that Stalin maneuvered Mao into a position in which the latter could hardly resist Kim's plan or avoid coming to the aid of North Korea if it ran into difficulty with the Americans. Not only had Stalin recently granted Mao his wish for a new treaty, but Mao needed continued Soviet air and naval assistance in executing his plan to seize Taiwan, and Kim had assisted him with Korean troops in the Chinese civil war. To deny Kim his wish would threaten Mao's relationship with both the North Koreans and, more important, the Soviets.

Stalin probably considered the North Korean venture in part as a means of further isolating China from the West. He was well aware of hopes in the United States for a Sino-Soviet split and that the prospects of American recognition of the new regime in China would rise considerably once the Nationalists had been eliminated on Taiwan. He also knew from the American press and perhaps from espionage sources that there existed substantial support both inside and outside the U.S. government for military assistance to the Nationalists to save Taiwan. Undoubtedly it occurred to him that the North Korean attack might shift the scales strongly in favor of such support. Long dubious of Mao's bona fides as a Communist and follower of Soviet leadership—so much so that in February he imposed secret protocols on the PRC that limited its sovereignty in dealing with Soviet citizens in China and excluded nationals of third parties from residing in Manchuria and Xinjiang—Stalin could not help but see advantages in the continued survival of the Nationalists on Taiwan.[37]

He also saw advantages in stepped-up Communist pressure in other parts of East Asia. Stalin had run into difficulties in Europe, where the Americans had drawn a clear line with the Greek-Turkish aid program, the Marshall Plan, the Berlin airlift, and the North Atlantic Treaty Organization (NATO). Moreover, the Communist Josef Broz Tito remained in power in Yugoslavia despite the Soviet leader's efforts to bring him down. With the success of the Communists in China and their ongoing struggle in Indochina against the French, however, the prospects in Asia seemed good for further revolutionary advances—especially since they could be encouraged without risking direct confrontation with the United States. During the first two months of 1950, as Stalin and Mao negotiated a series of agreements, China and the Soviet Union recognized the Communist-led government of Ho Chi Minh in Indochina, and, under Soviet pressure, the Communist Party in Japan abandoned its moderate approach for a militant line. Japan, of course, was part of the U.S. defense perimeter in the Pacific, and Stalin had no intention of openly contesting the American position there. Nonetheless, the Communists could create internal turmoil in Japan, which might give Washington further pause in using that country as a forward base for strong action in other parts of Asia. As for Indochina, Stalin could encourage China to assist Ho while himself staying in the background, thus achieving the twofold purpose of isolating Mao further from the United States and advancing the revolutionary cause against it and its allies.[38] Even if the forward course in Asia drew the United States more deeply into the region, Communist forces held a strong territorial and ideological base from which to resist—and in the process they might distract the Americans from Europe, the most critical theater of the Cold War.

The North Korean attack of June 25, 1950, and developments in the week that followed must be understood through an analysis of events and players interacting both on the peninsula and off. We have seen the crucial nature of the interaction of Stalin, Mao, and Kim. It is now time to examine the American side of the equation.

III

Why did the United States fail to deter the Communist side in Korea? Why, in light of this failure, did it decide to intervene militarily to repulse the North Korean attack? These are the key questions that remain in articulating the international dimensions of the war's origins.

Political and bureaucratic pressures within the United States are critical in addressing both questions. As noted in chapter 2, Congress was reluctant to provide adequate funding, either economic or military, to sustain the American position in Korea and, from September 1947 onward, leaders in the Pentagon were inclined to simply write off the peninsula. Despite these realities, the State Department tried valiantly to protect the U.S. position there, even opposing the final withdrawal of American troops after the ROK's inauguration.[39]

Still, at the end of 1948 the Soviets withdrew their own troops from the North, and in the new year the Pentagon continued its campaign for the Americans to do the same in the South. One of the military's growing concerns was that, with the Communists marching to victory in China, the tens of thousands of Koreans who had fought in their armies would return to the North and provide the DPRK with a decisive advantage over its enemy. Under such circumstances, the seventy-five hundred American soldiers in the South would be in a highly vulnerable position.[40]

Equally important, Washington remained glued to a Europe-first strategy. With tensions high in Europe over the Soviet blockade of the western sectors of Berlin, military planners were anxious to strengthen American reserves at home so as to prepare for an emergency across the Atlantic. The U.S. war plan at the time envisioned a conflict breaking out in Europe, with the initial American effort concentrating on an atomic air offensive against Soviet territory and on maintaining a foothold on the Continent, perhaps at the Pyrenees, and in the Middle East. In Asia operations would be restricted to a "strategic defensive" based on offshore islands.

This outlook grew partly out of the military's natural inclination to think in terms of preparing for a total war like World War II, but it gained reinforcement from the strict spending limits set by the president and Congress. This was an age in which people took balanced budgets and low taxes most seriously, and President Truman had domestic priorities to advance, which cost money. Moreover, atomic weapons appeared to provide for defense of America's foreign interests on the cheap.

With General Douglas MacArthur, the Far Eastern commander and head of the occupation of Japan, endorsing withdrawal from Korea, with the army budget increasingly strapped, and with conditions within South Korea improving somewhat, the State Department finally agreed in the spring of 1949 to go along with the pullout of the last American combat soldiers. By the end of June the withdrawal was complete.

The State Department did exact a price. The U.S. military advisory group in Korea was expanded and made permanent. Arms aid to the ROK continued, and now for an army of sixty-five thousand rather than fifty thousand. In early June the Truman administration presented to Congress an economic assistance bill calling for $150 million to the ROK for the approaching fiscal year, and its accompanying message from the president likened the aid program to that for Western Europe. Finally, the diplomats prepared a resolution for the fall session of the UN General Assembly that would extend the life of the UN commission on Korea created the previous year. They hoped that the presence of this observer group would help to discourage the North Koreans from launching a major attack.

Despite his and his department's ongoing concern about Korea, Secretary of State Dean Acheson failed to develop a course that deterred the Soviets from giving North Korea the green light or enabled the ROK to resist the enemy once it struck. The explanation rests in part on inattentiveness in the face of higher priorities in Europe and the limitations on intelligence, which viewed military attacks from the Communists as more likely against Taiwan and in Indochina than against South Korea. In the former cases, the United Nations was not involved, and there was no Soviet-American agreement dividing the territory. In addition, American ground forces were stationed in Japan, nearby Korea but hundreds of miles from Taiwan or Indochina. In any event, the balance of conventional military power on the peninsula itself was not altogether clear, and the North Koreans still were thought to have a chance of subverting the ROK through infiltration and guerrilla warfare. What information did come in of more aggressive North Korean intentions and military superiority tended to be from ROK officials who, it was feared, merely wanted more military aid so they themselves could take the offensive.[41]

Another explanation rests in the psychology of individuals who, as Harold Joyce Noble, the first secretary of the U.S. embassy in Seoul, later wrote, "had lived so long on the edge of a volcano . . . [that they] had become accustomed to it." "We knew it would explode some day," he recalled, "but as day after day, month after month, and year after year passed and it did not blow up, we could hardly believe that tomorrow would be any different."[42] Whether from the perspective of people on the scene or officials back home busy with other seemingly more pressing issues, warnings of an attack from the North had been circulating since 1946. By 1950 no official was willing to stick his neck out to predict an imminent invasion.

Domestic and bureaucratic politics also contributed to American unpreparedness in Korea. Despite the administration action of June 1949, new economic assistance was not passed by Congress until February 1950, and then only after the House of Representatives had rejected the legislation the previous month. Outside the State Department, the ROK had a limited constituency in the United States, and some members of the legislative branch were perfectly willing to hold aid to Korea hostage to the same for Taiwan. Acheson preferred no aid to Taiwan because he thought it would not save the island from the Communists while throwing them further into the hands of the Soviets. He remained willing to provide limited assistance, however, if it would help secure his Korean program. The Pentagon, in contrast, wanted more aid for Taiwan and, with the partial exception of the army, could not have cared less about Korea.[43]

Under the circumstances, it is understandable that Acheson did not do more on Korea than he did. He devoted considerable space to the peninsula in his National Press Club speech of January 12, 1950, hedging on the critical issue of U.S. aid to the ROK in the event it was attacked. Areas outside the American island defense perimeter in the western Pacific could not be guaranteed. In fact, "initial reliance must be on the people attacked to resist it"; but then they could look to "the commitments of the entire civilized world under the Charter of the United Nations, which so far has not proved a weak reed to lean on by any people who are determined to protect their independence against outside aggression."[44] Given the low level of the defense budget and the view in the military that Korea was relatively unimportant, the most he could do was attempt ambiguity.

By late June ambiguity was no longer possible. To Acheson and his boss, President Truman, who had previously devoted little attention to Korea, conditions had developed that clearly warranted the use of American forces. For one thing, North Korea had launched a blatant, all-out attack across the thirty-eighth parallel, one which could not have been executed without Soviet help and was not a direct response to a prior move from the South. This action represented aggression, a flagrant violation of the Soviet-American agreement of August 1945 and of UN resolutions recognizing the legitimacy of the ROK. For another, on June 29 General MacArthur, the commander in the field, reported that there was no hope of restoring the boundary without U.S. troops and that the very survival of the ROK was in jeopardy. He recommended that two American divisions from Japan be committed to the fray. Third, there was no indication of direct Soviet or Chinese Communist intervention in Korea or of impending Soviet or Soviet proxy moves in other, more important areas. The conflict in Korea appeared to be an isolated event, thus justifying thought outside the old category of total war. Fourth, broad support existed among allies abroad for strong American measures. If anything, such support was even stronger at home. Already the Joint Chiefs had supported the use of the U.S. Seventh Fleet to deter a possible Chinese Communist attack on Taiwan, and they showed no inclination to oppose a commitment of American soldiers to Korea. These conditions warranted decisive action, Acheson thought, "as [a] symbol [of the] strength and determination of [the] west." To do less would encourage "new aggressive action elsewhere" and demoralize "countries adjacent to [the] Soviet orbit."[45]

The logic that had been used by the State Department since 1947 for trying to save South Korea surfaced again, only now it dictated actually sending U.S. soldiers into combat. Such action had been considered in an army paper drafted the year before as the last American troops withdrew from the peninsula. Then it was concluded that sending ground units back into Korea, either through the United Nations or independently, would be "unsound militarily" but possibly "necessary on the basis of political considerations."[46] No decision emerged on the paper, probably because the State Department, which would have had the greatest interest in seeing it approved, saw no need for an immediate decision and was not sure it could prevail on the matter in a battle with the Pentagon.

How do we explain the willingness of the Joint Chiefs to go along with the intervention in June 1950? One key factor was President Truman's apparent inclination from the start to do whatever was necessary to stop the North Koreans. Another was a similar inclination on the part of Acheson, who was put in charge of deliberations in the crisis. Even so, military leaders held back on any recommendation for ground troops until it became clear that the situation was otherwise hopeless, that the commander in the field had requested them and given assurances that their deployment would not jeopardize the security of Japan, and that Communist moves outside Korea were unlikely. With sentiment elsewhere in the administration and in Congress heavily weighted toward intervention, the Joint Chiefs were unwilling to buck the tide.[47]

The United States jumped into the fray in Korea because aggression was being committed that reminded Americans of similar actions by Japan, Italy, and Germany in the 1930s and had led to World War II, and because domestic and other international conditions permitted it.[48] Given the Soviet-American agreement of 1945 and subsequent developments, the North Korean attack was seen not as a decisive act in an ongoing civil war but as a dangerous move that threatened world peace and stability.

WHO STARTED THE KOREAN WAR? TO BRUCE CUMINGS THIS IS THE wrong question, since "it is not a civil war question."[49] Another lead-

ing historian of the war, Burton I. Kaufman, labels the conflict "a gr
power struggle between the United States and the Soviet Union super-
imposed on a civil war between North and South Korea."[50] Cumings is
correct in asserting that the question of who started the war is not a
civil war question, or at least not exclusively that; but he is less per-
suasive in saying that it is the wrong question. Surely it is among the
many important ones that need to be addressed in an attempt to understand the overall event. How else, after all, can we grasp why the
outbreak of fighting on June 25, 1950, had such greater consequences
than the border clashes of the previous eighteen months? Or compre-
hend the relationship among North Korea, the Soviet Union, and China?
Or assess the American response? Kaufman may be challenged as well
because his description implies a clean separation of the great power
and civil natures of the war's origins. South and North Korea would
not have existed but for great power intervention on the peninsula in
1945. The subsequent internal conflict, to be sure, had roots in Korea
going back to the Japanese period and the ways in which the colonial
power used elements of the indigenous population as instruments of
its rule. Yet the particular course of the internal conflict from 1945
onward cannot be understood without constant reference to the foreign presence. And that particular course is critical in understanding
what happened in Korea between June 25, 1950, and July 27, 1953.

The Korean War can be understood only by integrating the internal
and external components of its origins. In this case integration often
reveals not so much a melting pot or a salad bowl as something in
between. The various ingredients in the mix always remained distinc-
tive, if broadly grouped in two, but the large event occurred only once
the elements in one of the groups blended together sufficiently with
the others to spark an explosion. That blend occurred, in turn, because the most powerful element in the other group left the weaker
element exposed.

"The Korean War" is an imperfect label, since it reflects only the
territorial boundaries, not the international dimensions, of the conflict. Yet, unlike "The Korean Civil War," it neither explicitly excludes
nor severely diminishes the importance of those dimensions. We can
bear the limitations of the former for lack of a better alternative. We
should reject the latter for its clear-cut distortion of reality.

PART II

COURSE

CHAPTER 4

The Road to Chinese Intervention,

July–November 1950

UNITED STATES GROUND TROOPS REENTERED KOREA IN EARLY JULY
1950 to restore the thirty-eighth parallel, a task that Washington
hoped would be achieved quickly and cheaply.[1] When MacArthur recommended the commitment of American soldiers to combat, he estimated that the job would require only two divisions, plus the air and
naval forces already involved.[2] Already the U.S. Far Eastern and soon-
to-be United Nations commander contemplated a counteroffensive
against the enemy at Inchon, the port for Seoul. The target date was
July 22.[3]

Quick and cheap or not, the objective articulated by Washington
conflicted with that of Syngman Rhee and MacArthur himself. In mid-
July the ROK president announced to the press that the North Korean
attack had "obliterated" the old boundary and that "no peace and
order could be maintained" in a divided Korea. MacArthur told visit-

ing members of the Joint Chiefs that he intended to destroy North Korean forces rather than merely drive them back behind the thirty-eighth parallel, thus making possible the unification of the entire country. The United States could use atomic bombs along the Korean border in the north to produce a radioactive barrier to outside interference. Soon a debate raged within the State Department on the issue of the original objective. On July 17 Truman directed the National Security Council to consider the matter of what to do once UN troops reached the thirty-eighth parallel.[4]

There was no hurry to decide. North Korean troops, far from being intimidated by the appearance of American combatants, had continued to push southward. By early August, with the aid of covert operations by guerrillas who had survived prewar ROK suppression campaigns, they had driven all the way to the Naktong River, often little more than thirty miles from Pusan on the southeastern coast (see map 3). United States and ROK solders now outnumbered the enemy, and American planes dominated the air, but for the moment North Korean troops possessed better equipment and a more aggressive spirit. Airpower was a limited advantage in the overcast skies of Korea's rainy season. At month's end DPRK forces launched an offensive across the front that, in the two weeks that followed, inflicted more casualties on U.S. troops than during any other comparable period in the war.[5]

Yet over the past two months the United States had built up supplies and personnel in Korea and Japan, and the DPRK army had suffered over fifty thousand casualties. Not all of the lost manpower could be quickly replaced, and neither could the captured and destroyed arms and expended ammunition. North Korea's lengthy supply lines produced increasing problems under clearing weather conditions in which the enemy had total control of the air and sea.

On September 15 UN forces launched a daring flanking operation at Inchon, catching the North Koreans completely off guard. Within four days UN forces had seized Kimpo airport outside Seoul; a week later they captured the capital city. Meanwhile, the UN Eighth Army had broken enemy lines around Pusan and was marching rapidly northward.

Washington was not unprepared for this swing of fortune. On September 11 President Truman had approved a major planning paper on

Korea, NSC-81. The paper anticipated granting MacArthur authority to move UN troops north of the thirty-eighth parallel "provided that at the time of such operations there has been no entry into North Korea by major Soviet or Chinese Communist forces, no announcement of intended entry, nor a threat to counter our operations militarily in North Korea." Prospects for such entry could be reduced, it was believed, if no American troops operated close to Chinese or Soviet borders. Thus, in addition to stating that all military operations would be prohibited beyond the peninsula, the paper stated that "it should be the policy not to include any non-Korean units" in operations in the provinces of North Korea "bordering the Soviet Union or in the area along the Manchurian border."[6] Sixteen days later, with no sign of direct Soviet or Chinese entry into Korea—or an intention to do so—and with UN ground forces approaching the thirty-eighth parallel, orders to this effect were dispatched to MacArthur in Tokyo. ROK units crossed the line on October 1; American and other UN units followed a week later.[7]

By the time of the latter crossing, the People's Republic of China (PRC) had issued an explicit warning of an intention to intervene if non-Korean troops entered the North. Actually, the United States, which lacked representation in Beijing, had begun during the last days of September to receive reports from British and Dutch representatives there indicating that China would throw its hat into the ring if American divisions moved beyond the thirty-eighth parallel. On September 30 Chinese premier and foreign minister Zhou En-lai declared in a speech that "the Chinese people absolutely will not tolerate foreign aggression nor will they supinely tolerate seeing their neighbors being savagely invaded by imperialists."[8] Then, at midnight on October 2, Zhou called Indian ambassador K. M. Panikkar to the foreign ministry and asked him to have his government convey to Washington that China would intervene in Korea if U.S. ground forces moved into the North. The State Department received the message on October 3.[9]

On October 8, with the warnings having failed to halt the Americans, Mao gave the preliminary order for the Chinese People's Volunteers (CPV) to move into Korea. Four days later, with Zhou and General Lin Biao conducting talks with Stalin at his vacation dacha on the

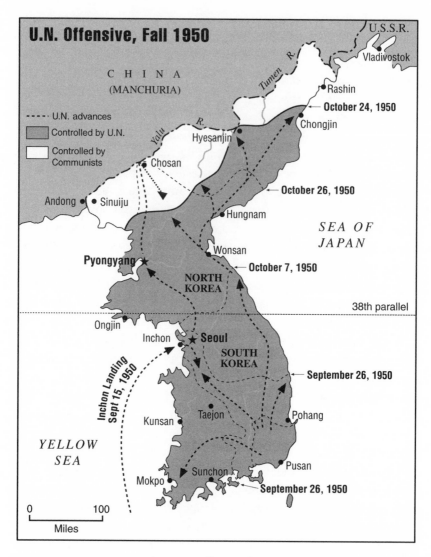

MAP 4. UN offensive, fall 1950.

Black Sea, he postponed implementation of the order. Only after a Politburo meeting on the thirteenth did the Chinese leader give the final go-ahead to CPV commander Peng Dehuai to send his forces across the Yalu River. The large-scale movement of Chinese troops onto the peninsula began on the nineteenth.[10]

FIG. 10. Ceremony of September 29, 1950, restoring the ROK government in Seoul. General Douglas MacArthur, the commander of UN forces in Korea, is to the right of the podium, President Syngman Rhee of the ROK to the left. Behind MacArthur, wearing a bow tie, is Ambassador Muccio.

FIG. 11. When UN forces captured Pyongyang, the North Korean capital, during the third week of October 1950, they found the capitol building heavily camouflaged.

Not only had U.S. troops crossed the thirty-eighth parallel in the face of Chinese warnings; on October 17 General MacArthur ordered them to move into provinces bordering Manchuria and the Soviet Union. A week later he removed all restrictions on their operations within Korea.[11] When the CPV first made contact with UN units on the twenty-fifth at Onjong, less than forty miles south of the Yalu in the northwest, American ground forces already had moved beyond the narrow neck of the peninsula just north of Pyongyang and Wonsan, which represented the best possible defensive line in North Korea.[12]

Although the first Chinese skirmishes were with ROK soldiers, Americans soon became involved, in both the western sector covered by the Eighth Army under the command of General Walton Walker and the eastern sector, a responsibility of the X Corps. After landing at Inchon and capturing Seoul, this army, commanded independently by General Ned Almond, had reembarked at Inchon to be transported by sea to Wonsan. Now, with a fifty- to one-hundred-mile gap over rugged mountain terrain separating the two main UN forces, advance units of the CPV probed for weaknesses. By November 6 a disturbed MacArthur wired home that "men and material in large force are pouring across all bridges over the Yalu from Manchuria. This movement not only jeopardizes but threatens the ultimate destruction of the forces under my command."[13] He requested permission to bomb the Yalu bridges.

Washington allowed him to attack only the Korean side of the bridges, a nearly impossible task given the sinuous course of the river. The Truman administration considered halting the UN advance, but ultimately it declined to revise MacArthur's orders, a decision made easier by the break of Chinese contact with UN forces after November 7.[14] So the UN commander continued to prepare for a final offensive aimed at clearing Korea of the enemy.

On the twenty-fourth, a day after American troops had celebrated a Thanksgiving dinner with all the trimmings, MacArthur flew in for a quick visit of his forces in the western sector. They were beginning an operation that he hoped would be sufficiently decisive and sufficiently swift to enable them to spend Christmas at home with their families.

After taking off to return to Tokyo, he ordered his pilot to swing northward and then eastward along the Yalu. All he saw, he wrote later, "was an endless expanse of utterly barren countryside, jagged hills, yawning crevices, and the black waters of the Yalu locked in the silent death grip of snow and ice."[15] Upon arriving in Tokyo several hours later, he announced to the press the commencement of a new offensive. United Nations air action over the past three weeks had "sharply curtailed" the movement of Chinese troops and "markedly limited" the influx of supplies from Manchuria, thus isolating the battlefield and enabling friendly forces to position themselves for an operation that "if successful . . . should for all practical purposes end the war."[16]

Four days later, as hundreds of thousands of CPV soldiers slashed mercilessly through overextended and outnumbered UN units in both sectors, MacArthur wired home despondently that "Chinese military forces are committed to North Korea in great and ever increasing strength. . . . We face an entirely new war."[17]

Why had the war in Korea reached this point? Why did the United States, as head of the UN command, alter its original objective of restoring the thirty-eighth parallel and attempt to unify the country, even in the face of Chinese warnings? Why did the Chinese decide to intervene to prevent unification by hostile forces? Why, after the initial Chinese contact with UN units, did Washington refuse to halt offensive operations, thus exposing its overextended and divided forces to dangerous counterattack? These are the questions to be addressed in this chapter.

I

Since its intervention in 1945, the United States had never abandoned the objective of Korean unity. The only questions were when and how it might be achieved. Because the objective of containing the Soviets had always held priority, the Americans—in the State Department at least—had rejected unification through abandonment. Unification by force, on the other hand, was ill-advised given America's priorities elsewhere and the desire to avoid war. Before June 25, 1950, Washington policy makers regarded the end of Korea's division as a long-term goal unlikely to be achieved at any time in the foreseeable future.

The North Korean attack soon reopened the issue. The intervention by the United States signaled its continuing unwillingness to lose South Korea through the use of naked force. But some officials in Washington quickly developed the argument that the North Korean move fundamentally changed the case against *U.S.* military action to achieve unity. John Allison, head of the State Department's Division of Northeast Asian Affairs, took the lead in this endeavor, arguing, first, that Korea's continued division would make "impossible" fulfillment of the UN Security Council resolution of June 27, which called for restoration of "peace and security in the area."[18] That is, a North Korea merely pushed back behind the thirty-eighth parallel could lick its wounds and, once they were healed, launch another attack. Second, Allison contended that restoration of the old dividing line would anger and demoralize the South Koreans, who had recently placed their forces under the UN command. This would greatly diminish prospects for future American cooperation with the ROK. Finally, to "leave the aggressors . . . unpunished" in this instance would encourage others to make similar moves at other times and at other places. To deter aggression in the future, in short, it must be not only repulsed but punished in the present.[19]

As for the possibility that an effort to unify Korea by force would provoke a direct clash with the PRC and/or the Soviet Union, Allison believed there existed "grave danger" of such a confrontation "whatever we do from now on." He denied that the United States would gain any advantage by compromising "with clear moral principles and a shirking of our duty to make clear once and for all that aggression does not pay." He recognized that "this may mean war on a global scale" and that the government should set about to inform the American people of "what it will mean to them."[20]

This line of thought grew naturally out of the fears and frustrations engendered by international events of the past year, in particular the successful Soviet test of a nuclear device the previous August—several years ahead of what most American analysts had anticipated—the

Communist victory on mainland China, and the subsequent creation of the Sino-Soviet military alliance. In this context, the North Korean attack appeared as a manifestation of increasing Soviet aggressiveness, as a willingness, in the words of President Truman on June 27, to "use armed invasion and war" in advancing its goals.[21] Several days later the *New York Times* remarked that "the Soviets can choose to put pressure on almost any point on the periphery [of the Eurasian heartland], sucking in American strength now here, now there, 'bleeding the United States in a long campaign of attrition.'"[22] To some American officials, including Secretary of Defense Louis Johnson, Secretary of the Navy Francis B. Matthews, and the influential Senator Richard B. Russell, all-out war with the Soviet Union before it could build up its nuclear arsenal and delivery capability represented the only escape from such a fate.[23]

The Joint Chiefs of Staff rejected preventive war, but they saw the prospect of uniting Korea as a method of reversing "the dangerous strategic trend in the Far East." "Penetration of the Soviet orbit," they believed, "would disturb the strategic complex which the USSR is organizing between its own Far Eastern territories and the contiguous areas." "The pivot of this complex" was Manchuria, and "a free and strong Korea could provide an outlet for [its] . . . resources and could also provide non-communist contact with the people there and in North China." Beijing might even reassess its "dependent" relationship with Moscow.[24]

The prevailing view within the executive branch in Washington, nonetheless, was that the Soviet Union or China, or both, would send forces into Korea to prevent UN troops from marching into the northern reaches of the peninsula. From the start of the conflict, U.S. officials had assumed that a direct Soviet-U.S. confrontation in Korea would lead to world war. By August they recognized that the escalating commitment in Korea, which now included units not just from the occupation in Japan but from continental North America, had left the United States in a poor position to execute its war plan. In any case, U.S. forces were so weak as to raise doubts about the final outcome of an all-out war. Even before the North Korean attack, the National Security Council had produced a document, NSC-68, warning of the heightened risk of U.S. military weakness and calling for major increases in defense spending over the next four years.[25] For the moment it was believed that, at best, Soviet defeat in war would come only after a long and costly struggle in which the U.S. homeland might suffer extensive damage from air attack. The result of a Sino-U.S. clash in Korea was less certain, but it surely would increase the risk of global conflict and tie up key U.S. resources on the peninsula for a substantial period. By mid-August even the hawkish Allison conceded that American unpreparedness for war with the Soviet Union, combined with uncertainties regarding Moscow's and Beijing's intentions, made premature any commitment of the United States to a campaign above the thirty-eighth parallel.[26]

Still, the option received ongoing consideration, so much so that the administration began laying the political groundwork for its implementation. On August 10 Warren Austin, the U.S. ambassador to the United Nations, asked rhetorically in a speech before the Security Council, "Shall only part of the country [Korea] be assured freedom?" "I think not," he answered. "The United Nations has consistently worked for a unified country, an independent Korea. The United Nations will not want to turn from that objective now." A week later he made a similar pronouncement. Then, at the end of the month, President Truman declared in a radio address that "Koreans have the right to be free, independent, and united." Under UN "guidance," he concluded, the United States would "do [its] part to help them enjoy that right."[27] Meanwhile, U.S. diplomats had probed European allies on a UN military venture above the thirty-eighth parallel and received a tentative but affirmative response.[28] Increasingly the State Department viewed the unification of Korea as a method of seizing the offensive in the Cold War. As a departmental position paper concluded, a total victory on the peninsula would be "of incalculable importance in Asia and throughout the world." The accomplishment would keenly impress Japan and "stimulate any latent or active differences between Peiping [Beijing] and Moscow." Even "Soviet satellites in Europe" would take notice.[29]

Yet the dominant opinion in Washington was that the United States should seek to avert a direct clash with the Soviets or Chinese, and this thinking represented an integral part of NSC-81. Then the Inchon landing and its rapid follow-up helped to produce a momentum that proved impossible to reverse over the short term.

The first thing to understand about Inchon is that it was a very personal victory for General MacArthur. The city's harbor possessed narrow and winding channels, strong currents, and one of the highest tidal ranges on earth. The Joint Chiefs had strong reservations about it as a landing site, in part because of its physical features, in part because it was located so far north that, even if UN forces made it ashore, they might be so isolated that the enemy would destroy them. But MacArthur insisted that the risks were worth taking. The unlikely location would ensure surprise and would enable a sufficiently wide envelopment of the main DPRK forces to cut off their escape routes back across the thirty-eighth parallel. In the end, MacArthur's position as the longest-serving officer in the armed forces, his supreme self-confidence, and the tradition of granting the commander in the field considerable latitude in tactical operations won out. The Washington brass approved his plan but only with great reluctance. When the Inchon operation proved a brilliant success, they were unlikely anytime soon to again question his judgment.[30]

A second point to remember is that MacArthur was a highly political general, a man who had permitted his name to be placed on the ballot in the Republican presidential primary in Wisconsin in 1948. A rabid Asia-firster, he held views that were of great interest to Republicans intent on attacking the Truman administration's policies toward East Asia in the developing congressional election campaign in the United States. Attacks had been mounting for over a year, as the Truman administration tried to avoid too deep an embroilment in the region as the Communists solidified their hold on mainland China. Criticism of that caution gained momentum in early 1950 with new revelations of Communist spying in the U.S. government and the conclusion of the Soviet alliance with the Communist regime in China. Beginning in February, Senator Joseph R. McCarthy (R., Wisc.) gained headlines nationwide and considerable support from Republican leaders for his charges that the State Department employed dozens of Communist sympathizers. The North Korean attack in June merely added fuel to the claim that Democratic leadership on Asian policy was a disaster.[31] Policy toward Taiwan was another source of complaint, and in late August MacArthur publicly took issue with the U.S. position there, which was that the American Seventh Fleet would protect the island from attack only until the war in Korea ended.[32] Although most of the press and public appeared to agree with Truman on this issue, the Korean case was different: whereas Taiwan was seen as part of China and the conflict over it as part of a civil war, the ROK was viewed as being under attack from an aggressive Communist regime that deserved to be punished. Furthermore, the president had cultivated domestic restraint on the Taiwan issue but had failed to do so on Korea, even encouraging public expectations of a UN campaign to unite the peninsula. After Inchon any effort to halt MacArthur was sure to generate a public response from the imperious general and sharp Republican attacks under conditions disadvantageous to the Democrats.

Yet even without the domestic political equation, Inchon produced strong momentum for aggressive action. Rather than generating a slow, methodical, and costly advance against the enemy, it reversed the military situation overnight and at little expense in lives and equipment to friendly forces. If followed up rapidly, Inchon appeared to present an opportunity for a quick and total victory on the cheap. On the other hand, should UN forces hesitate in pursuing their advantage, North Korean troops would have an opportunity to regroup and perhaps gain reinforcements from the outside.

Sentiment among European allies might have produced restraint in Washington. All had strongly supported the initial U.S. course in Korea, as they saw in North Korea's attack an event that might be replicated in a divided Germany. By the end of the summer, several of them had offered concrete support for the UN effort there. Great Britain even rushed two battalions of troops to the peninsula, despite limited resources and important commitments elsewhere. Contributions were made, however, in part because the NATO allies saw them as instruments of influence on a benefactor who might, under the pressure of the moment, become overcommitted to Asia at the expense of Europe.[33]

Still, the British, who with Canada often took the lead in dealing with the Americans, were particularly sensitive to the risks of restraining the leader of the Western camp. In a cabinet paper of August 30, Foreign Minister Ernest Bevin wrote that

> American opinion is in a highly emotional state, which is attributable in part to the Korean situation itself and in part to the sense of frustration induced by the feeling that, in fighting North Koreans, Americans are not coming to grips with the real enemy. In such a state of mind the American public is likely to be irrational . . . towards the United Kingdom where our policy diverges from that of the United States.[34]

In the aftermath of Inchon, Bevin, now in New York for NATO talks and the opening of the UN General Assembly, worked cautiously to encourage U.S. moderation in Asia while solidifying the Anglo-American relationship. He broke with Washington on Chinese representation in the General Assembly, voting in favor of an Indian resolution—which still lost—to seat the PRC; but he compensated by persuading the British cabinet to accept *in principle* the controversial American initiative to rearm West Germany.[35]

He also worked with U.S. diplomats to craft a resolution on Korea for the General Assembly. Read broadly, the Security Council resolution of June 27 permitted UN ground action above the thirty-eighth parallel. Interpreting it in that manner represented the easy way out, as in August the Soviets had returned to the Security Council and surely would veto any new U.S.-sponsored resolution there. Yet the June 27 resolution had passed at a time when supporters had not anticipated more than an effort to repulse the North Korean attack. Since the United States still normally mustered large majorities behind its measures in the General Assembly, Washington considered it prudent to present a new resolution to that body endorsing American plans in the North. Knowing this, on September 23 British officials presented the outline of such a resolution to their American counterparts. The outline called for overtures to North Korea on unification prior to any ground campaign above the thirty-eighth parallel and new elections throughout the country to achieve a unified government. The Americans objected on both counts, and Bevin quickly accommodated his ally, despite qualms from the British chiefs of staff in London about any ground offensive into the North. When the resolution finally moved to the General Assembly on the twenty-ninth, it had eight cosponsors and broad backing among non-Communist delegations.[36]

Nonetheless, events over the next several days created potential problems for the resolution. On October 2 the Soviets presented a counterresolution calling for a cease-fire in Korea, withdrawal of foreign troops, free elections throughout the country arranged by a joint North-South commission, and the observance of this process by a UN committee that included representatives from the nations bordering on Korea. The Indian delegate, who had never supported the first resolution, immediately proposed an effort to reconcile the two. Despite ominous signals from Beijing regarding PRC intentions in Korea, the United States fought off the Soviet and Indian efforts, and with the support, if reluctant, of its NATO allies.[37]

Technically, the explicit threat of Chinese intervention that reached Washington on October 3 should have brought American troops to a halt at the thirty-eighth parallel. This was clear in NSC-81 and the new instructions to MacArthur of September 27. That the Chinese threat did not have such an impact is explicable partly in terms of the momentum that had built up for the northern campaign by the time of its appearance and the liabilities in the United States and Korea of postponing the offensive or even restricting it to ROK troops. Two other elements must be added to the equation, however, the method by which the threat was transmitted and the American attitude toward the PRC.

The United States had lacked official representation in China since April 1950, when O. Edmund Clubb, the consul general in Beijing, had been ordered home due to his harsh treatment by government authorities.[38] Now the Chinese could communicate with the Americans only indirectly. In this case they chose the top Indian representative, probably because he was of higher rank than any diplomats from Western countries, which had not established full relations with the PRC. Unfortunately, Ambassador Panikkar was considered in the West to be an unreliable reporter, having, among other things, predicted a

Chinese Communist assault on Taiwan during the previous summer. The fact that the direct threat came through private channels rather than being stated publicly also compromised its impact, as the Americans regarded the former as more likely than the latter to be a bluff.[39]

Yet the problem went deeper than the method of the threat's transmittal. China had been divided for over a century, and most American observers doubted that the Communists or any other group could unite and rule the country. By the fall of 1950, American leaders accepted the likelihood that the PRC would be a permanent fixture there. They knew, though, that it still faced hostile guerrillas in parts of the south and west and huge tasks of internal reconstruction and modernization after many years of civil war and foreign occupation. They assumed as well that Mao wanted to avoid becoming more dependent than he already was on his Soviet ally, which remained a presence in China's northern provinces. As Acheson remarked in a September 10 interview with CBS news commentator Eric Sevareid,

> I give the people of Peiping [Beijing] credit for being intelligent enough to see what is happening to them. Why they should want to further their own dismemberment and destruction by getting at cross purposes with all the free nations of the world who are inherently their friends and have always been friends of the Chinese as against this imperialism coming down from the Soviet Union I cannot see.[40]

This attitude combined arrogance, condescension, and naïveté, but it was balanced by fear of the PRC as a revolutionary force in border areas, especially Southeast Asia, where France and Great Britain struggled to maintain a foothold for the West. If the Americans backed off in Korea so palpably in the face of this belated Chinese threat, the PRC might become emboldened to act aggressively at other times and in other places, to question the will of the United States to maintain a firm course when challenged. By early October Acheson believed that a show of "hesitation and timidity" would increase rather than reduce the danger to the United States. Despite the risk involved, circumstances dictated a "firm and courageous" stand.[41]

In the end, the risk posed by Chinese embroilment in Korea was not of the same magnitude as that of the Soviet Union. The drafters of NSC-81 concluded that Soviet intervention would indicate "that global war is probably imminent," although the desirability of avoiding such a conflict would "warrant every effort . . . to localize the action," even perhaps through "a direct approach to the highest Soviet leaders." In contrast, while the United States should seek to avoid "a general war" with China if it intervened in Korea, "appropriate air and naval action" might be taken early on against the PRC, and the matter might be taken to the Security Council "with the purpose of condemning the Chinese Communists as aggressors."[42] China did not possess the capacity to wage global war against the United States, or even to strike in Europe; the Soviet Union did. This fact made caution in the face of a threat by the latter both more necessary and less dangerous than by the former. The momentum of early October was breakable, but by the Soviets, *not* the Chinese.

II

Why did the threat come from the Chinese rather than the Soviets? Why did the Chinese wait so long to issue their threat? Why, in the end, did the Chinese intervene in Korea?

An answer to the first question is relatively simple: Stalin regarded direct intervention by his country as too risky, given its relative weakness in atomic weapons, delivery capability, and economic potential and the likelihood that such intervention would lead to all-out war with the United States. To be sure, he recognized that China's intervention, for which he pressed, might draw the Soviets in as well, and this chance he was willing to take. In early October he wrote to Mao that

> together we will be stronger than the USA and England, while other capitalist European states with the exception of Germany, which cannot now render any kind of assistance to the USA, do not represent a serious military force. If war is unavoidable, then let it be now, and not after several years, when Japanese militarism will have been revived as an ally of the USA.[43]

This assessment, of course, was part of a campaign to persuade Mao to intervene. Clearly, Stalin's preference was to avoid war with the United States—and if it was to come, he wanted to make absolutely certain that the Chinese already were fully engaged with the Americans. Even a *threat* of Soviet intervention before the Chinese committed would put him in an excessively exposed position.

The lateness of the Chinese threat is more difficult to explain, although as in the Soviet case a sense of vulnerability and the complexity of alliance politics go far in providing an answer. It first must be remembered that, during the previous May, Stalin had maneuvered Mao into a position in which it was virtually impossible to veto Kim Il-sung's desire for an early attack across the thirty-eighth parallel. Then Mao had assumed the role of team player, offering Kim his assistance. But Kim wanted to carry out the task of unification as much as possible on his own. Insofar as he needed assistance from the outside, he preferred it from the Soviets rather than the Chinese, since there remained an important element within his own Communist Party that he regarded as too closely tied to Beijing. Kim not only declined Chinese assistance beyond the return of Korean units that had fought in the Chinese civil war; he did not inform Mao of the date of his planned attack on the South.[44]

After the war began, the Chinese moved quickly to bolster their representation in Pyongyang, establishing an embassy in July that included several military and intelligence officials to report on battlefield developments. When in August Beijing attempted to send the high-ranking general Deng Hua to the North Korean capital, however, the DPRK blocked the move. Late in the month Mao warned the North Koreans of a possible U.S. counterattack at Inchon, but he was ignored. As it turned out, key North Koreans and their Soviet advisers were not quick to grasp the significance of the UN landing at Inchon, even once it occurred, and so they failed to execute a timely retreat of DPRK troops from the Pusan perimeter. Once they did begin to move northward, enemy envelopment had trapped most of them in the South. Having lost contact with his field commander, Kim Il-sung did not recognize the desperation of the situation until September 28.[45] A direct request for Chinese intervention from Pyongyang did not reach

Beijing until late on October 1, virtually simultaneously with a similar plea from Stalin, who was willing to supply substantial matériel but not combat forces.[46] Only now, as historian Chen Jian has suggested, did Mao possess the "moral justification" and potential "effectiveness" needed to intervene.[47]

That said, the Chinese took considerable action well before October to prepare for intervention in Korea. In July 1950 Mao established the Northeast Border Defense Army and redeployed three Chinese armies to the region. He also launched a political mobilization campaign at home against the United States and domestic "reactionaries."[48] In a Politburo meeting on August 4, he told his top subordinates that "we must lend them [the North Koreans] our hands by sending our military volunteers there."[49] The timing of intervention could be decided later, but on the next day he instructed his generals in the northeast to be prepared to fight within a month. Later he extended the period of preparation to the end of September and called for twelve Chinese armies to be stationed along the Yalu, an increase by eight over his order of July.[50]

Mao's ideology predisposed him to believe the worst of the United States. The change in American policy toward Taiwan after the outbreak of war in Korea reinforced his view that, if the military situation on the peninsula changed, so, too, would the U.S. attitude toward halting at the thirty-eighth parallel. Ambassador Austin's remarks at the United Nations in mid-August provided additional confirmation. On August 20 Foreign Minister Zhou addressed a message to the United Nations, declaring that "Korea is China's neighbor. . . . The Chinese people cannot but be concerned about solution of the Korean question."[51] Six days later an article in the Chinese journal *World Culture* asserted that "the barbarous action of American imperialism and its hangers-on in invading Korea not only menaces peace in Asia and the world in general but seriously threatens the security of China in particular. The Chinese people cannot allow such aggressive acts of American imperialism in Korea."[52] As we have already seen, private and public statements by high Chinese officials during the last days of September followed closely the theme of the above declaration. If the warnings lacked the specificity of Zhou's to Panikkar on October 2–3, they certainly provided a solid foundation for it.

Those warnings aside, Mao had two interrelated reasons to avoid a definitive commitment to intervene, even after the North Korean request. The first was the absence of a clear-cut agreement with Stalin on the nature and level of Soviet matériel assistance. As early as July 5, Stalin had suggested to Mao that he "concentrate immediately 9 Chinese divisions on the Chinese-Korean border for volunteer actions in North Korea in case the enemy crosses the 38th parallel." He also stated that "we will try to provide air cover for these units."[53] Eight days later, having received no reply, Stalin inquired about the Chinese position and stated that, if they had decided to move the units as suggested, he would dispatch 124 jet fighter planes to cover them. He also noted that Soviet teachers hoped to train Chinese pilots within two or three months and then transfer all equipment to them.[54] Mao replied on July 22, accepting Stalin's offer but also expressing concerns that the time period allotted for training Chinese pilots was too short.[55] Stalin then approved Mao's suggested training period as lasting until the spring of 1951.[56] The Soviet air division arrived in Manchuria in early August 1950, yet Stalin refused to commit these forces to action in Korea if Chinese troops entered that country.[57] Although there is a substantial gap in the available record on both sides regarding Sino-Soviet exchanges on Soviet aid—air and ground alike—the matter clearly remained unresolved in early October.

Compounding the problem for Mao were divisions in the Politburo at home, where such leading members as Zhou En-lai and General Lin Biao, and probably a majority of the entire body, expressed reservations about intervention.[58] By early October Mao was strongly inclined to send troops into Korea, and he was the final authority in the government and party, possessing impressive credentials as the intellectual, military, and political leader of his country. Even so, his style of governance at this point included collegial elements. He understood that a decision to take on the Americans in Korea involved grave risks and that these would be graver still if they were accompanied by neither detailed agreements on Soviet aid nor a consensus within the top leadership at home. His movement toward a final decision did not even begin until early October, and the process was anything but linear. It is not surprising, therefore, that an explicit warning to the Americans came over two weeks after Inchon.

What is more surprising is that Zhou's warning through Panikkar occurred virtually simultaneously with Mao's transmittal of a telegram to Stalin stating that a preliminary decision had been made that China would *not* intervene in Korea. Actually, on October 2 two telegrams had been drafted to Stalin, one in Mao's own hand. One had Mao informing the Soviet leader that his forces would intervene under the name of the CPV. Although the draft message expressed the desire "to annihilate the invaders from the United States and other countries [of the UN command]," it stated that initially the CPV would engage only enemy forces that crossed the thirty-eighth parallel and use "defensive tactics" while "awaiting the arrival of Soviet weapons." When Chinese forces became better equipped, they would, "in cooperation with the Korean comrades, launch a counteroffensive to destroy the invading American forces."[59] This message was not sent, however. In the one that was sent, Mao emphasized the fears of many of his comrades about taking on the Americans with such poorly equipped forces. It also requested that Stalin receive Zhou and Lin at his vacation residence at Sochi to discuss the matter.[60] Obviously, Mao wanted to bargain with Stalin for Soviet aid, a course made all the more necessary by widespread doubts in China about intervention. Mao's warning to the Americans through Zhou probably was designed, first, to try to deter them from crossing the thirty-eighth parallel and, second, to demonstrate to his comrades at home that he had done all he could to avert intervention.

A crucial step toward the initial order for the CPV to move into Korea on October 8 was Mao's call of General Peng Dehuai to Beijing from his position as head of the First Field Army in the northwest. The purpose of the call was to ask that Peng assume command of the CPV in Korea. Lin Biao had declined the position due to ill health, and Su Yu, who had been in charge of preparations to liberate Taiwan, was ruled out for the same reason. Mao needed a commander who both was up to the task and supported his interventionist view. Peng was a resourceful military leader from Mao's home province of Hunan. The men's relationship had been strained at times in the past and would eventually land Peng in prison. But soon after arriving in the Chinese capital late on October 4, Peng swung his weight behind Mao with the still dubious Politburo. That support altered the mood of Mao's top advisers.[61]

Still, the matter of Soviet aid remained unresolved, even on October 8 as the preliminary order for intervention was sent to Manchuria, and Zhou and Lin flew to the Soviet Union. Mao had informed Stalin a day earlier that he would send nine divisions to Korea, but not immediately.[62] The Zhou-Lin talks with Stalin beginning on the tenth did not go as well as Mao had hoped. Available records are sparse here, but the best evidence indicates that the Soviet leader agreed to equip twenty Chinese divisions immediately and many more later, but he stated that Soviet air units would not be ready to support Chinese troops in Korea for two to two and a half months. With this news, and under pressure from Peng for specifics on antiaircraft artillery and air support to be made available for his forces, Mao suspended his order of intervention on the twelfth only to reinstate it a day later.[63] He had gotten all he could from Stalin, and, with UN ground forces moving rapidly northward in Korea, the time had arrived to finalize the decision he had been predisposed to make all along.

Why did Mao choose as he did? The traditional view, advanced by Allen S. Whiting in his 1960 classic *China Crosses the Yalu*, emphasizes Mao's concern about China's physical security posed by the advance of UN, especially U.S., forces to the Yalu frontier. This interpretation remains plausible, although new evidence suggests a need to broaden the analysis. As early as August 4, Mao told members of the Politburo that, "if the American imperialists won the war, they would become more arrogant and would threaten us."[64] On October 2, in the message he drafted to Stalin but did not send, he stated, "If Korea were completely occupied by the Americans and the Korean revolutionary force were fundamentally destroyed, the American invaders would be more rampant, and such a situation would be very unfavorable to the whole East."[65] With the United States intervening in Korea, Taiwan, the Philippines, and Indochina, China would be on the way to being encircled. Under such conditions, it was a pipe dream to think, as the noninterventionists contended, that China could devote its attention to reconstruction and development at home if only it refused to confront the Americans in Korea.[66] Clearly, Mao viewed the Americans as aggressive and Korea as a potential stepping-stone for an attack on China, just as it had been for the Japanese earlier in the century. Almost as clearly, opposition to intervention within the Chinese leadership and Kim Il-sung's reluctance to have China intervene would have deterred Mao from doing so short of a UN ground campaign above the thirty-eighth parallel. Had only ROK troops marched into the North, he may have avoided sending Chinese troops, although he surely would have assisted the North Koreans with supplies and refuge on Chinese territory to enable them to mount a guerrilla resistance.

Mao did not lack reinforcing motives for intervention. As Chen Jian has pointed out, from the start Mao analyzed the war in Korea in the context of "the dialectic Chinese strategic culture," which defined "crisis as a combination of danger and opportunity." In this light, U.S. intervention in Korea and Taiwan provided a chance to further mobilize the Chinese people and to purge remaining reactionary elements. For the PRC to shy away from protecting Korea, on the other hand, would only encourage the reactionaries.[67]

Furthermore, intervention would fulfill an obligation to the North Koreans created by their support for the Communists in the Chinese civil war.[68] Mao saw this obligation in terms of both his country's historic role in the region and his responsibility to promote international revolution. Prior to the nineteenth century and its weakening relative to the great powers, China had enjoyed a special protective relationship with Korea. As an intense nationalist, one of Mao's highest goals in foreign policy was to restore China's traditional influence in border areas. In the context of the global struggle of the Cold War, his nation was part of a vast "intermediate zone" between the Soviet Union and the United States, where the crucial battles were likely to be fought.[69] One such battle was now upon him, and he had no intention of shirking his duty.

Even so, Mao was not suicidal. To insist upon intervention, he had to believe that his China could prevail. He was the man, after all, who in 1927 had coined the phrase "power grows out of the barrel of a gun."[70] The Americans could make more powerful weapons—and more of them—than could China, including atomic bombs. So how did Mao reconcile China's relative material weakness with his belief that his country could actually defeat the United States in a war in Korea?

In the deepest sense the answer rests in the psyche of a man of extraordinary talent, energy, and determination who had a problematic relationship with the authority figure of his childhood, his father, and who had survived, indeed prevailed, as a revolutionary through tumultuous decades in which China had been ripped apart by internal strife and foreign invasion.[71] As a young man Mao had published an article emphasizing physical training and individual will as the key instruments of national renewal. For many years hence, he was forced to adapt to circumstances in which his enemies—whether the Nationalists from the inside or the Japanese from the outside—possessed superior material resources.[72] Through that process Mao had developed ideas, grounded most prominently in the theories of the ancient Chinese strategist Sun Tzu, as to how in war a physically weak power could ultimately defeat a physically strong one. He had implemented them sufficiently deftly to enable the Communists to emerge victorious on the mainland, and at a pace far more rapid than even he had thought possible.[73]

While acknowledging the importance of "objective" factors such as size of population, quantity and quality of military equipment, and economic resources, those ideas reserved a prominent place for "subjective" considerations. Only men could fight and win wars, and their intelligence in mobilizing and deploying material elements and their spirit in executing strategic and tactical plans could result in victory for the objectively weak over the strong.[74] With Mao's ideas and recent battlefield experiences in mind, a group of Chinese field commanders meeting in late September 1950 expressed confidence in the PRC's ability to defeat U.S. forces, the key being their deficiencies in a variety of subjective areas. American troops lacked political motivation because they had invaded another people's country and fought an unjust war; combat effectiveness because they were inexperienced in

such operations as night battles and close-in fighting; tactical flexibility because of adherence to strict military codes and regulations;
and physical and mental toughness because they were products of a
soft, corrupt society. Add to these the objective problem of relative
distance from the actual scene of battle, which would create huge
logistical problems for the Americans, and the commanders saw victory as well within their grasp.[75]

But what of the atomic bomb? Here was a weapon that could level
an entire city in a matter of seconds. There can be little doubt that the
Chinese Communists worried about America's possible use of atomic
bombs. Yet Mao had addressed this issue only a week after the United
States destroyed Hiroshima in August 1945. Mao told his colleagues
in Yanan that such weapons could not "decide wars"; if they could,
Soviet intervention would not have been necessary to bring about
Japan's surrender. A year later he made his first reference to the atomic
bomb as "a paper tiger."[76] By 1950, of course, the Soviets had the
bomb, and the Chinese believed that this would reduce the likelihood
that the Americans would employ it in an Asian war far removed from
Europe, the leading area of U.S. concern. In any event, the objective
advantage of China in possessing the largest population of any nation
on earth made unlikely a U.S. victory through atomic warfare. The
essentially rural nature of the population meant that atomic weapons
could not be used efficiently against China, and even if millions of
people were killed, there would be hundreds of millions still left.[77]
The American atomic capability, in other words, was worrisome, but
not so much so as to dictate against intervention in Korea. A combination of objective and subjective factors still made a glorious victory for
China the likely outcome.

Despite his general confidence, Mao did decide that China should
at first employ defensive tactics in Korea, waiting until objective factors were more in its favor before initiating an offensive. Although no
announcement of Chinese entry would be made, he surmised that the
CPV presence in Korea might be discovered by the enemy before
major engagements occurred. If this discovery brought a halt to the
UN advance, the CPV would spend six months building defensive
lines in the northern mountains, during which time it would train

pilots in the use of Soviet planes and integrate Soviet tanks and artillery into their ground forces. It would consider taking the offensive during the spring of 1951, but only after "having achieved an overwhelming air and land superiority over the enemy's troops."[78] If, on the other hand, enemy forces continued their northern march, the CPV would attempt to engage them primarily in the east, where the more vulnerable ROK troops led the advance.

By the fourth week of October, Chinese troops were pouring across the bridges over the Yalu River into Korea. The only questions that remained were, When would UN forces discover them? and What would be their response?

III

What we now know about Mao's intentions in Korea in mid-October demonstrates the momentous nature of MacArthur's decision to continue an all-out offensive and Washington's decision to permit him to do so. Had non-Korean forces stopped at the narrow neck, only ROK units would have confronted the Chinese during the fall and winter. Those units would have been badly mauled, and whatever was left of them would have retreated behind UN lines, which would have been solidifying well south of the Yalu. Thus UN forces could have dug in over the winter and prepared for enemy offensives in the spring. Meanwhile, the United States could have searched for a diplomatic solution. Whether or not such a solution would have emerged is highly uncertain, but it can be said that, whatever happened in the spring of 1951, the United States would have been in a stronger position, both politically and militarily, to counter Communist action than it actually was when the Chinese launched their counteroffensive in late November 1950. So I now turn to the questions of, first, why Washington did not prevent MacArthur from moving non-Korean troops into the northernmost provinces before the Chinese presence was detected and, second, why it failed to order his retreat, or even a halt to his offensive operations, once that presence was obvious.

There is no simple answer to either of these questions, although a starting point in addressing both is to acknowledge the limitations of U.S. intelligence. When MacArthur's orders of non-Korean troops into the northernmost reaches of North Korea occurred on October 17 and 24, the Chinese decision to intervene directly on the peninsula was not known, even though, by the time of the second order, CPV forces had already crossed the Yalu in large numbers. Before the UN commander launched his offensive in late November, Washington did not know that over two hundred thousand Chinese troops were in Korea. General Charles Willoughby, the UN intelligence chief in Tokyo, never previously acknowledged that more than sixty thousand Chinese soldiers had entered the peninsula. The care taken by the Chinese to camouflage the extent of their presence in Korea, most notably through restricting their daytime movements, clearly influenced American decision making.

Yet *how much* is open to dispute, as a host of other factors contributed to the U.S. debacle of late November. One was MacArthur's personality and aura in the aftermath of Inchon. At Wake Island, where on October 15 President Truman had met the victorious general to discuss the evolving situation in Korea, MacArthur expressed confidence that the Chinese would not intervene. Even if they did, he predicted, UN forces would easily prevail, in large part because of their superiority in the air.[79] Whether on the eve of Japan's attack on Pearl Harbor and the Philippines in 1941, in the aftermath of North Korea's invasion of the South in mid-1950, or in the wake of his own operation at Inchon in September, MacArthur was inclined to overestimate the capacity of his own forces, and now no one in Washington was inclined to challenge him. The Joint Chiefs did request an explanation for the field commander's order of October 24 giving non-Korean ground forces the authority to operate anywhere on the peninsula. MacArthur quickly replied that the move derived from military necessity and that his instructions of September 27 had not prohibited it. In addition, a message two days later from the new secretary of defense, George C. Marshall, and the discussion at Wake Island had made it clear that he possessed the freedom to use his ground forces as he thought necessary within Korea. Military leaders back in Washington did not dispute the man who, against their better judgment, had pulled off the Inchon landing.[80] The advance of American troops in this instance meant that, when they first made contact with Chinese units, they would be well north of the best defensive line above the thirty-eighth parallel. Henceforth, a move to that line would represent a substantial retreat in the face of enemy pressure rather than a prudent precaution to avoid overextension and reduce Chinese anxieties. Given the Truman administration's fears about appearing weak in the face of pressure from the PRC, this difference was of some moment.

MacArthur's persona became all the more important in early November, by which time UN forces had captured and interviewed Chinese soldiers from several different armies. This should have led analysts to the conclusion that a major Chinese intervention was under way. That it did not is best explained by the atmosphere existing in the high command. Seventy years old in 1950, MacArthur surrounded himself with men who would not disturb the dreamworld of self-worship in which he often chose to live. General Willoughby was representative of this pattern. Imperial in demeanor to those below him, he was quite the reverse to his boss, who he knew was determined to continue the UN advance to the Yalu. Some officers in that command in Korea worried deeply about the level of Chinese intervention, but their concerns never got through Willoughby to the man who most needed to know.[81]

Yet MacArthur would not have been easy to persuade, especially if persuasion meant giving up on his offensive plans. When late in the first week of November he did become concerned about the movement of Chinese troops across the Yalu, he asked Washington for permission to attack the bridges there rather than to halt his movement northward. Since he knew that NSC-81 left open the possibility of attacks on China in the event it intervened on a large scale in Korea, he viewed the events of early November with a degree of equanimity. Washington's message of November 8 informing him that his mission of destroying North Korean forces might have to be modified led him to plead "with all the earnestness that I possess that there be no weakening at this crucial moment and that we press on to complete victory which I believe can be achieved if our determination and indomitable will don't desert us." He told his superiors that "with my air power, now unrestricted so far as Korea is concerned except as to hydro-electric installations, I can deny reinforcements coming across the Yalu in sufficient strength to prevent destruction of those forces now arrayed against me in North Korea."[82] In reality, he probably calculated that, if this estimate turned out to be false and his ground forces did become threatened by the Chinese, he could persuade Washington to use air and naval power against China—and that would prove decisive.[83]

In the end, it was President Truman and his top advisers, especially Acheson and Marshall, who most needed to know of the massive Chinese presence in Korea. Unlike MacArthur, they were Europe-firsters, and they genuinely wanted to avoid a confrontation with China. Had they known the magnitude of the Chinese presence in Korea, they might well have stopped UN ground forces during the second week of November.

Still, these men *did* have access to an intelligence report of November 8 by the Central Intelligence Agency, which contrasted with Mac-Arthur's optimism. This report estimated that combined Chinese and North Korean ground forces on the peninsula could compel their UN counterparts to withdraw to "defensive positions further south." Whatever the current number of PRC troops already committed, Beijing probably could make available 350,000 soldiers "for sustained ground operations in Korea . . . within thirty to sixty days." On the other hand, if the military situation in North Korea became stabilized, the Chinese might decide "that, with advantageous terrain and the onset of winter, their forces now in Korea are sufficient to accomplish their immediate purpose."[84] Although this report received the endorsement of the intelligence agencies of the State Department and the armed services, the most that the National Security Council was willing to do the next day was propose efforts by Acheson to seek contacts with the Chinese. He met no opposition to a suggestion that the PRC be offered a demilitarized zone of ten miles on both sides of the Yalu, but it was agreed that there should be no alteration of MacArthur's mission to clear Korea of enemy forces.[85]

Had the secretary of state lived in a political and bureaucratic vacuum, he probably would have called for a halt to the UN offensive at some point over the next two weeks. During that time of preparation for MacArthur's final offensive, Acheson tried unsuccessfully to contact the Chinese. He attempted as well to shore up support for American policy at the United Nations and, along with President Truman, to provide public reassurances to the PRC that the United States had no intention to carry the war into China.[86] Yet neither the propaganda emanating from Beijing nor reports from non-Communist diplomats there inspired confidence regarding Chinese intentions. On November 17 John Paton Davies, a China specialist on the State Department's Policy Planning Staff who also had served in Moscow, advised that "the bulk of the evidence . . . [indicates] that the Kremlin and Peiping [Beijing] are committed to at least holding the northern fringe of Korea—and, that, against our present force they have the military capability of doing so." He thought it best to halt "major military operations and seek the establishment of a demilitarized zone south of the Yalu."[87]

Yet the Pentagon, including the much-admired Marshall—who had preceeded Acheson as secretary of state—insisted that MacArthur's mission not be changed. Acheson was a bold, even arrogant, man. Recent developments on the domestic scene, however, had placed him on the defensive. On November 7 the Republicans made substantial gains in congressional elections after sharply attacking the secretary of state and his Asian policies. Some Democrats even blamed the aristocratic and sometimes acerbic Acheson personally for the losses.[88] Under the circumstances, even if he had been able to persuade Truman to bring MacArthur to a halt, a divided administration would have faced a fierce public debate during which "the sorcerer of Inchon" would have made his views known. Unfortunately, if understandably, Acheson chose to follow rather than to speak up, a course that he would come to regard as the low point of his service to the president.[89]

In most government settings, short of a disastrous turn of events or overwhelming evidence of such a turn on the horizon, policy makers tend to hold to rather than alter established policy. Regarding the U.S. course in Korea during November 1950, the evidence that indicated a halt to offensive operations included Chinese internal propaganda that seemed to be mobilizing the nation for war with the United States, the presence already of an undetermined number of Chinese troops on the peninsula, and the possibility, given the buildup north of the Yalu, that hundreds of thousands more would enter the fray. There was also known to be a substantial buildup of Soviet planes in Manchuria—and Soviet pilots did show a willingness to fly them against their UN counterparts in limited missions along and slighly south of the Yalu.[90] This evidence was not sufficiently definite in identifying Chinese intentions and capabilities to override a willful general who had recently led his forces to a brilliant victory and now promised another if only the folks back home would let him finish the job. Among those folks were professional military men accustomed to giving a good deal of freedom to the commander in the field. As in early October, they and others continued to fear the consequences of showing weakness in the face of a Chinese threat. From the president on down, they shied away from the public spat with MacArthur that was sure to follow any change in his orders. The result was, as Acheson later put it, "one of the most terrific disasters that has occurred to American foreign policy, and certainly . . . the greatest disaster which occurred to the Truman administration."[91]

FROM THE START OF THE KOREAN WAR, THE SOVIET UNION AND the United States had wanted to avoid a direct clash on the peninsula. That desire had not changed by late November. Nonetheless, with the second team on the Communist side now fully engaged, with the Soviets building up their airpower in Manchuria and from November 1 onward giving the Chinese limited fighter support in the air over the Yalu, and with U.S. and allied forces reeling in the face of the enemy onslaught, a pattern of escalation could easily emerge that would end in superpower confrontation.[92] Such a scenario is not difficult to construct: an angry, despondent MacArthur demanding that his superiors at home grant him authority to bomb Chinese bases in Manchuria; a beleaguered Truman administration giving in to the pressures of the moment; a cornered Stalin expanding Soviet air action to protect his ally; the Americans frustrated with at best a stalemate in Korea, at worst a defeat, lashing out with atomic weapons; the Soviets taking advantage of their conventional superiority in Europe and disarray among America's allies to launch a military attack there. To many at the time this scenario appeared close to reality on November 30, when in a press conference President Truman stated that he had not ruled out the possibility of using atomic weapons.[93]

CHAPTER 5

Why the War Did Not Expand beyond Korea,

November 1950–July 1951

THE CHINESE SECOND-PHASE OFFENSIVE BEGINNING ON NOVEMBER 25, 1950, was to the Communist side what the Inchon landing had been to the United Nations. Like the Americans before September 15, the Chinese prior to December had given considerable thought to a military campaign to unify Korea. Mao's unsent telegram to Stalin of October 2 had emphasized the desirability of quickly wiping out the Americans on the peninsula. Such an outcome, rather than a prolonged stalemate, would reduce the prospects of the United States waging a major war against the Chinese mainland. Yet the expulsion of UN forces from all Korea would require large-scale Soviet matériel assistance, and Mao was prepared to fight a holding operation until such aid arrived and the CPV was fully prepared to use it.[1] Mac-Arthur's final offensive made it impossible to avoid a direct military confrontation with the United Nations through the winter. Even then,

Mao's initial objective in the second-phase offensive was to push the enemy back to a line from Pyongyang to Wonsan.[2]

The rapid retreat of enemy units opened to Mao the possibility of achieving total victory more rapidly than anticipated. On December 4, after Kim Il-sung had visited Mao and pressed for that goal, Beijing wired CPV headquarters that, although the war "might be protracted," it also might "be resolved quickly." Negotiations with the United States should occur only after it agreed to withdraw entirely from Korea. Meanwhile, the CPV and its North Korean ally should seize not only Pyongyang but Seoul as well.[3] Stalin soon wired support for this position from Moscow.[4] By midmonth the UN Eighth Army in the west had retreated all the way to the Imjin River just south of the thirty-eighth parallel, and the X Corps in the east was evacuating by sea from Hungnam and Wonsan. Mao had received an intelligence report that General J. Lawton Collins, the U.S. army chief of staff, had concluded after a trip to Japan and Korea that the United States could not "retain a long-term defense" on the peninsula.[5] Under the circumstances, the Chinese leader was anxious to avoid granting either political legitimacy to the thirty-eighth parallel or UN forces a respite that would enable them to regroup. On December 22, under pressure from Mao and despite concerns about excessive optimism, General Peng Dehuai gave the order for a third-phase offensive to commence on New Year's Eve.[6]

On that night CPV troops, along with restored DPRK units now under Chinese command, attacked all along the front. In the west, UN forces quickly abandoned Seoul, crossed the Han, and retreated all the way to Pyongtaek, seventy miles below the thirty-eighth parallel. Farther east, North Korean soldiers broke through ROK divisions and penetrated deep into the South, where they joined anti-Rhee guerrillas. Reports flowing into Washington from the UN command led to fears in the Pentagon that friendly forces soon would have to evacuate the peninsula.

In fact, since early December, MacArthur's estimates of the Korean situation had been extremely pessimistic. General Collins had met with him on the sixth in Tokyo after returning from consultations with U.S. field commanders in Korea. Supremely optimistic only weeks

MAP 5. The Chinese advance, 1950–51.

before, the UN commander was now quite the reverse. He urged that reinforcements be sent immediately from the United States, that an earlier offer from Chiang Kai-shek to provide Nationalist troops be accepted, that the U.S. Navy institute a blockade of the China coast, and that air and naval bombardment of the Chinese mainland com-

FIG. 12. Chinese troops captured by the First U.S. Marine Division in North Korea on December 9, 1950. Note especially the difference between the footwear of the captives and captors. Chinese soldiers often wore tennis sneakers or rags on their feet. The inadequacy of their clothing in the harsh Korean winter proved an important factor in their inability to sustain their offensive in South Korea in early 1951.

FIG. 13. Turkish troops generally fought tenaciously in the retreat of UN forces in late 1950 and early 1951. Here a Turkish unit rests on a mountain road in western Korea.

FIG. 14. General Matthew B. Ridgway, commander of the Eighth Army in Korea, honors a French unit for its heroic stand against the Chinese at Chipyong-ni in February 1950. The battle was a key in halting the Chinese advance on the central front.

mence, with the goal of destroying the PRC's capacity to wage war. Otherwise, unless the Chinese agreed to an armistice at the thirty-eighth parallel, UN forces should withdraw from the peninsula.[7] On December 30, with leaders at home as yet unwilling to provide him with reinforcements or to expand the war, MacArthur delivered a similar assessment. In pleading to Washington for attacks on the Chinese mainland, he declared that, since the PRC was already fully committed in Korea, the United States could do nothing to "further aggravate" Sino-American relations. He believed that "a Soviet decision to precipitate a general war [probably] would depend solely upon its own estimate of relative strengths and capabilities" rather than on U.S. action outside Korea. Furthermore, a forced evacuation of Korea without direct military action against China "would have the most adverse effect upon the people of Asia," would require "a material reinforcement of the forces now in this theater" in order to hold the offshore island chain, and "would at once release the bulk of the Chinese forces now [in Korea] . . . for action elsewhere."[8]

On January 3, 1951, Admiral Forrest Sherman, the chief of naval operations, proposed measures to the Joint Chiefs that bore similarities to MacArthur's. Sherman wanted to reexamine present limitations on operations related to Korea, keeping in mind only the need to avert hostilities with the Soviet Union until the United States was more fully armed. "As soon as our position in Korea is stabilized, or when we have evacuated Korea," the United States should institute a naval blockade of China. Air and naval attacks on the mainland should occur only if the Chinese Communists attacked U.S. forces beyond Korea. For now the United States should remove restrictions on Nationalist Chinese operations against the mainland, provide logistic support to anti-Communist guerrillas there, and initiate periodic aerial reconnaissance over Manchuria and along the China coast. If the United Nations refused to support these measures, Washington should act unilaterally.[9] Nine days later, in the midst of another testy exchange with Tokyo, the Joint Chiefs "tentatively agreed" to Sherman's proposals, and Secretary of Defense Marshall placed them on the agenda of the NSC meeting scheduled for January 17.[10] Four days prior to this meeting, Truman sent a personal message to MacArthur in which he stated that, if UN forces were evacuated from Korea, "it should be clear to the world that that course is forced upon us by military necessity and that we shall not accept the result politically or militarily until the aggression has been rectified."[11]

The Truman administration never adopted MacArthur's or Sherman's proposals. On April 11 the president removed MacArthur from all his commands. In early May the Americans began secret peace feelers to the Soviets and the Chinese, indicating that they were willing to end the fighting in Korea in the general area where it had begun the previous year.[12] On June 23 Jacob Malik, the Soviet ambassador to the United Nations, made a radio address in New York in which he stated that "as a first step" toward halting the war, the belligerents should discuss "a cease-fire and an armistice providing for the mutual withdrawal of forces from the 38th parallel."[13] Finally, on July 10, armistice talks began between the two military commands in Korea at Kaesong near the thirty-eighth parallel. The period of highest risk of an expanded war had passed.

Why, in the face of the Chinese counteroffensive of late 1950, and especially the Communist advance south of the thirty-eighth parallel early the next year, did the United States refuse to expand the war to China? Why did the two sides eventually agree to commence negotiations without either having achieved a clear-cut victory? Answers to these questions are critical to understanding why the Korean War fell short of escalating into a direct confrontation between the United States and the Soviet Union and, quite possibly, another world war.

I

The main reason the war did not expand is that the top leaders of the two nations with the greatest capacity to do so, the United States and the Soviet Union, preferred to contain the fighting. Unlike MacArthur, Truman believed East Asia was secondary to Europe in the U.S. struggle with the Soviet Union. He understood as well that U.S. forces were poorly prepared for all-out war with the primary enemy, which in the midst of the increased danger led him in mid-December to declare a national emergency and create the Office of Defense Mobilization, with sweeping powers to build up U.S. military capabilities.[14] Meanwhile, the more the United States expended its resources in Korea and China, the less would remain for a potential conflict in Europe. The presence of Soviet air divisions in Manchuria gave the Communists a substantial capacity not only to resist U.S. incursions beyond Korea but also to extend operations over the peninsula and even to Japan.[15] Finally, and perhaps most important of all, Washington's European allies were scared out of their wits at the thought of an expanded war. In mid-November Acheson had contacted the British and several other allies about the likelihood, in light of enemy air operations into Korea from Manchuria, that UN planes would be given the right of "hot pursuit" north of the Yalu. The response to the prospect of this relatively limited action was distinctly negative.[16] The Europeans were far from certain to remain supportive of the United States should a larger war occur, unless it was initiated by the other side. Since the bulk of any U.S. nuclear attack on the Soviet Union and operations to supply friendly conventional forces on the Continent would have to be launched from the United Kingdom, Washington could ill afford to alienate London—or, for that matter, any of the other NATO governments.[17]

Truman's understanding of this situation became clear in the aftermath of his statement to the press of November 30 that use of atomic weapons in Korea was under consideration and that such weapons were under the control of the commander in the field, that is, MacArthur.[18] Despite a quick corrective statement from the White House on the latter point, Truman's faux pas sent British prime minister Clement Attlee hurtling across the Atlantic for consultations. Howard K. Smith, London correspondent for the *Nation*, described the circumstances as "one of the most amazing political upheavals in Europe since the [second world] war[,] . . . a rebellion of free Europe against the kind of leadership America was giving the West on the Korean issue."[19] Truman made no effort to discourage Attlee's visit, although he resisted his guest's pressure to make concessions on Taiwan and China's seat at the United Nations to achieve an armistice in Korea. The president agreed, however, to seek negotiations to end the fighting there and to attempt "to keep the Prime Minister at all times informed of developments" that might lead to the use of atomic weapons.[20] To bolster the European military front, Truman also agreed to the "early completion of plans for integrated forces in Europe and appointment of a supreme commander for NATO."[21]

The Attlee meeting represented merely the beginning of intense allied pressure on the United States. Until the Chinese counteroffensive, Washington had largely had its way on Korea in the United Nations. That event brought a major change, as the international body shifted from being largely an instrument of U.S. policy to one of allied and neutral nations to restrain the world's strongest power.

The setting was the General Assembly, since in the Security Council the Soviet Union alone could block action with its veto. This it did on November 30 when it killed a six-power resolution calling upon China to withdraw from Korea. The United States wanted to take the measure immediately to the General Assembly. Yet with India in the lead among Asian neutrals and the United Kingdom and Canada guiding the allies, Washington was forced to give priority to a thirteen-power resolution that called for creation of a group of three persons "to determine the basis on which a satisfactory cease-fire in Korea can be arranged."[22] The resolution passed on December 14; on the next day Acheson authorized the U.S. delegation at the United Nations to communicate to the cease-fire group "a generalized statement of conditions" for an armistice in Korea that provided for establishment of "a demilitarized area across all of Korea approx[imately] 20 miles in width with the southern limit following generally the line of the 38th parallel."[23] The United States had been exploring the possibility of such a settlement for two weeks, but its formal expression to the cease-fire group added to its solidity as the U.S. position. The secretary of state also conceded that negotiations with the Chinese could deal with issues beyond the peninsula so long as Korea came first and was not connected with other matters.[24]

Still, the Communist side opposed the thirteen-power resolution all the way through the General Assembly and then refused to engage the cease-fire group. Statements in the Chinese press and by a PRC delegation temporarily observing proceedings at the United Nations indicated that Beijing would not end the fighting without a settlement of the Taiwan and UN representation issues in its favor and perhaps even participation in negotiations for a peace treaty with Japan. PRC diplomats departed from the United States on December 19. Three days later Zhou En-lai publicly condemned the resolution as illegal, demanded the withdrawal of all foreign troops from Korea, and characterized a cease-fire as serving no other purpose but to secure time for U.S. forces on the peninsula to regroup for another offensive. Clearly, the Communists intended to exploit their military advantage to the full.[25] That decision, and the early success of the Communist offensive below the thirty-eighth parallel, put great strain on efforts in the American polity and at the United Nations to limit the war.

The most important factors in bolstering restraint in Washington were the petering out of the enemy offensive during the second week of January and the rebuilding of the fighting spirit of UN ground forces by General Matthew B. Ridgway, who had taken command of the Eighth Army late the previous December after the death in a jeep accident of General Walton Walker. Forty miles below Seoul and in the rugged mountain terrain of central Korea, the CPV, hampered by extended supply lines, the absence of air support, a paucity of mechanized ground transport, and severe winter weather for its poorly clad and fed troops, temporarily exhausted its capacity to advance.[26] Between January 15 and 18, General Collins and General Hoyt Vandenberg, the air force chief of staff, visited the front in Korea and reported home that there was no immediate danger of friendly forces being driven from the peninsula.[27] By February 11, when the CPV finally launched a new offensive on the central front, UN units already had executed limited counteroffensives of their own. In the west they were even closing in on the Han River just south of Seoul.[28] The momentum in Washington for expanding the war had subsided. MacArthur's reports on Korea would never be trusted again.

American allies and neutrals had continued in the new year to work to restrain Washington, and the UN General Assembly continued to be their primary forum. The CPV offensive across the thirty-eighth parallel sent the allies and the United States off into opposite directions in New York. The allies wanted to continue the efforts of the cease-fire group to seek negotiations with the Communists, while the United States pushed for consideration of a resolution condemning the PRC as an aggressor and endorsing sanctions. In the end, the British and the Canadians carried out a delaying action against rather than outright opposition to an aggressor resolution in hope that the military situation in Korea would stabilize and lead to a moderation of U.S. sentiment.[29]

As early as January 5, Acheson told British foreign minister Bevin that failure to condemn China would "be the beginning of the end of the UN just as the end of the League of Nations started with their [sic] failure to take any action against Japan and Italy in similar circumstances." In the United States, he warned, "a failure of the UN to recognize this aggression would create a wave of isolationism . . . which would jeopardize all that we are trying to do with and for the

Atlantic Pact countries."[30] In fact, public opinion polls showed broad sentiment in favor of withdrawal from Korea; former president Herbert Hoover received widespread attention for his view that the United States should develop a military strategy focused on the Western Hemisphere; and many Republican politicians—joined by some Democrats—openly opposed sending more U.S. troops to Europe, thus sparking a "great debate" in Congress. Acheson's warning was hardly an empty one.[31]

Yet Acheson grasped the seriousness of allied and neutral sentiment on Korea, as well as the risks of flouting the United Nations after having initiated its involvement in Korea in both 1947 and 1950. With British commonwealth prime ministers gathering in London to discuss efforts in the cease-fire group—led by India's Benegal Rau—to advance a series of principles for a settlement of the war, the U.S. secretary of state opted for patience. It took until January 11 for the prime ministers and the cease-fire group to agree on five principles to present to the Chinese. These principles linked settlement of issues regarding Taiwan and Chinese representation at the United Nations to a Korean cease-fire, a linkage that the Truman administration wanted to avoid. But despite the risks of such a course on the domestic political front, where sentiment against concessions to China ran high, Acheson thought that the United States should support them in the First Committee of the General Assembly. The president went along.[32] Their assumption was that the Chinese, fearful of negotiations that might force a halt to advantageous military operations, would reject the principles. This, in turn, would open the way for passage by the General Assembly of a resolution condemning China.

The assumption was largely correct. The First Committee, in which all UN members were represented, passed the principles on January 13. Four days later the Chinese rejected them. On the twentieth the United States presented to the First Committee a resolution condemning China as an aggressor and calling for "a committee . . . as a matter of urgency to consider additional measures to be employed to meet this aggression and to report thereon to the General Assembly."[33] Then Zhou En-lai threatened to upset the U.S. applecart by sending a message on the twenty-second that narrowed the gap between the Chinese position and the five principles. Finally, after the British cabinet actually voted against supporting the U.S. resolution as drafted, Washington revised the measure to include creation of a "good offices committee," which would continue the efforts of the cease-fire group to close the gap between the PRC and the United States. If this committee reported "satisfactory progress in its efforts," the committee considering additional measures against China could postpone its report to the General Assembly.[34] Ambassador Austin also stated in floor debate that the resolution would confer no new authority on the UN commander and that any report on additional measures to the General Assembly would constitute a recommendation only. On February 1 that body approved the amended resolution, with India and Burma alone outside the Communist bloc voting nay.

Although the United States had had much of its way in the United Nations, fears of an expanded war had produced delay in passage of the resolution and modification of it in a manner that reduced prospects of early action against China beyond Korea. The delay gave time for UN forces to stabilize the front on the peninsula. The modification, by further delaying the prospects of sanctions against the PRC, left open nonmilitary measures, such as an economic embargo, as a possible response to a future major Chinese offensive in Korea. That offensive would be a while in coming, but when it did, the United States was in the midst of an orgy of internal recrimination over MacArthur's dismissal. The existence of relatively limited sanctions to impose against China represented a convenient safety valve for both the Truman administration and the United Nations.

II

In the weeks following passage of the aggressor resolution, UN forces in Korea gradually recovered most of the ground they had lost below the thirty-eighth parallel. After blunting the Communist offensive on the central front in mid-February, they slowly worked their way northward, recapturing Seoul in mid-March. By the end of the month, except in the extreme west, they had virtually restored the ROK to its prewar boundaries. Three weeks later, UN lines were slightly above the thirty-eighth parallel nearly everywhere other than on the Ongjin Peninsula.[35]

This advance greatly diminished support for an expanded war in the executive branch in Washington, but it did not satisfy MacArthur's thirst for total victory. Despite Truman's order of the previous December that U.S. representatives abroad avoid all but the most innocuous public statements without prior clearance from home, during February and March the UN commander made a series of comments indicating discontent with restrictions to Korea on his use of airpower and with the possibility of a military stalemate.[36] Washington did not rebuke him until March 24, when he issued a press release that taunted the Chinese for their alleged lack of military prowess, declared his forces as fully capable through an expanded war to threaten China with "imminent military collapse," and invited the commander of enemy forces to meet with him to agree upon the means of achieving UN political objectives in Korea, that is, unification, "without further bloodshed."[37] Coming after MacArthur had been informed of an impending presidential peace initiative, this statement represented, as Acheson later put it, "sabotage."[38]

It was not until April 5, when three more dissenting statements by MacArthur hit the press, that sustained deliberations began in Washington leading to his dismissal.[39] On the previous day the Senate, following a three-month-long debate, had passed a resolution endorsing the dispatch of four U.S. divisions to Europe, a key element of the administration's plan to strengthen NATO. In addition, intelligence reports from Korea indicated a massive buildup of Chinese forces for a spring offensive. Given the number of enemy planes reportedly stationed in Manchuria, the Communists now had the potential to expand air operations well beyond the current level of contesting UN air and naval missions directed at North Korea. In mid-January the Communists had expanded their air operations to include more planes and areas well south of the Yalu.[40] Now, it was feared, substantial attacks might be launched against UN forces on the ground, on UN supply lines, on South Korean ports, or even on Japan. To counter such operations, which could easily shift the balance of military power back in favor of the Communists, the UN commander would have to act quickly, and this would require his possession of authority to order his planes to pursue enemy aircraft back to their bases in Manchuria. On April 5 the Joint Chiefs drafted a new directive to MacArthur doing precisely this, but although the president gave his approval, they never dispatched it to Tokyo. Decision makers in Washington feared that, under conditions of heightened tension, MacArthur would use the directive to expand the war when it was not really necessary.[41] Thus on April 8 the Joint Chiefs and Secretary of Defense Marshall advised the president that, "from a military point of view," MacArthur should be recalled.[42] With Acheson already on board, Truman informed his advisers of his decision on the next day. Meanwhile, he had ordered an air force squadron armed with atomic weapons to the western Pacific.[43]

As in January, allied opinion influenced the process. American leaders realized that granting new authority to the UN commander would be a hard sell to other NATO members. It might be impossible while MacArthur remained in the post, a point made clear on April 6 by the "preliminary" British response to a U.S. overture regarding retaliatory bombing across the Yalu. The British believed that two steps should precede such action: consultations among the allies at the ministerial level, and a warning to the Chinese "for the immediate cessation of their air attacks." Military leaders in London questioned the likelihood of an escalated Communist air war. Foreign Minister Herbert Morrison summarized the British view with the remark that "MacArthur's rashness and political irresponsibility, rather than massive air attacks from outside Korea," represented the greatest danger of an expanded war.[44]

Even with MacArthur gone, the British refused to agree to retaliatory attacks outside Korea without prior consultation. The firing produced vicious Republican attacks on Truman and Acheson, including calls for their impeachment, and public opinion polls indicated widespread sympathy for the deposed general. Now the British worried that domestic pressures would reduce the administration's restraint in Korea.[45]

Washington held off on giving the new UN commander, General

Ridgway, expanded authority until several days after the first stage of the Chinese spring offensive began on April 22. By this time Beijing and Moscow probably believed such authority had been granted—or would be if they expanded the air war—since speculation to this effect had appeared in the American press earlier in the month.[46] After the twenty-sixth they surely understood this, because at that time the information leaked out through the U.S. delegation at the United Nations.[47] Yet even when the authority was sent to Tokyo, it was on a very restricted basis. "If at all possible," the Joint Chiefs instructed Ridgway, "you should seek JCS advice before taking action and in any case you should inform the JCS immediately and withhold publicity until notification of the allies has taken place."[48] Despite considerable lobbying in private by the State Department, the British never agreed to the bombing of Manchuria without prior consultation at the governmental level.[49]

Another issue that reached its climax after MacArthur's dismissal was economic sanctions against China. With the failure of the good offices committee of the General Assembly to deliver the Chinese to the negotiating table, pressure from the United States for the additional measures committee to recommend economic sanctions had been building for some time. Washington had imposed a total embargo on trade with the PRC during the previous December, and it hoped to persuade the rest of the non-Communist world to follow suit. To Acheson, the importance of an early move in this direction became all the more important after Truman called MacArthur home. Now more than ever the administration needed, first, to convey to the enemy that there was no U.S. weakening on Korea and, second, to show an aroused public at home that it possessed a plan for ending the conflict other than the risky strategy of expanded military operations.

Matters came to a head in early May. On May 3 General MacArthur, who two weeks before had delivered a moving address to Congress, began testifying before a joint session of the Senate Armed Services Committee and Foreign Relations Committee. He was the first witness in for the most part open hearings that would last into June and would include appearances by all the administration's top foreign and military policymakers except Truman himself. Among other things,

MacArthur fueled nationalist sentiments by referring to U.S. allies' contributions to Korea as "token"—in fact, the United States and the ROK were providing over 80 percent of the ground troops—and by asserting that large quantities of strategic materials were flowing into China through British Hong Kong.[50] The otherwise anti-MacArthur *New York Times* applauded him on the latter point, declaring that "no one in his senses can urge that the way to deal with aggression is to arm it."[51] An amendment soon appeared to an appropriations bill in the Senate that would end U.S. economic assistance to countries selling war-related materials to Communist nations.[52]

By this time, the additional measures committee of the General Assembly was in session, and the United States had submitted a proposal for an embargo on petroleum, atomic energy materials, arms, ammunition, and implements of war, including articles useful in making such products. Allied members did not like the proposal, both because of its timing—the first phase of the Chinese spring offensive had been blunted, and the time appeared ripe for peace overtures—and because its categories were too broad. Yet U.S. pressure proved decisive. On May 10 the British announced support for the measure, and four days later the committee went along. Four days after that, a resolution encompassing the U.S. position passed the General Assembly without a single negative vote.[53]

The beginning of the second phase of the Chinese spring offensive on May 16 helped to produce this result, but it also fueled allied worries that the United States was not through in escalating pressure on the PRC. Already the Truman administration had announced the dispatch of a military mission to Taiwan, an increase in military aid to the Nationalist regime there, and the establishment of a priority for such aid equal to that for NATO countries.[54] On the seventeenth Nationalist leader Chiang Kai-shek called for the opening of a second front on the Chinese mainland. On the next day Dean Rusk, the assistant secretary of state for the Far East, delivered a belligerent speech in New York in which he characterized the PRC as a mere puppet of the Soviet Union and pledged that the United States would "not acquiesce in the degradation which is being forced upon . . . [our friends in China.]"[55] At the Senate hearings General Omar Bradley, the chairman of the Joint Chiefs of Staff, indicated that the United States had no intention of restricting military operations to Korea if the war continued indefinitely. The present strategy was to persuade the enemy to accept an end to the fighting by making it excessively costly to continue. If the desired result did not emerge within a reasonable period, then a more aggressive course might be adopted. To top policy makers, in other words, restraint was a relative, not an absolute, virtue.[56]

III

Moscow and Beijing closely followed the American press, which provided massive coverage of the Senate hearings. The testimony included that of General Vandenberg, who estimated that U.S. airpower could not destroy China's war-making capacity without severely undermining its ability to launch a major atomic offensive against the Soviet Union.[57] Combined with allied opposition, also heavily covered in the press in the United States and Western Europe, there were strong reasons for Washington *not* to expand the war. Yet Communist leaders surely understood that, so long as the fighting went on in Korea, its escalation was always a possibility. From what we can gather from the American side, the possibility would have increased had UN forces been driven from the peninsula, and in December 1950 and April 1951, Stalin supported CPV plans to launch offensives aimed at achieving such a result. In mid-March 1951 he even approved a proposal to move some Soviet air units into North Korea so they could better protect CPV supply lines.[58] Apparently that proposal was never executed because the airfields in North Korea could not be protected against enemy attack. Nonetheless, another Soviet air division was sent to operate from Manchuria, and air action in northwestern Korea again escalated in early April.[59] That said, Stalin consistently refused to commit Soviet troops to combat or to permit Soviet air forces to engage in operations against UN ground forces or supply lines. Had he desired, Stalin easily could have provoked an expanded war by increasing Soviet military action in northeast Asia or even by launching a Soviet invasion of Western Europe. Why did he avoid such adventures while clearly encouraging the Chinese to push aggressively in Korea?

Evidence from the Soviet press of December 1950, from official circles in Moscow, and from a U.S. State Department report on a meeting of Soviet foreign minister Andrei Vishinsky with Communist bloc delegates at the United Nations (obviously acquired through a mole in the Polish delegation) provides a clear picture of Soviet thinking at the early stages of the Chinese counteroffensive in Korea.[60] The Soviets regarded the United States in particular and the West in general as confused and divided and, as a result, likely to act weakly in the face of the Chinese challenge. The State Department characterization of Vishinsky's statement succinctly outlined this point of view:

> There will be no war at this time because we do not intend to go to war and the United States cannot afford to do so . . . because it is faced with political and economic disintegration. The isolationist movement is rapidly gaining ground and disunity is spreading. The American people are growing more and more convinced that the United States has no real allies and that they cannot control the situation themselves. . . . The United States is trying to dominate the countries of Western Europe, which have to give ground to a certain extent because of their internal economic conditions . . . . But they are very much opposed to the present American policy, which they realize would only bring about a catastrophe if pursued to its final conclusion.[61]

There was a substantial kernel of truth in this analysis, although it was surely influenced by the predisposition of Marxist-Leninists to emphasize the "internal contradictions" within and among capitalist nations. Under the circumstances, Stalin regarded a forward strategy by the Chinese and North Koreans on the peninsula as more likely to promote disarray than unity in the Western camp. If to stem disunity the Americans made concessions on Korea, Taiwan, Chinese representation at the United Nations, and/or a Japanese peace treaty, the outcome was bearable to him. If the Americans hung on militarily in Korea and became even more adamant in their political and economic opposition to the PRC, that was bearable as well, probably even preferable on the second point. Even an expansion of the war to China in the manner MacArthur wanted could be advantageous, as it could only tear asunder the Western alliance and leave the United States weaker, both politically and militarily, to act in Europe. The biggest danger was an all-out nuclear attack on the Soviet Union, but it seemed unlikely that such a move could be carried out without substantial prior warning or crucial allied support. Thus Stalin chose to hold direct Soviet involvement in Korea to a minimum while encouraging Mao and Kim to push forward aggressively. In Eastern Europe he pressed Communist governments to increase the mobilization of their economies for military production and intensified a propaganda barrage in NATO countries indicating that West German rearmament, which the Americans advocated, would result in war.[62] This basic approach continued well into the spring.

By early June, however, the spring offensives of the CPV had failed, with Communist forces suffering well over one hundred thousand casualties. Although the Chinese possessed almost endless reserves of manpower, their losses had decimated many of the most experienced and highly motivated units. Increasingly, the PRC called upon former soldiers of Nationalist Chinese armies who, when faced with a lack of food and ammunition and superior enemy firepower, often surrendered. At the end of the first week of June, UN ground forces had not only recovered all territory lost during late April and May but also advanced to positions nearly forty miles above the thirty-eighth parallel in extreme eastern sectors and from fifteen to twenty-five miles north of the line in all other areas east of the Imjin River.[63]

Moreover, the Western alliance had held firm and even showed signs of consolidation. In December 1950 Truman had named General Dwight D. Eisenhower as the first NATO commander, and the arrival in Europe of the great soldier-statesman early the next year had helped calm the worst fears in the alliance. So had the U.S. retreat from its earlier position of insisting upon moving forward simultaneously with West German rearmament and new deployments of American troops to Europe. In early April the congressional debate on the latter ended, and in May a U.S. division arrived on continental Europe. Plans for three more divisions from the United States and two from Great Britain continued, as did progress toward the expansion of NATO to Greece and Turkey. The United States, Great Britain, and France also committed military assistance to Tito's wayward Communist regime in Yugoslavia. The steady advance of rearmament programs on both sides of the Atlantic promised to reduce fears among the European democracies of the rearming of West Germany, thus making it more likely.[64]

Progress also had occurred toward a generous peace treaty with Japan, which would exclude the Soviet Union and China, provide for a continued U.S. military presence in the islands, and permit a Japanese contribution to its own defense. Australia and New Zealand had been bought off with the prospect of a security treaty with the United States. The same prospect existed for the Philippines, and the British grudgingly went along in exchange for U.S. agreement to leave Nationalist China out of the process and to restrict Japan's right to build ships to challenge Britain's role in Asian trade.[65]

While increasing cohesion characterized the Western alliance, strains developed not far below the surface among the Communist powers. Mao was never satisfied with Soviet matériel support to the war effort, whether in the air or on the ground. Chinese analyses of the failure of the spring offensives emphasized superior enemy firepower. Not only did the CPV lack air cover for its troops and heavy artillery equal to that on the other side, but much of the Soviet equipment was also of poor quality, sometimes even inoperable. Adding to the resentment was Stalin's insistence that the aid be purchased—albeit on credit. Finally, for the Soviet advisers—technical, economic, and military alike—Stalin demanded special privileges, including extraterritoriality in the event they broke Chinese laws.[66]

Stalin, of course, possessed a global perspective on military matters rather than a regional one like Mao. Soviet productivity had distinct limits, and Communist forces in the European theater were engaged in an intense process of modernization. When on June 21 Mao asked him to equip sixty CPV divisions by the end of the year, Stalin replied that this was "physically impossible and totally unthinkable," that it would take through the first half of 1954 to meet such a request.[67] In addition, the Soviet leader remained dissatisfied with the pace at which Chinese pilots were entering the fray. On June 13 he wired Mao that eight Chinese air divisions should be committed immediately to the fight in Korea. Three days later Stalin complained to the chief Soviet military adviser in China that Mao was trying "to make professors out of the Chinese flyers, not pilots."[68] Clearly, neither side was content with the performance of the other.

The Chinese and North Koreans had problems as well. Kim Il-sung and Peng Dehuai had clashed in January over continuing the offensive below the thirty-eighth parallel, with Kim insisting on pressing southward. Mao and eventually Stalin had supported Peng on the matter.[69] Peng and other Chinese generals tended to look down on Kim as a military leader, especially for his failure to take precautionary measures late the previous summer after Beijing warned him of a possible U.S. counterattack at Inchon. For his part, Kim complained of the overbearing influence of Mao through Pak Il-u, the North Korean army's representative to CPV headquarters and a member of the Chinese faction of Korean Communists.[70] Kim also expressed discontent with CPV treatment of the Korean populace. Although Mao had sent strict orders to CPV commanders on this matter, implementation was less than perfect. Most important here was the fact that CPV units faced frequent shortages of food in an area where the indigenous food supply was often less than adequate even under normal conditions. Thus Chinese soldiers sometimes faced the choice of going hungry or collecting food from the locals in a manner that generated friction.[71] Circumstances aside, Chinese leaders had difficulty treating their Korean brethren as equals, just as Stalin did the Chinese.

The Communist allies had too much at stake in remaining together to risk an open split, and in June they finally agreed on a shift in tactics in Korea. At the end of May and in the first days of June, fear existed in China that the CPV might be forced to retreat as far north as the Pyongyang-Wonsan line, that UN forces might even try another amphibious assault deep in North Korea. Reinforcing such fears were conditions at home, where a shortage of raw cotton—in part a result of the drying up of sources in the West—had halted work in textile mills for over two weeks; where a massive public donation campaign had proven necessary to finance purchase of heavy weapons from the

Soviet Union; and where anti-Communist guerrilla activities in the south and west, though weakened, continued to deny the PRC complete physical and ideological control over the country. Mao now advanced a strategy of trying to wear down the enemy over time with a series of concentrated attacks at specific points on the battlefront while, at the same time, exploring prospects for a cease-fire through negotiations.[72]

Although Kim arrived in Beijing on June 3 and initially opposed an early beginning of talks, his dependence on the Chinese eventually led him to agree to negotiations based on an armistice at the thirty-eighth parallel. On June 5 Mao wired Stalin requesting that he receive in Moscow Chinese Politburo member Gao Gang and Kim for talks on Korea. The Soviet leader agreed. Nine days later, after meeting with his guests, he cabled Mao that an armistice would be advantageous.[73] By this time the enemy had halted its northward advance; Acheson had indicated in the Senate hearings that the United States would accept an end to the fighting at or near the thirty-eighth parallel; and George Kennan, a prominent U.S. diplomat now on leave from the State Department, had contacted Jacob Malik, the Soviet ambassador at the United Nations, with a similar message.[74]

In response to Stalin's judgment of June 13, Mao suggested either that the Communist side wait for the proposal of an armistice by the adversary or that Moscow request an armistice on the basis of Kennan's overture. The Chinese leader showed a new flexibility on terms. "In the interests of peace," he wrote, "let's solve the question of Korea first." The issue of PRC entry into the United Nations could be ignored, and, although Taiwan's fate should be raised, it could eventually be dropped as a condition. On Korea, he made no mention of the withdrawal of foreign troops, but regarding an armistice line Mao appeared adamant: the border at the thirty-eighth parallel must be restored, with "a small neutral zone on both sides. It is absolutely impossible that the neutral zone will be only on the side of North Korea."[75] This statement was a response in part to the stance of Kim Il-sung and in part to the announced position of the United States the previous December, which had the demilitarized zone entirely above the thirty-eighth parallel.[76] Mao also told Stalin that "we are getting prepared to deliver a stronger blow to the enemy in August."[77] He was willing to take a major first step toward ending the fighting, but he was not counting on the Americans to agree on acceptable terms anytime soon.

MORE THAN ANY OTHER SINGLE FACTOR, CHANGING MILITARY conditions in Korea had led Stalin and Mao to reassess their aims, just as the United States had done in both September and December of the previous year. What was different between the Western and the Communist alliances was that in the former the main secondary powers, the Western Europeans and Canada, had served as restraints on the leader, whereas in the latter the leader provided a restraint on the secondary powers. That is, China and North Korea wanted deeper Soviet involvement in the Korean fray—most important, they desired direct Soviet air support for their troops in battle. The impact on the military situation aside, such support would have been impossible to hide, as some Soviet planes with Soviet pilots would have been shot down over enemy territory and identified. As it was, Stalin permitted Soviet pilots to operate in a narrow area sufficiently distant from the battlefront that the fiction of noninvolvement was publicly maintained. As for the Americans, had it not been for allied opposition, as early as November 1950 they probably would have instituted hot pursuit into Manchuria of enemy planes operating just inside North Korea.[78] It is unlikely that such limited action alone would have led to major Soviet counteraction, but without ongoing allied pressure, this move might have been only a first step in a process that eventually spun out of control.

Such a process would have been fine with leaders on Taiwan and in the ROK. For the Chinese Nationalists, an expanded war represented the only realistic chance for recapturing the mainland from the Communists. For Rhee and his supporters, it represented the best chance for unification of Korea in the face of PRC intervention. Both of these parties were perfectly willing to risk global war to achieve their objectives.

Neither of them was able to influence the United States on the matter. The Nationalists did gain support, including covert American operatives, for minor forays against the mainland from offshore islands still in their possession, but these neither threatened the PRC's survival nor engaged Soviet forces.[79] While constantly lobbying against an end to the war without unification, Rhee focused on securing U.S. support for an expanded ROK army rather than an extension of the UN effort to China.

Yet with the approach of armistice talks, ROK influence threatened to take on new dimensions. In late May and early June, while Kim Il-sung lobbied quietly with the Chinese for new military action that would at least reestablish the thirty-eighth parallel, the South Korean government launched a massive effort to mobilize the public against any halt in the fighting short of the Yalu. Rhee made veiled threats of drastic action should the United Nations attempt to deny his countrymen in their quest for unity, and cabinet members joined in. The National Assembly managed a rare show of unity with the president by unanimously passing a resolution endorsing a continuing fight for an "independent and unified country." Mass demonstrations occurred in Pusan, the wartime seat of government.[80] At the end of June, as the UN and Communist commanders moved rapidly toward the commencement of negotiations, the ROK cabinet announced that a ceasefire must include a Chinese withdrawal from Korea; the disarming of the North Korean Communists and a UN guarantee that no third power would assist them either militarily or financially; and recognition of "the national sovereignty and territorial integrity of the Republic of Korea."[81] Ambassador Muccio wired home on the day the armistice talks began that he doubted the "ROK Govt will take overt action of [a] serious nature. On the other hand, Rhee has committed himself so far in opposition [to the] whole idea of [a] ceasefire that he cannot [very] well publicly reverse himself when faced with a *fait accompli.*"[82] With Rhee operating on his own turf and ROK troops constituting over half of UN ground forces, he had the potential for making considerable mischief.

Still, the ROK was dependent on American support for its survival, and to the United States and its most important allies, unification was simply not critical. Despite their superior firepower, UN forces had little capacity to augment their ground units from the outside, whereas the Chinese possessed nearly 750,000 reserves in nearby Manchuria.[83] Having been burned badly as a result of its earlier effort to unify the peninsula, the United States was now determined to seek an armistice short of clear-cut victory. With the Soviets and the Chinese of the same mind, and the North Koreans willing, if grudgingly, to go along, the risks of an expanded war had virtually disappeared for the short term.

CHAPTER 6

Negotiating an Armistice, July 1951–July 1953:

Why Did It Take So Long?

AT THE END OF JUNE 1951, SECRETARY OF STATE ACHESON BELIEVED there was "at least [a] fifty-fifty" chance for an early armistice in Korea. Recent Communist propaganda had downplayed demands on Taiwan, PRC admission to the United Nations, and the withdrawal of foreign troops from Korea. The Soviet Foreign Ministry had indicated a desire for talks on military issues between field commanders, a venue more conducive to straightforward discussion of an armistice than the previous Soviet brainchild of a multilateral conference including at least one neutral and a U.S. ally, Great Britain, that sympathized with parts of the Communist position.[1]

In early July Chairman Mao guessed that "it would take ten to fourteen days to prepare and go through the negotiations." While he ordered continuing precautions against possible new UN military moves, an end to enemy offensive action nearly a month earlier and the be-

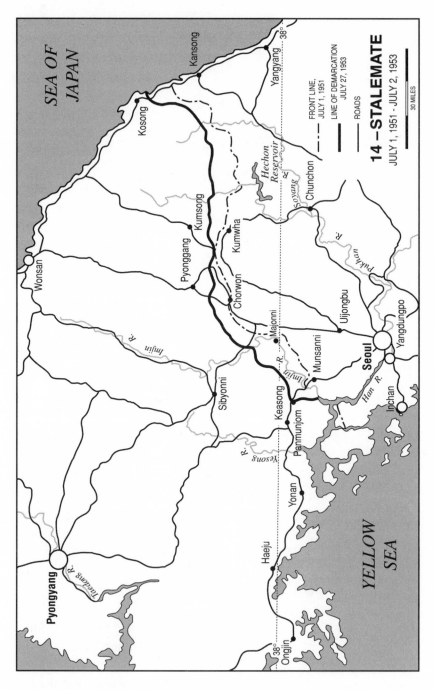

MAP 6. Stalemate on the battlefield.

14—STALEMATE

JULY 1, 1951 - JULY 2, 1953

— · — · — FRONT LINE, JULY 1, 1951
————— LINE OF DEMARCATION JULY 27, 1953
————— ROADS

30 MILES

ginning of the resupply of CPV forces had buoyed his optimism. Anticipating early achievement of an armistice, Chinese negotiators who traveled from Beijing to Korea to assist in the talks carried only summer clothing.[2]

Few people thought that the war would drag on for over two more years and that casualty figures would nearly double, despite the absence on either side of an effort to alter the military balance. Indeed, the preliminary armistice line was agreed to on November 27, 1951, less than five months after the commencement of talks. When the armistice was finally signed on July 27, 1953, the battle line rested within a few miles of its location two years before.

Why did it take so long to conclude an armistice? Was it because the continuing military balance relieved both sides of a compelling reason to halt the fighting? Or were there deeper reasons—circumstantial, ideological, and/or political—for the prolonged deadlock? Why, ultimately, did the war end? Answers to these questions reveal a good deal about the nature of the Korean War, and of the larger Cold War of which it was a part.

I

A deep ideological and cultural divide separated the contestants in Korea. The two sides bore intense animosity and distrust toward each other, and they recognized that a halt to the fighting would not end the worldwide or even the regional struggle between the West and the Soviet bloc. They also realized that an armistice in Korea would influence this larger struggle. By late August 1951, a pattern had emerged that ensured an intense contest of wills over every issue addressed in the talks.

American leaders feared that an armistice in Korea would produce escalating action by the Communists in other areas, most notably Southeast Asia, and compromise military preparedness in the West. Lieutenant General O. P. Weyland, the commander of U.S. air forces in the Far East, opined to General Ridgway on July 3 that UN forces were "in an excellent military position" in Korea, and the fighting provided "an invaluable training area" for the U.S. military, as well as an ideal climate at home for a continued defense buildup. The Communists, on the other hand, would gain from an armistice in Korea, since they could shift attention to Indochina, where the PRC already provided Ho Chi Minh's revolutionary forces with aid against the French. Increased Chinese assistance to Ho might lead to a French defeat, and this might result in a Communist advance westward through Southeast Asia, the Indian subcontinent, and all the way to the Middle East.[3] General Ridgway worried especially about a letdown in the rearmament program at home. "I can hardly imagine a greater tragedy for America and the Free World," he told the Joint Chiefs on July 4, "than a repetition of the disgraceful debacle of our Armed Forces following . . . World War II."[4] With raw materials becoming increasingly scarce, inflation threatening to get out of control, and many in Congress and the private sector pressing for a loosening of controls on the economy, Secretary of Defense Marshall echoed similar thoughts at a cabinet meeting in Washington.[5]

Despite his concerns, Ridgway recognized the disadvantage of tying down hundreds of thousands of American troops in Korea while the military balance in Europe was advantageous to the Soviets. He instructed his negotiating team to show sensitivity toward the Oriental concern about face. They must provide enemy negotiators with easy avenues of withdrawal from stated positions.[6]

Less than a month later, however, Ridgway wired home a blistering description of the enemy and a proposal on tactics that was anything but sensitive to the fine points of Chinese culture:

> Communists . . . understand only what they want to understand; . . . [they] consider courtesy as concession and concession as weakness; . . . [they] are uninhibited in repudiating their own solemn obligations; . . . [they] view such obligations solely as means for attaining their ends; . . . [they] attained . . . power through murderous conspiracy and . . . [they] remain in power by that and other equally infamous practices.
>
> To sit down with these men and deal with them as with representatives of an enlightened and civilized people is to deride one's own dignity and to invite the disaster their treachery will inevitably bring upon us.

I propose to direct the UNC [United Nations Command] delegation to govern its utterances accordingly and while remaining . . . scrupulously factual and properly temperate in word and deed, to employ such language and methods as these treacherous savages cannot fail to understand, and understanding, respect.[7]

The early interaction of representatives of the military commanders on both sides at Kaesong had served to highlight their ideological and cultural differences.

Problems began when, prior to the July 10 commencement of talks, CPV forces seized the Kaesong area, which had been in "no-man's-land" between the opposing forces when the UNC had agreed on the conference site. This action left the Communists in control of movements by and physical arrangements for the enemy delegation. On the tenth the Communists detained for an hour the convoy of jeeps carrying most UNC personnel to the conference site while they completed arrangements in Kaesong to create an impression that the United Nations was suing for peace. As the convoy entered town, each of its vehicles showing a large white flag as previously agreed, three jeeps occupied by Communist officers appeared to lead the procession. It then wound through the war-torn streets with, as one U.S. participant later recalled, the officers assuming "the demeanor of conquerors." Communist cameramen snapped dozens of pictures for distribution throughout Asia.[8]

Vice Admiral Turner Joy, the head of the UNC delegation, traveled to Kaesong by helicopter. On landing he encountered a "reception committee . . . armed to the teeth." He and his top assistants joined their jeep convoy waiting nearby and were led to what was designated UNC headquarters in Kaesong, a building atop a hill with armed North Korean soldiers "dotting the grounds."[9] Presently, members of the UNC party got back into their jeeps and proceeded, again in Communist tow, to the negotiating site, a building that once had housed the most expensive restaurant in town. Inside, Admiral Joy met General Nam Il, the chief North Korean negotiator. Stiffly, the two men and their subordinates exchanged introductions and credentials. Once seated, Joy found himself peering northward—in Oriental cultures, the victor faced south—and directly into the eyes of the much shorter

FIG. 15. UN motorcade halted at Kaesong checkpoint, July 1951.

FIG. 16. UN delegates to the Armistice Conference at the main entrance of the conference house, July 16, 1951. Left to right, Rear Admiral Arleigh Burke; Major General (ROK Army) Paik Sun Yup; Vice Admiral C. Turner Joy (head of the delegation); Major General Laurence C. Craigie; Major General Henry I. Hodes.

Nam. The Communists had provided the leading enemy spokesman with an abnormally low chair, their own with an exceedingly high one. Joy soon retrieved a chair of normal size, but, as he later recalled, "not before Communist photographers had exposed reels of film."[10]

Members of the UNC delegation had no freedom to move about. When during a recess Joy attempted to send a courier to communicate with his base camp at Munsan-ni, twenty-one miles away by road, Communist guards delayed him sufficiently to prevent his completion of the mission.[11]

Ridgway quickly instructed Joy to insist upon, first, "free [UNC] access to the conference site from the Imjin River area during daylight hours" and, second, the right to attach twenty newsmen to the UNC delegation. It took until late on July 14 for the two sides to reach agreement on these issues. The Communists conceded the second point only after the UNC delegation refused to continue direct talks without having the newsmen present. On the first point the two sides agreed to a five-mile neutral zone around Kaesong and a smaller area, one-half mile in radius, around the actual conference site. No military forces, "except those necessary for military police duty and armed only for this function," were to enter the larger area; in the smaller one there were to be no armed personnel at all.[12]

Twelve more days of acrimonious maneuvering passed before the parties agreed on an agenda, which following its adoption would proceed with item 2, the negotiation of a military demarcation line and a demilitarized zone.[13] The absence of reference to the thirty-eighth parallel represented a concession by the Communists, who nonetheless insisted that that point represented the only acceptable demarcation line.

On June 26 Acheson had indicated publicly that the thirty-eighth parallel could serve as the basis for an armistice, so at first the Communists had not anticipated that their stand would create a problem.[14] Yet on July 27 Admiral Joy put forth a line that was not only for the most part north of the thirty-eighth parallel but was even well north of the existing battle line. Joy claimed that, since a cease-fire would include an end to military operations in the air and sea as well as on the ground, and since the UNC enjoyed huge advantages in the first two areas, the Communists would gain more than the UNC when the fighting ended. Hence, they should provide compensation on the ground. Although privately the Americans expected to retreat from this opening position, U.S. military leaders insisted that, because the thirty-eighth parallel was indefensible, it was unacceptable as the final line.[15]

UNC negotiators reasoned that their opening position would ease an enemy concession on the thirty-eighth parallel, as the Americans would retreat as well, thus making the existing battle line a reasonable compromise. The Communists, though, were outraged. Nam Il labeled Joy's proposal "incredible" and "naive and illogical." Maintenance of the current battle line by the UNC, he asserted, depended on its superiority in the air and sea. Since that line shifted "all the time" north and south of the thirty-eighth parallel, even it did not represent "military realities," and this fact made the line prior to June 25, 1950, the logical point on which to establish an armistice. Concluding with a flourish, Nam asked, "Seeing that you make such a completely absurd and arrogant statement, for what actually have you come here? Have you come here to negotiate for peace or just to look for an excuse for extending the war?"[16] Joy characterized Nam's response as "a rude and graceless act" and lectured him on the proper comportment of people "whose military organizations are respected throughout the world."[17]

After another week of acrimonious exchanges, an incident in the conference area threatened to end the negotiations altogether. As members of the UNC delegation returned to the conference house at the end of a lunch break, a company of heavily armed Chinese soldiers marched past them,[18] a clear violation of the July agreement that permitted no armed personnel in the conference area and only lightly armed military police in the larger neutral zone. The incident infuriated Ridgway, who wanted to "demand" an immediate explanation of "this flagrant violation" of past agreements, "a statement satisfactory to me of the corrective action taken, and acceptable guarantees against a recurrence." Washington softened the response but retained its insistence on corrective action.[19] The incident stalled the talks until August 10.

The Chinese already planned a new military offensive. General Peng had concluded as early as July 24 that the Americans were unlikely to conclude an armistice under current battlefield conditions. The CPV, therefore, needed to push enemy forces south of the thirty-eighth parallel. Mao agreed, and preparations began for a "sixth-phase offensive" in September.[20]

As August progressed, however, military conditions worsened for the CPV. The UN bombing badly hurt its logistics, as did floods, which destroyed hundreds of bridges in North Korea and damaged many storehouses.[21] What is more, in the middle of the month the UNC began its own limited offensive, pushing opposing forces slightly northward at several points on the central and eastern fronts. Mao ordered reconsideration of the planned offensive, while his negotiators at Kaesong advised abandonment of their stand on the thirty-eighth parallel.[22]

By August 22 indications of flexibility existed in both camps. The UNC had proposed meetings of subdelegations from each side to create a setting for less formal interaction. The Communists agreed, and such meetings began on the sixteenth. Soon the Communists hinted that they would abandon insistence on the thirty-eighth parallel if the UNC would first drop its insistence on compensation.[23]

Then, on the night of August 22–23, an incident occurred that temporarily wiped out any progress toward agreement. The Communists contacted the UNC, claiming that the conference site had been bombed and strafed, and pressed its representatives to participate in an immediate investigation. Two hours later, in the darkness and rain, two UNC liaison officers arrived at the site of the alleged incident and confronted a barrage of charges and evidence of a UNC air attack. The physical evidence appeared to UNC personnel as manufactured, inconclusive, or both. Eyewitness accounts were no better, although a plane of other than UNC origin may have flown over or near the conference site around the time of the reported incident. The head Communist liaison officer declared from written notes that future meetings at the delegation, subdelegation, and liaison levels were off until the UNC took responsibility for the incident. The Communists subsequently refused to permit an investigation during daylight hours.[24]

Their propaganda intensified on alleged UNC violations of the conference area and neutral zone.

The decision to suspend negotiations came from leaders in Beijing, who recognized that it could lead to their prolongation or termination.[25] Why, at a time of relative weakness on the battlefield—which on August 26 would cause Mao to cancel plans for a large-scale September offensive[26]—did the Communists suspend the talks?

The act was part of a psychological warfare campaign by people striving to overcome an appearance of weakness. The PRC and DPRK were new governments unrecognized by the United States, the world's most developed and powerful nation. They represented populations that for generations had been exploited by foreigners. Their ideology and their regimes alone represented rebellions against that exploitation. Now they faced the current leader of the capitalist oppressors as equals across the negotiating table, itself a giant achievement. Only in material terms the contest was far from equal, a fact illustrated by Mao's unsuccessful efforts in June, in the aftermath of the CPV's crushing defeat in its spring offensives, to persuade Stalin to take charge of the negotiating process and increase Soviet aid to Korea.[27] Communist maneuverings at the beginning of the armistice talks were the acts of revolutionaries contemptuous of diplomatic niceties and the will of their well-heeled adversary, but also trying desperately to seize every advantage in a largely disadvantageous situation.[28]

The sharp UNC reaction to the tactics of the Communists, and their ineffective response to it, reinforced concern in Beijing and Pyongyang. Initially Mao had intended to stand firm on UNC demands regarding procedural issues. On July 13, for example, he wired Stalin that the American insistence on "the presence of correspondents at the conference" was "a stupid trick, and we will easily reject it."[29] Yet he soon conceded the point. He did the same when the UNC refused to include the withdrawal of foreign troops on the agenda.[30] *Time* magazine, the leading American news weekly, described the series of events with the headline "Red Backdown."[31] Early in August the *New York Times* characterized U.S. negotiators as believing "that the Communists . . . will pay a high price" to secure an armistice, this at a time when the UNC was demanding an armistice line well north of what had been won in combat.[32]

The flouting of the agreement on the neutral zone by Communist soldiers on August 4 represented a show of strength toward an opponent who was considered arrogant on the surface but soft underneath. Already the Communists had accused the UNC of violating rules on the neutral zone and restrictions on air attacks on convoys in North Korea seeking to supply the Communist delegation. Those accusations continued after substantive talks resumed on August 10. The UNC denied blame for any of the alleged incidents in the neutral zone and insisted that convoys attacked from the air had not been protected by the agreed-upon procedures. The denials continued after August 19, when a CPV military police platoon patrolling the neutral area was ambushed and its leader slain. A UNC investigation concluded that, while an attack had occurred, no UN military units were in the area at the time. The attack might have been by South Korean partisans, for whom the UNC disclaimed responsibility.[33]

This incident set the stage for the Communist response to the alleged strafing three days later. The Communists could not let stand the UNC claim that it was not responsible for partisan activity from its own side in the neutral zone, for this could lead to all kinds of mischief. In any event, conspiratorially minded as they were, the Communists surely did not believe that South Koreans could (or would) act independently of U.S. desires. So, when a plane of unknown origin but flying from the south entered the neutral zone and dropped explosives, the Communists responded quickly and sharply.[34]

For their part, the Americans were disinclined to accept any unproven enemy claim. The Communists were believed untrustworthy, and admissions were undesirable that could be used to advance their worldwide propaganda. Cultural conditioning reinforced such considerations. Americans lived under a system of rule by law and the presumption of innocence. Theoretically if not always in fact, this meant that, when charges were made against a party, they had to be investigated carefully and impartially. If no strong evidence of guilt appeared, the charges had to be dropped. The Chinese and North Koreans were unbridled by such conditioning, and they viewed as stonewalling the refusal of the UNC to accept their own version of events. Tired of being pressured and harassed and ever suspicious that the Communists were manufacturing evidence, the UNC dug in its heels.

If local conditions accentuated the ideological and cultural divide between the parties, developments beyond the peninsula also contributed to Communist suspension of the negotiations. The conference on a Japanese peace treaty was to convene on September 4, and the treaty's signing was likely to be followed by establishment of a Japanese-American military alliance. The United States stood on the verge of pulling together a broad coalition of non-Communist states behind a treaty that excluded China, left the Taiwan issue unresolved, dampened prospects for aggrieved nations to collect reparations, and paved the way for both an indefinite U.S. military presence on the archipelago and eventual Japanese rearmament. Still, many outside the Communist world remained lukewarm or hostile toward U.S. designs. British commercial circles worried about competition from a resurgent Japan, already lurching forward due to the increased demand for finished goods provoked by the Korean War. In the Philippines, Burma, and Indonesia, the reparations issue stirred popular emotions. Plans for continued U.S. military bases in Japan nourished regional sentiments of "Asia for the Asians," as did the fact that the draft of the peace treaty was largely an Anglo-American product. By mid-August Burma had declined to attend the conference, India leaned in the same direction, and Indonesia had accepted only tentatively.[35]

To the Communists, the combination of danger and opportunity inherent in the final stages of the treaty-making process dictated a sabotage effort. First, on August 11 the Soviet Union announced that it *would* attend the San Francisco conference. Moscow and Beijing then escalated their propaganda campaign to undermine support for the treaty.[36] Breaking the armistice talks represented in part a ploy to alarm U.S. allies and jolt Asian neutrals, who might press for a great power conference to resolve outstanding issues in Asia.[37]

II

Suspension of the talks lasted until October 25 and proved advantageous to the UNC. Ridgway used the negotiations over resumption to insist on a shift in conference site, establishment of joint respon-

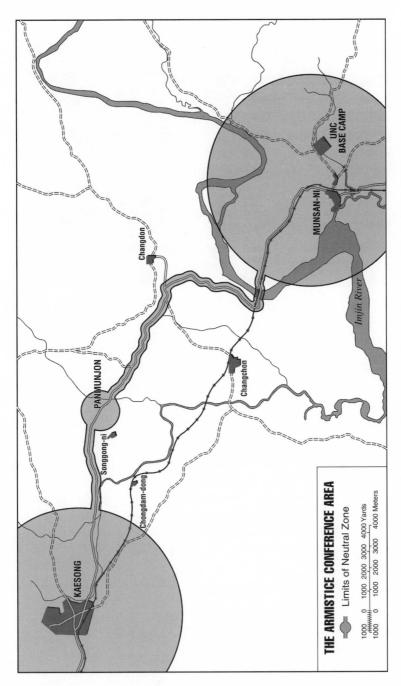

MAP 7. The new conference area and neutral zone as of October 25, 1951.

THE ARMISTICE CONFERENCE AREA

Limits of Neutral Zone

1000 0 1000 2000 3000 4000 Yards
1000 0 1000 2000 3000 4000 Meters

KAESONG

Chongdam-dong

Songgong-ni

PANMUNJON

Changchon

Changdon

Imjin River

MUNSAN-NI

UNC BASE CAMP

FIG. 17. Tents and huts at the second conference site, Panmunjom, March 1952.

sibility for its security, a reduction of the neutral zone around Kaesong, and an acknowledgment of no UNC responsibility for acts by
South Korean irregulars. He achieved all four, although not without
compromise on specifics. Meanwhile, forty-nine countries, including
Indonesia and five other Asian and Arab nations, signed the Japanese
peace treaty. In limited military offensives from the beginning of September through the first week of October, UN forces pushed the battle
line slightly north at several points and inflicted tens of thousands of
casualties on the enemy. The Communists, in turn, gained face when
in mid-September the UNC expressed regret over an incident of several days earlier in which an American jet had strayed over the conference area and fired on several buildings. A month later another such
incident occurred, resulting in the death of a twelve-year-old boy.
Again the UNC accepted responsibility and expressed regret.[38]

The resumption of talks, now in tents outside the tiny village of
Panmunjom several miles east of Kaesong, brought no end to the acri-
mony between the negotiators, but it did lead in just over a month to
tentative agreement on an armistice line. That agreement was based
on the "line of contact" in the middle of a 4-kilometer demilitarized

zone, which was to stand if the parties resolved other agenda items within thirty days.[39]

The UNC advantage of late November was only slight, and it derived solely from the ability of its armed forces to capture small bodies of territory along the front. Under orders from Washington, and despite pleas for "more steel and less silk," Ridgway conceded Kaesong to the enemy and granted the thirty-day provision, which he believed would relieve the Communists from military pressure during that period and perhaps even longer. This was so because public opinion at home was unlikely to tolerate increased American casualties for territorial gains that might have to be returned at a later date. Worse still, he surmised, should the talks not succeed in a month, strong pressure would build to extend the thirty-day provision. The Communists would bolster their defensive positions, making future UN military pressure far more difficult and costly.[40]

The Truman administration insisted that Ridgway give ground for political reasons, both domestic and international. American forces had suffered over one hundred thousand casualties in Korea, and, at home, the "die for a tie" strategy was an increasingly hard sell. In Western Europe impatience grew with the economic consequences of rearmament. People there also showed frayed nerves over the testing of atomic weapons on both sides and talk in the American press of a third world war. Europeans understood that the first step in reducing Cold War tensions was to stop the fighting in Korea, and they doubted the U.S. commitment to that goal. The convening in early November of the Communist World Peace Congress in Vienna and the UN General Assembly in Paris led to fears in Washington that Soviet propaganda soon would gain the upper hand in the key region of its competition with Moscow.[41]

Strains in the Western camp encouraged Stalin to advise Mao against rushing to conclude an armistice in Korea. On November 19 the Soviet premier wired his Chinese counterpart that "the overall international situation" put the United States in a position of greater need to end the fighting than the Communist side. As a result, "a hard line" was the appropriate course in the negotiations.[42]

Mao did not disagree with Stalin, but the heavy burden endured by his country and Chinese-occupied North Korea led him to emphasize the advantages of peace. Korea, he told Stalin, consumed nearly one-third of the PRC budget, while poor crop yields produced widespread famine in north China, and people nationwide staggered under the weight of a mass collection campaign to aid Korea and resist American imperialism. With the U.S. compromise on the armistice line, Mao hoped by year's end to settle remaining issues and to halt the fighting. Yet he recognized the possibility that the conflict would "be drawn out for another half year or year," so he was "economizing" on Korean military operations through "tactics of a long, active defense," which would secure current positions while "inflicting great manpower losses on the enemy." He also pursued austerity measures at home, including army reorganization, reductions in the bureaucracy, and a strengthening of the mass mobilization campaigns to increase production and assist Korea.[43] Mao remained determined to resist any "bullying . . . by foreign imperialists."[44]

Mao's worries about enemy bullying diminished at the end of November, when General James Van Fleet, Ridgway's successor as commander of the Eighth Army, ordered the reduction of UN military operations "to the minimum essential to maintain present positions." "Offensive action" was permissible only "to regain key terrain lost to [future] enemy assault." The order leaked to the press and, despite Washington's denials that a de facto cease-fire was in effect, the Communists were granted temporary relief from enemy pressure—unless they initiated offensive action. Van Fleet issued the order without Ridgway's foreknowledge or approval, a reflection of the less than ideal relationship between the two commanders.[45]

The significance of the order should not be overrated. Without augmenting resources, the UNC had little chance for a major advance northward. The priorities of the United States and its European allies made such a buildup impossible. Moreover, sentiments in the UN General Assembly ruled out an expansion of sanctions against China—either economic or military. Finally, the Chinese could increase their own ground forces in Korea just as the Soviets could step up their support to the CPV. Already, with the completion of the training of Chinese pilots in the use of Soviet jet fighters, the enemy had substantially improved its capacity to contest UNC air action over North Korea. At most, UNC ground forces could have inched slightly northward, inflicted thousands more casualties on the enemy, and prevented it from digging in firmly on a static line. Yet such action also would have produced more UN casualties, which would have generated new pressure at home to either bring the war to an early end or fight on to total victory. And the continuing high level of international tension would have perpetuated doubts among NATO allies regarding the wisdom of U.S. leadership.[46]

Since neither side possessed both the capacity and the will to fundamentally alter the military balance on the peninsula, prospects for an early armistice rested on the magnitude of the unresolved issues at Panmunjom. With this in mind, I turn to an examination of the three remaining agenda items.

III

Agenda items 3, 4, and 5 read as follows:

> 3. Concrete arrangements for the realization of [a] cease fire and armistice in Korea, including the composition, authority and functions of a supervising organization for carrying out the terms of a cease fire and armistice.
> 4. Arrangements relating to prisoners of war.
> 5. Recommendations to the governments of the countries concerned on both sides.[47]

The last item was a sop to the Communists, who had wanted to include "withdrawal of all armed forces of foreign countries from Korea." The Americans resisted negotiations on this matter before fighting ended, but they agreed to their inclusion at a postarmistice conference.[48] As merely an agreement to negotiate on the issue at some later date, item 5 was unlikely to delay an armistice. Items 3 and 4, however, were another story.

The Americans lacked confidence in future Communist intentions, which explains their insistence upon a defensible armistice line. The

United States also considered as paramount restrictions on the buildup of military forces on both sides, since maintenance of the balance of power in Korea would reduce prospects for the renewal of hostilities. This made essential a continuing American advantage in the air and inspection of the other side's military facilities to enforce the limitations placed on armed forces. American officials anticipated Communist resistance on these issues, as well as ROK objections to Communist inspectors moving freely in its territory.[49]

A possible substitute for broad inspection, Washington believed, was a statement upon conclusion of an armistice that, if the Communists resumed hostilities, the military response would not be limited to Korea. An important element in the credibility of this "greater sanctions" statement was the support of key allies. The State Department did not approach the British on the matter until November 21. Since the action anticipated if the Communists breached an armistice included bombing and a naval blockade of China, agreement was far from assured.[50] With Communist press correspondents at Panmunjom indicating that their negotiators would resist inspection of key installations behind their lines, quick agreement on item 3 appeared unlikely.

The prisoners-of-war (POW) issue also held the potential to create problems. Mao had anticipated the previous July that the Americans would propose a one-for-one exchange of POWs, but he expressed determination to secure an all-for-all exchange. The letter of international law favored him on the matter. The Geneva Convention of 1949, which the United States had signed and both the UNC and the Communists had announced they would honor, stated that "prisoners of war shall be released and repatriated without delay after the cessation of hostilities."[51] Yet many U.S. policy makers regarded an all-for-all exchange as unfair and repugnant in the Korean context. For one thing, the Communists had not actually abided by the Geneva Convention, failing to submit lists of prisoners held by their side to the International Committee of the Red Cross (ICRC), to permit visits to POW camps by members of that organization, or to reveal the location of those camps.[52] The Communists, it was suspected, had committed numerous atrocities against UNC prisoners.[53]

Furthermore, an all-for-all exchange would provide the enemy with a much larger source of manpower than the UNC, as the latter held over 150,000 prisoners, many more than the other side. This disparity was potentially disruptive of the balance of military power in Korea.[54] The UNC could reduce this danger by reclassifying some of the Koreans held in its camps, roughly 40,000 of whom had been residents of South Korea in June 1950 and had been impressed into the North Korean army either from civilian life or after serving in the ROK armed forces and being captured by the Communists.[55] The UNC also could give Chinese POWs a choice of whether or not to return to the mainland. Many of these men had been Nationalist soldiers in the Chinese civil war and had been impressed into Communist armies against their will. American observers estimated that more than half of them would opt against repatriation.[56]

Finally, UNC adherence to the principle of no forced repatriation might provide a psychological victory for the West in the Cold War. The United States would derive the advantage in future wars of confronting enemy soldiers who were more likely to surrender because they felt confident of not being repatriated.[57] If the civil aspects of the present fighting in Korea and the recent conflict in China provided an immediate context to apply the principle to the West's advantage, a possible war in Europe matching NATO forces against Soviet bloc armies added a future case with at least equal potential for exploitation.[58]

Still, by mid-November 1951 the trend in both Washington and Tokyo was to accept an all-for-all exchange, with the exception of the forty thousand South Koreans mentioned previously, who would be reclassified as "civilian internees." Otherwise, it was feared, the return of prisoners held by the Communists would be jeopardized.[59] The wild card here was President Truman, who expressed doubts about forcing repatriation on prisoners likely to be "immediately done away with" by the Communists. At minimum, he believed that the UNC should receive "some major concessions" in return for an all-for-all exchange.[60]

The simple fact was that neither the Communists nor the United States had made firm decisions regarding their positions on items 3 and 4. Their resolution at Panmunjom promised to be difficult, but how difficult, how long the difficulties would take to resolve, and how they would be resolved remained very much in doubt.

The two sides moved quickly after the November 27 agreement on the armistice line toward serious discussion of the remaining issues. By December 19 considerable progress had been made on item 3. The two sides had agreed that troops could not be augmented after the armistice, but that they could be rotated in and out of Korea. Differences remained over the replenishment of matériel and the extent and nature of inspection, although Admiral Joy believed these resolvable through further negotiations. The repairing of old and the building of new airfields in North Korea was the major sticking point, "the key issue of the armistice," Joy opined to Ridgway, and this might be resolved if the United States and its allies agreed on a greater sanctions statement.[61]

Joy's judgment came before the two sides had examined each other's POW lists, which they agreed to exchange on December 18.[62] The Communist list, it turned out, included a mere 11,559 prisoners, roughly one-ninth the number of soldiers UNC had classified as missing in action and one-sixth of those the Communists claimed in news releases and radio broadcasts to have captured. The UNC list included 132,000 prisoners and 37,000 civilian internees, whereas the Communists claimed 188,000 of their soldiers missing. On December 22 UNC negotiators explained that an additional 16,000 of the men on their POW list had been discovered to be ROK citizens and also would not be returned. The UNC hoped that the enemy would eventually concede this reclassification, as the North Koreans had forcefully inducted tens of thousands of captured ROK citizens and soldiers into their army, a practice contrary to international law that could be used against the Communists in the ongoing propaganda war.[63]

Even with the reclassification of 53,000 of its captives, the UNC stood to return more than ten times the number of men put forth by the Communists, which magnified feelings about the unfairness of an all-for-all exchange, concerns about its impact on the balance of forces in Korea, and suspicions of enemy mistreatment of POWs. President Truman continued to express opposition to an all-for-all exchange, and he also harbored fears that an early armistice would compromise the rearmament program in the United States.[64]

As the thirty-day stipulation on the armistice line agreement ran out in late December, the negotiators at Panmunjom approved a fifteen-day extension. The reality was, however, that thorny issues remained unresolved, and behind the scenes the U.S. president leaned in a direction on POWs that could produce deadlock. That possibility gained weight early in January 1952, when the UNC introduced the principle of voluntary repatriation at Panmunjom. The Communists responded with such epithets as "absurd," "useless," and "ridiculous."[65]

In raising the question of individual freedom of choice, voluntary repatriation struck at the heart of ideological and cultural conflict between East and West. For Americans raised in the Lockean tradition, the rights of the individual preexisted the state and thus could not be denied by it. The Confucian tradition acknowledged no such rights, and neither did Marxist-Leninism.

The issue also possessed serious implications in the ongoing civil conflicts in China and Korea. If significant numbers of UNC prisoners chose not to return to North Korea or mainland China, the Beijing and Pyongyang regimes would receive blows to their claims of sole legitimacy over their countries. The Chinese showed particular sensitivity on this point. When the UNC stated on January 15 that Chinese prisoners should have the choice of going to Taiwan, the PRC negotiator replied that, "if anybody dares to hand over any of the personnel of the CPV captured by the other side to the deadly enemy of the Chinese people [the Nationalists], the Chinese people will never tolerate it and will fight to the end."[66]

Stalin was unlikely to counsel accommodation here. Although prior to World War II the Soviets had concluded agreements based on the principle of voluntary repatriation, at the end of that conflict they insisted on total repatriation of prisoners and displaced persons. In early 1945 more than five million Soviet citizens were under foreign authority, some of whom had defected from Soviet armies or fled Soviet territory and had collaborated with Germany, a reflection of the Stalin regime's unpopularity in some regions of the USSR. Stalin was determined to retrieve these people. With U.S. assistance, over five million people eventually were returned to the Soviet Union, many against their will.[67] Application of the principle of voluntary repatriation in Korea would set a dangerous precedent, with implications not only for the future loyalty of Soviet soldiers and citizens but also for satellite populations in Eastern Europe, where U.S. encouragement and aid to dissenting groups were on the rise and ongoing purges indicated a continued Soviet concern.[68]

Despite the impasse on POWs at Panmunjom, progress continued on item 3. On January 9 the Communists agreed to replenishment of military equipment. Two days later the Joint Chiefs informed Ridgway that the UNC should drop its objection to the rehabilitation and construction of airfields if all other issues were resolved. The move reflected Washington's confidence in the effectiveness of the greater sanctions statement and its ultimate acceptance by U.S. allies. By the middle of the month, the Pentagon contemplated putting forth a "package proposal," with the UNC conceding on airfields and the Communists on POWs.[69] Secretary of State Acheson thought an armistice likely around the end of the month.[70]

Even so, administration officials recognized that the POW issue might become a breaking point in the talks, and they strove to establish a final position on it. State Department analysts raised several objections to holding fast on nonforcible repatriation, beginning with anticipation that neither allied nor domestic support would prove firm on the matter. Another concern derived from conditions in POW camps of the UNC. Because the UNC had cut corners in its assignment of personnel there, it had limited control over the camps' internal workings. Prisoners themselves controlled many of the barracks and created gangs to enforce discipline. Pro-Nationalist soldiers forced into Communist armies and then captured in Korea controlled some barracks, where they terrorized potential dissenters, making it impossible for them to freely express their opinions. Communist-controlled barracks had similar conditions, but with the opposite side providing the terror.[71]

Despite these and other concerns, on February 8 Truman endorsed the UNC stand at Panmunjom on the POWs.[72] He instructed his subordinates to explore ways of finessing the matter, but the most the UNC could suggest was to screen the prisoners and then remove from the list any who said they would forcibly resist repatriation. The revised list would be presented to the Communists with the offer of an all-for-all exchange.[73]

Why did Truman hold firm on the issue? First, the president may not have been fully informed of conditions in the camps, either of how difficult it would be to discover the true opinions of the POWs or of the degree of unrest that had developed there over recent months. On the other hand, Truman was in a particularly surly mood regarding the behavior of Communist leaders worldwide, and he was fully briefed by Secretary Acheson on the moral and pragmatic objections to forcing POWs to return to the Communists against their will.

A passage of January 27 in Truman's private journal reveals the state of mind of the man who would soon make the final decision on POWs. "The communist governments," he wrote, "have no sense of honor and no moral code." The PRC had requested a cease-fire during the previous summer merely in search of an opportunity "to import war materials and resupply their front lines." The president thought it time for "an ultimatum with a ten day expiration limit, informing Moscow that we intend to blockade the China coast from the Korean border to Indo-China, . . . destroy every military base in Manchuria, . . . and if there is further interference we shall eliminate any ports or cities necessary to accomplish our peaceful purposes." To prevent such action, the Chinese must withdraw their troops from Korea, and the Soviet Union must halt shipments of war materials to China. Having warmed to the task, Truman proceeded to expand the scope of the ultimatum to include a withdrawal from Eastern Europe by the Soviet Union and its halt of aid "to the thugs who are attacking the free world." Otherwise, he declared, there would be "all out war. . . . Moscow, St. Petersburg [Leningrad], Mukden, Vladivostok, Pekin[g] [Beijing], Shanghai, Port Arthur [Lushun], Dairen [Dalian], Odessa, Stalingrad, and every manufacturing plant in China and the Soviet Union will be eliminated."[74] The president never took these ideas to his advisers, but his private expression of them indicates a depth of anger and frustration toward the Communists that surely influenced his stance on the POW issue.

Acheson reinforced Truman's thinking with a memorandum arguing that an agreement requiring U.S. troops "to use force to turn over to the Communists prisoners who believe they would face death if returned would be repugnant to our most fundamental moral and humanitarian principles on the importance of the individual, and would seriously jeopardize the psychological warfare position of the United States in its opposition to Communist tyranny."[75] Ideology and advantage had joined to dictate a firm stand.

Nonetheless, by early April the two sides had narrowed their differences to a point where a final trade-off on items 3 and 4 appeared within the realm of possibility. On item 3, division remained only on the repair and construction of airfields and membership on the neutral nations supervisory body. The stage seemed set for a UNC concession on airfields and the Communists' withdrawal of their insistence on Soviet membership as a neutral on the supervisory organ. On item 4, the Communists had tacitly accepted the UNC position on civilian internees and indicated that further removals might be made from original lists on the basis of residence in South Korea prior to the war. That is, while the principle of nonforcible repatriation remained unacceptable, it *might* be implemented in practice by adjusting the lists presented the previous December. The keys were the size of the final UNC list and the number of Chinese on it. When U.S. negotiators indicated that their side's list might be in the neighborhood of 116,000, but that this could not be determined without a screening of prisoners on Koje Island off the south coast of the peninsula, the Communists proposed a recess to enable both parties to check their final lists. With little change having occurred in the line of contact since the agreement on item 2 and with the two sides having essentially agreed on item 5, prospects for an early armistice had never seemed better.[76]

Those prospects collapsed on April 19, 1952, when American negotiators presented to their counterparts an estimate of 70,000 returnees from their side, including only 25 percent of the roughly 20,000 Chinese. The surprised and outraged Communist representatives stammered that this figure "absolutely by no means can be a basis for further discussion" and threatened to revert to the initial lists as the focal point for negotiation.[77] Over the next fortnight the opposing sides exchanged package proposals, but to no avail. The Chinese prisoners remained a stumbling block on which neither side was willing to bend.[78]

The Americans erred in advancing both the 116,000 and the 70,000 figures. The latter number was based on a screening of only half of the POWs. In early May it was raised to between 80,000 and 85,000 merely by counting as prospective repatriates all the North Koreans in compounds that resisted screening, but the new estimate was not immediately presented to the Communists.[79] Furthermore, despite UNC efforts to devise a screening process that would produce the highest possible number of repatriates, prisoners in compounds dominated by pro-Nationalist Chinese were so intimidated that all they were willing to say was "'Taiwan' over and over again."[80]

Ridgway rejected immediate rescreening, in part because of the delay involved, the messiness of a process that already had produced hundreds of casualties, and the likely need as a result to reassign more UNC troops from the front to the POW camps.[81] An additional factor may have been the UNC commander's ongoing outrage at enemy behavior, which had been fueled since February by the emergence of a Communist propaganda campaign claiming that the United States engaged in bacteriological warfare in North Korea and Manchuria by dropping infected insects from airplanes.[82] Ridgway considered the charges outrageous lies. Surely they encouraged him in his long-standing desire to present the Communists with a final, inflexible position in the talks.[83]

Still, a recount probably would not have produced a number satisfactory to the Communists. In June 1952 Zhou En-lai hinted to an Indian diplomat visiting China that a 100,000 figure would be acceptable, but that was a substantial distance from the revised UNC estimates. Even then, neither Zhou nor any other Chinese official showed flexibility on Chinese prisoners.[84] With U.S.-assisted Nationalist raids on the mainland from offshore islands picking up again in March, the PRC faced constant reminders of the ongoing Chinese civil war.[85] Mao remained determined not to give a victory to his mortal enemy, Chiang Kai-shek, by agreeing to the return of thousands of Chinese prisoners to Taiwan.

Mao was in a stronger position to resist UNC pressure than during the previous fall. First, Chinese manpower in Korea had grown to over seven hundred thousand, and soldiers were better armed with Soviet equipment. Although the ROK army had expanded as well, the growth in UNC forces had not kept pace.[86] Second, the Chinese had taken advantage of the low level of enemy ground action to expand a system of trenches and tunnels that greatly reduced vulnerability to UNC artillery and air action.[87] During March the CPV also had inoculated most of its troops against plagues, typhoid, and smallpox, thus reducing the danger that epidemics would weaken its military position.[88] Finally, on the propaganda front the Communists were well positioned to counter the American stance on the POW issue. They already had begun to take advantage of loose UNC control on Koje Island by maintaining a communications network in barracks with sympathetic, well-organized prisoners. In February they even prevented an initial screening effort in an uprising that cost the lives of seventy-seven brethren.[89] Increasingly, unrest on the island represented a method for undermining the high moral position of the UNC on POWs. So was the bacteriological warfare campaign, which by mid-March took up 20 percent of PRC broadcasts aimed at foreign audiences.[90] Mao probably preferred an armistice in Korea during the spring of 1952, but he was hardly desperate.

He might have been closer to that state had the UNC continued its military pressure of the previous fall. It did not because of a desire to hold down casualties, as well as fears of domestic and allied dissent. Had the Joint Chiefs in Washington and the UNC in Tokyo anticipated the final U.S. position on POWs and the difficulties it would cause in the negotiations, however, they might have ordered more aggressive battlefield tactics through the winter of 1951–52. As it was, the UNC focused on air action in North Korea, which hampered enemy logistics and constantly reminded DPRK and CPV leaders of the costs of a continuing war but did not threaten the military status quo.[91] By April 1952, short of a sizable UNC buildup on the ground or an expansion of the war beyond the peninsula, the UNC had little to offer but more of the same.

IV

Nearly a year passed before movement reappeared at Panmunjom. The Chinese continued to increase their presence in Korea, stationing some 1.35 million troops there by early 1953. They also stepped up their exploitation of conditions on Koje-do. In May 1952 Chinese prisoners managed to capture the U.S. commandant and to maneuver his successor into signing a statement implying that the UNC had failed to provide humane treatment to prisoners and to abide by international law.[92] The UNC quickly disassociated itself from the statement and appointed a no-nonsense commandant who reestablished order and took firm control of recalcitrant prisoners. The process generated considerable violence and hundreds of casualties, however, which enhanced a Communist propaganda offensive calling into question the UNC screening and, indeed, its entire stand on the POW issue.

Washington pointed out that it had proposed a rescreening by neutrals after an armistice, but this failed to avert criticism from allied governments and doubts among their constituents of U.S. veracity. A political crisis within the ROK growing out of President Rhee's effort to stay in office for another term added further doubts about the prudence of continuing the fight in Korea. Rhee's autocratic behavior and Washington's tolerance of it undermined U.S. efforts to sell the war as a struggle of freedom and democracy against slavery and authoritarianism.[93]

Yet the Truman administration refused to budge on the POW issue, even though the Democratic Party's prospects in the November elections were hurt by the ongoing war. In May UNC air expanded its campaign of interdicting enemy supply routes and storage areas in North Korea. General Mark W. Clark replaced Ridgway as UN commander on May 12 and commenced a search for new targets north of the battle line. In late June, with Washington's approval, his planes attacked heretofore untouched dams and power plants along the Yalu. The offensive produced a two-week power blackout in the DPRK. Between mid-July and the end of August, the UNC launched three intensive attacks against Pyongyang and its surroundings, merely the most spectacular operations in an air war broadened well beyond previous interdiction efforts.[94]

By mid-July Communist negotiators at Panmunjom wanted to make concessions on the POW issue based on the estimate of eighty-three thousand returnees recently passed on by the UNC. Mao demurred, lecturing his subordinates about the need to avoid concessions under political and military pressure.[95] In fact, the Chinese leader had made concessions under such circumstances before, and he would do so again. Now, though, the issue at hand was sufficiently momentous to make him stand firm, the pressure insufficiently so to make him bend.

The Americans strove diplomatically on two fronts during the summer and early fall. At Panmunjom they sought to devise a method of implementing nonforcible repatriation acceptable to the Communists. With NATO allies they sought to prepare the way for tightening economic sanctions against China at the UN General Assembly scheduled to convene in October. Neither effort bore fruit. The Communists showed only marginal interest in finessing the POW issue, and the UNC, seeing no chance for progress, recessed the talks on October 8. NATO allies, already upset with U.S. clumsiness on the POW and bombing issues, responded coolly to the idea of imposing new sanctions on the PRC.[96]

In the fall of 1952, Korea became the focal point of the UN General Assembly in New York, much to the discomfort of the United States. Acheson soon confronted difficulties in passing even a simple resolution supporting the American position at Panmunjom. Pressure to consider a compromise resolution increased after November 4, when General Dwight D. Eisenhower won election as president of the United States. Although his leadership of Allied forces in Europe during and after World War II gave him strong credentials as a statesman, he won on a Republican platform that attacked the Truman administration's defensiveness in foreign policy, and he drew in on his coattails a GOP majority in both houses of Congress. The candidate was less shrill than some of his supporters, but he occasionally talked about liberating Eastern Europe from the Communists, and John Foster Dulles, his presumed choice as secretary of state, was among the leaders in bombastic rhetoric. Eisenhower was vague on Korea while doing well in polls among voters who inclined toward an offensive strategy to end the war. American allies and neutrals alike gained a sense of urgency over the prospect that a window was rapidly closing for a peaceful solution in Korea.[97]

Although numerous proposals circulated on the POW issue, interest focused on one by the Indian V. K. Krishna Menon, which called for a "neutral" repatriation commission, made up of Sweden, Switzerland, Poland, and Czechoslovakia, that would take custody of POWs once they were transported to the demilitarized zone. The commission would interview POWs and decide their fate by majority vote, with an "umpire" deciding individual cases if the regular members deadlocked. By mid-November Menon had refined his proposal, but Acheson remained fearful that its implementation would lead to an indefinite retention of prisoners who resisted repatriation.[98]

The process of drafting and amending an Indian resolution produced a spat between Acheson and his British and Canadian counterparts, but the Soviets helped rescue the alliance by denouncing the measure. Eventually, the Americans accepted it, despite vagueness on the final disposition of prisoners. The resolution also went beyond the U.S. position at Panmunjom in placing prisoners in the custody of a neutral commission. Perhaps the greatest result of the exercise was to stall any U.S. effort to impose additional sanctions on the PRC. Activities of the Arab-Asian bloc, the Latin Americans, and key NATO allies revealed broad opposition to such a move in the General Assembly.

That reality cut two ways: in discouraging the Truman administration from expanding the war, it encouraged the Communists to continue their test of Western endurance. A new group of leaders in Washington would soon decide whether or not objections at the United Nations or, more narrowly, among NATO allies should continue to dictate against new pressure on the enemy in Korea.

V

If NATO allies were concerned about Eisenhower's approach to the war, so, too, were the Chinese. During the previous summer Mao had articulated several advantages to continuing the war: an ongoing boost to PRC prestige derived from fighting the Americans to a standstill; the promotion of unity at home; and the provision of valuable experience to the Chinese army. The Americans, on the other hand, lacked China's manpower reserves, and their Europe-first strategy made disadvantageous a prolonged war in Korea.[99] In meetings with Stalin in

Moscow, Zhou initiated exploration of possible concessions on the POW issue, but this was in part a ploy to induce the parsimonious dictator to loosen Soviet purse strings to assist further in Korea and in implementing the PRC's first Five-Year Plan. When Zhou made some progress in the latter area and Stalin advised firmness on the POW issue, Mao offered no dissent.[100] Still, he ordered a study of Eisenhower's statements on Korea and a projection of his course there if elected. The conclusion was that the general-turned-politician would escalate militarily.[101] Eisenhower's preinauguration activities—a December trip to Korea, talk of resolving the stalemate with "deeds" rather than "words," and a highly publicized meeting with General MacArthur to hear his plan to end the war—reinforced this expectation. Stepped-up amphibious training maneuvers off the coasts of North Korea and China and Nationalist Chinese raids from offshore islands on PRC-held territories opposite Taiwan had already stirred concern in Beijing, which recognized the strong pro-Chiang sentiment within the GOP.[102]

Mao surmised that, because of world opinion and the Soviet capacity to retaliate, the Americans were unlikely to employ atomic weapons in or beyond Korea. Nor was the United States likely to concentrate action against the well-fortified CPV ground positions. Rather, he anticipated amphibious assaults on the west and east coasts of Korea and diversionary attacks on the China coast. These moves would come in the spring of 1953, he thought, and he ordered preparations to counter them. If UNC military moves could be repulsed with large casualties, he concluded, conditions on the peninsula "would become more stabilized and more favorable to us."[103]

Mao's attitude continued into the new year in the face of ongoing indications of U.S. military escalation. Two weeks after his inauguration on January 20, Eisenhower announced that the U.S. Seventh Fleet would no longer prevent Nationalist attacks on the mainland from Taiwan. Chiang quickly reaffirmed his determination to recapture the mainland, and Major General William C. Chase, chief of the U.S. military advisory and assistance group on Taiwan, bragged that Nationalist forces had doubled their fighting efficiency over the past year. Back in Washington, Senator William Knowland, chairman of the Republican Policy Committee, pressed for a naval blockade of China, and the new president approved an expansion of the ROK army from fourteen to sixteen divisions, with a future move to twenty a distinct possibility. In early March Eisenhower called top advisers and congressional leaders to the White House to hear General Van Fleet, the retiring Eighth Army commander, outline his well-publicized belief that the way to end the war was through military escalation.[104] Yet on February 8 China's Communist Party daily published a speech by Mao in which he declared that "we desire peace, but as long as U.S. imperialism does not discard its barbaric and unreasonable demands, and its plots to expand its aggression, the resolution of the Chinese people can only be to continue to fight together with the Korean people to the end."[105] Later in the month Mao decided that the PRC should await an initiative by the other side before reopening talks at Panmunjom.[106]

On February 22 General Clark sent a letter to Kim Il-sung and Peng Dehuai that could be interpreted as such a move. Back in December the executive committee of the League of Red Cross Societies in Geneva had called on both parties in Korea to repatriate sick and wounded POWs. Neither side responded immediately, but the U.S. State Department anticipated that the matter would be raised at the UN General Assembly, scheduled to reconvene in late February. Anxious to move before pressure built in New York, American diplomats pushed Clark to advance the proposal directly to the Communists, and he acceded to their wishes.[107]

The Communists did not rush to respond, but on March 5, 1953, an event occurred in the Soviet Union that could not help but produce a flurry of activity in the Communist world. After a brief illness, Stalin died at his suburban home at Kuntsevo.

VI

Stalin consistently advised Mao to take a tough position in the armistice talks. At the same time, the Soviet premier always showed determination to avoid direct Soviet embroilment with the Americans over

Korea. With the Eisenhower administration appearing to gear up for military escalation in Korea and China, the possibility that Stalin was on the verge of advising the Chinese to end the war cannot be ruled out, but no reliable documentation has surfaced to confirm it.[108] What is certain is that Stalin's successors moved quickly to advocate moves to end the war, and the Chinese offered no resistance.[109] All indications are that they were pleased with the Soviet decision, as were the North Koreans.

The decision for new moves to end the war came while Chinese and North Korean delegations were in Moscow to attend Stalin's funeral. On March 19 the Soviet Council of Ministers passed a resolution with draft letters to Mao and Kim Il-sung that called for a positive response to General Clark's overture of February 22. This action should be followed by the statement of a high government official in Beijing, preferably Zhou En-lai, "that the time has arrived to resolve the entire question of prisoners and, consequently, to secure the cessation of the war in Korea and the conclusion of an armistice." When the negotiations reconvened at Panmunjom, the Communists should propose an immediate exchange of all prisoners who insisted upon repatriation and the turning over of the remaining prisoners "to a neutral country in order to secure a fair resolution of the question of their repatriation." The resolution closed with the comment that "we cannot foresee all the steps and measures which the governments of the USSR, PRC and DPRK will need to make" to achieve an armistice.[110] The clear message was that the Communists must strive to bring the war to an end.

It still took over four months to conclude an armistice, nearly three of which were consumed reaching agreement on POWs and on details regarding the armistice line. Zhou's message to the United Nations on POWs did not come until March 30, and formal talks at Panmunjom did not resume until April 26. On June 4 the Communists finally accepted UNC insistence on release from custody of nonrepatriate POWs within 120 days of an armistice and without their shipment to a third country. They also agreed to a Neutral Nations Repatriation Commission of five members, with a simple majority empowered after

FIG. 18. North Korean general Nam Il, the head of the Communist delegation at Panmunjom, walks from a meeting of the reconvened talks, May 8, 1953. Photo by Associated Press

an interview process to decide whether or not individual POWs would be repatriated.

The Communists did so only after the UNC made clear on May 25 that, despite allied objections, it would terminate the talks if its proposal was not accepted and void agreements on the neutral areas around Panmunjom, Kaesong, and Munsan. The latter move would enable the UNC to bomb the Kaesong area, which was believed to be a major storage center of supplies for Communist forces. Commencement of air attacks on several irrigation dams in North Korea on May 13, which resulted in the flooding of thousands of acres of spring plantings and the disruption of rail traffic north of Pyongyang, added pressure on the Communists.

For their part, at the end of May and in early June, the Communists launched tactical offensives along the front that achieved small territorial gains and helped cushion the impending concession at the negotiating table. While in March the Communist side had largely decided to end the war, the precise timing and terms for its conclusion emerged only after intense bargaining that included military pressure by both sides.[111]

Pressure was more ominous to the Communist side because the UNC possessed the greater capacity to escalate. To be sure, American military leaders calculated that a successful UN offensive to the Pyongyang-Wonsan line would require not only a substantial buildup on the ground but also nuclear attacks on Manchuria. Such attacks would reduce the U.S. nuclear stockpile and bomber fleet, threaten the NATO alliance, and perhaps even lead to Soviet air attacks on Pusan, Inchon, and key Japanese ports. The worst-case scenario was a Soviet nuclear offensive against the United States, which might inflict as many as nine million civilian casualties and reduce by half the sortie rate of the Strategic Air Command.[112] Yet the United States now possessed over one thousand nuclear weapons and the previous fall had successfully tested a hydrogen bomb, which held a destructive power hundreds of times greater than the weapons used against Japan in 1945. In addition, should the Americans continue to bomb irrigation dams in North Korea and add to their targets the heretofore neutral area around Kaesong, the Communist supply network might become all the more strained. With the Chinese anxious to get on with implementation of their Five-Year Plan, with the Soviet leadership in turmoil in the aftermath of Stalin's death, and with the economies of both the Soviet Union and its Eastern European allies facing the strains of a prolonged arms buildup, the Communist camp prudently chose to avoid the risk of escalation.[113]

That prudence was soon tested. In the early hours of June 18, only days before the expected signing of an armistice, President Rhee defiantly released from custody over twenty-five thousand Korean POWs who said they would resist repatriation to the Communist side. Rhee's consistent opposition to an armistice without unification of Korea had finally manifested itself in concrete action.[114]

The Communists responded to Rhee's action with a letter to Clark.

FIG. 19. U.S. and ROK officials meet at President Syngman Rhee's Seoul residence on June 13, 1953, only days before Rhee's release of Communist prisoners threatened an early armistice. Left to right, Admiral Arthur Radford, chairman-designate of the Joint Chiefs of Staff; Rhee; U.S. ambassador Ellis Briggs; ROK foreign minister Pyun Tung Tai; Lieutenant General Maxwell, commander of the Eighth Army.

Characterizing the prisoners as having been coerced into leaving the camps by "the South Korean Government and Army directly controlled by your side," the letter posed three questions: "Is the United Nations Command able to control the South Korean Government and Army? If not, does the armistice in Korea include the Syngman Rhee clique? If it is not included, what assurance is there for the implementation of the armistice agreement on the part of South Korea?" The letter concluded with an ominous assertion: "If it [the ROK] is included, then your side must be responsible for recovering immediately all the 25,952 prisoners of war . . . who were released and retained under coercion and to be press-ganged into the South Korean Army, and your side must give assurance that similar incidents absolutely will not recur in the future."[115] Although the UNC quickly reinforced the camps with U.S. soldiers, who recaptured a few hundred of the escapees and, in preventing further breakouts, inflicted nearly two hundred casualties, it considered impossible the recapture of most of the escapees.[116]

The Communists did not threaten to end the talks, however, and unlike the response to incidents of August 1951, Chinese propaganda concentrated attacks on Rhee and his government rather than the United States.[117] The Soviets hinted to the Americans that the demand for recapture of the released POWs "should not be taken literally."[118]

Conditions in Korea aside, developments during June in the Soviet Union and Eastern Europe put the Communists in a weak position to continue the war. In Moscow the Soviet troika that succeeded Stalin— Lavrentii Beria, Georgii Malenkov, and Nikita Khrushchev—mired itself in intrigue. In late June Beria disappeared from public view and soon thereafter was arrested and removed from all his posts.[119] Only weeks earlier, overt unrest had emerged in Czechoslovakia and East Germany, and it seethed just below the surface in Poland and Hungary as well.[120] The time for a prolonged test of strength over Korea had passed.

When General Clark outlined the U.S. position in a letter to Communist commanders on June 29, he received a measured if delayed response. Clark insisted on the impossibility of recovering all the escaped prisoners and that he could not guarantee ROK acceptance of an armistice. He promised, though, that the UNC would strive to achieve ROK cooperation. The Americans were already engaged in such an effort, led by Walter S. Robertson, the assistant secretary of state for the Far East, who had rushed to the peninsula after the release of the Korean POWs. The Communists, while intensely argumentative, agreed to resume the recessed talks at Panmunjom.[121]

The Communists did not bargain seriously until they had launched an offensive on the central front with six CPV divisions. The focus, as with the limited offensives of late May and early June, was on punishing ROK units, which retreated up to six miles before U.S. reinforcements stopped the enemy advance and recovered most of the lost territory. The lesson administered, on July 19 Communist negotiators commenced bargaining at Panmunjom.[122]

By this time Rhee had agreed not to obstruct an armistice "so long as no measures or actions taken under [it] . . . are detrimental of our national survival." Although Rhee hinted that he would use force if a postarmistice political conference failed to achieve unification, Washington emphasized that he would not have its support in such action.[123] The final roadblock for an end to the fighting had been overcome.

The signing of the armistice on July 27, 1953, took place in a large bamboo and wooden structure at Panmunjom built especially for the ceremony. It was far from a joyous moment. "There was no pretense at an exchange of courtesies, or even of civility," the London *Times* reported.[124] The principals on both sides barely glanced at each other. The South Koreans did not even appear. Since the armistice went into effect only twelve hours after the signing, the contestants continued to pound each other, the Communists with their ground artillery at the front, the UNC with their air and naval power penetrating well into North Korea.[125] "Seldom in the long story of human conflict," James Reston wrote in the *New York Times*, "has an armistice rested on such bad faith."[126]

The end reflected poignantly the depth of the situational and ideological divide between the opposing parties in Korea—between the leader of the West, which for generations had ridden the wave of technological advance to house the dominant imperial nations on earth, and representatives of the former colonial world, now awakened in a nationalist surge that sought to overthrow old patterns of power; between the leader of a liberal, capitalist bloc, which sought either the status quo or evolutionary change, and representatives of its authoritarian, socialist opposite, which sought to tear down what it considered a corrupt, exploitative, and aggressively acquisitive system. These divisions go far to explain the length of time it took to end the war, even after both sides had accepted the existing military balance.

That the war finally did end is explained in part by the apparent willingness of one of those sides to expand the fighting if it could not be stopped, in part by the death of the leader of the other side. That death not only eliminated the hardest of the hard-liners on the armistice negotiations; it brought to the surface tensions within that side which could be addressed more comfortably in a less tense international climate.

Whatever the "bad faith" of the contestants in the Korean War, the circumstances of its end, both internal and external, gave hope that the armistice would last. Here Rhee's rhetoric about forceful unification, which continued after July 27, could easily mislead. The ROK leader had played his cards fully on the eve of the armistice, and the Americans had refused to budge on either ending the fighting or resuming it again at a later date. Meanwhile, the CPV had administered a sharp reminder to the ROK army that it had no chance of achieving advances without U.S. aid.

As for the Communist side, indications are that Kim Il-sung had wanted peace for over a year. His ambition to unite the peninsula under his rule never died, but the pounding his nation had taken from the air gave him pause when considering any initiative to resume hostilities. Other factors deterred him as well. Unlike the thirty-eighth parallel prior to the North Korean attack of June 1950, the new line dividing the peninsula was defensible. Behind it were not only a beefed-up, experienced ROK army but also U.S. forces that showed no inclination to withdraw completely as they had done in 1949. As if this was not enough, Secretary of State Dulles flew to Seoul after the armistice to conclude a mutual defense pact with the ROK.[127]

The Soviet Union and China had much reason as well to avoid a resumption of hostilities. If the Korean people themselves had been the primary victims of the war, losing in killed or wounded roughly 10 percent of their brethren, the Soviets and the Chinese also had made sacrifices that they were not anxious to repeat. The Soviets had expended or committed themselves to hundreds of millions of dollars in military and economic assistance to the PRC and DPRK while provoking a greatly intensified arms race with the Americans, whose economy outproduced their own by a factor of three or four to one. The war had solidified China's isolation from the West, but it also had strengthened Beijing's international prestige and sense of itself as a great power.

From Mao's perspective, however, these developments were bittersweet. The CPV suffered hundreds of thousands of losses in Korea and failed to overcome the huge U.S. advantages in firepower, even with Soviet aid, which was often slow in coming and limited in both quantity and quality. China also had failed to force a settlement of the

Taiwan issue in its favor—indeed, Taiwan's very existence as a separate entity was largely a result of the war. Ultimately the PRC made an embarrassing concession on the POW issue. What is more, in the immediate aftermath of the armistice, the nations participating in the UN enterprise issued a "greater sanctions" statement indicating that, if the Communists initiated a resumption of hostilities, the ensuing conflict probably would not be limited to Korea. Despite the reluctance of NATO allies to go along with the statement, U.S. determination that it be issued accentuated the risks to the Communists of any new military venture on the peninsula.

In sum, although the war had left the peninsula bitterly divided, an armed camp licking severe wounds, the circumstances of its end made unlikely a repeat performance. The Cold War would not depart anytime soon, but there was reason to hope that its most devastating impact on Korea was in the past.

PART III

BROADER ISSUES

CHAPTER 7

The Korean War and the American

Relationship with Korea

THE U.S. OCCUPATION OF KOREA AFTER WORLD WAR II MOVED THE
American relationship with the peninsula onto an entirely new plane.
In the late nineteenth century the United States had established formal relations with Korea, but despite the urging of some Americans in
the field, Washington studiously avoided taking sides in that nation's
increasingly tumultuous politics. During the first decade of the new
century, the United States stood aside as an aggressive Japan grabbed
Korea for its empire. A generation later, Korea remained uncontested
as American businessmen and missionaries were squeezed in that
country and the United States moved toward confrontation with a
Japan expanding into other areas. This all changed with Japan's defeat
in 1945, as the United States finally assumed a primary role in northeast Asia.

Yet, on the continent itself, that role remained uncertain. Whereas the American position in occupied Japan seemed well established, after 1946 Washington refused to become directly involved in the civil war in Manchuria, and it scaled down its presence in Korea, ending the occupation in 1948 and withdrawing its last combat troops the following year. The U.S. commitment was sufficiently ambiguous to enable North Korean premier Kim Il-sung to persuade his Soviet over-lord Joseph Stalin to support a conventional attack on the despised Republic of Korea below the thirty-eighth parallel. This act and the train of events that followed moved the Korean-American relationship dramatically toward the one of today: a political, military, and even economic alliance that has survived by a decade the larger Cold War from which it grew.

My purpose in this chapter is to analyze the impact of the Korean War on the bilateral relationship between the United States and the Republic of Korea. I organize my presentation into the three broad categories of military, economic, and political affairs and employ the method of examining the relationship before and after the event with an eye toward weighing its influence.

I

In Korea the bilateral relationship with the United States is often re-ferred to as "an alliance forged in blood." In general, the phrase ap-pears to have its origin many centuries ago in a Chinese novel in which friends sealed their relationship by cutting their skin and ex-changing blood.[1] Although its first use to describe the Korean-American relationship remains a mystery, there can be no doubt that it refers to the situation that grew out of the Korean War. Nearly thirty-seven thousand Americans died in that conflict, and South Korean losses were many times that. American veterans of the war who visit Korea are treated with a reverence unheard of in their homeland. What is largely forgotten in the United States (it was, after all, a first-generation Korean American who was responsible for the Korean War Memorial in Washington, D.C.) is very much a living memory in Korea. The alliance manifests itself to the present day in two very concrete forms, the presence of some thirty-seven thousand U.S. military personnel and numerous military bases and installations on South Korean soil, and the existence of a mutual defense treaty. The linkage of these phenomena to the war could not be more clear-cut. A year before its outbreak, American troops withdrew from the peninsula, leaving behind under five hundred officers in a military advisory group intended to help train the fledgling ROK army. The ROK regime of Syngman Rhee "moved heaven and earth to have withdrawal deferred," U.S. ambassador John J. Muccio remarked soon after its completion.[2] Short of a continued American military presence, Rhee demanded creation of a Pacific pact similar to NATO, a bilateral agreement for mutual defense against "aggressive nations," or a public pledge from Washington to defend the ROK.[3] He received none of these. In his famous speech to the National Press Club of January 12, 1950, Secretary of State Acheson left Korea out of the American defense perimeter in the Pacific.[4] Less than four months later, when Senator Tom Connally remarked in a published interview that, "whether we want it or not," the ROK might have to be abandoned to the Communists, Acheson responded weakly.[5] Other statements by the secretary and the president that expressed U.S. support against aggression to areas from Europe to Indochina often left out Korea.[6] Despite increasing reports of a growing military imbalance on the peninsula in favor of North Korea, no one on the American side suggested a redeployment of U.S. troops or a military commitment.[7]

To the surprise of many, including Rhee, Stalin, Kim Il-sung, and Chinese Communist leader Mao Zedong, the blatant North Korean attack of June 25, 1950, *did* lead to a rapid commitment of American forces to the peninsula. Had the ROK been placed in jeopardy as a result of guerrilla activity aided through the infiltration of arms and manpower from above the thirty-eighth parallel, Washington's response probably would have been less decisive. Under such circumstances, the fall of an American client could have been seen as comparable to the case of China, where the corrupt and unpopular regime of Chiang Kai-shek had recently fallen to the Communists. The conventional, well-coordinated nature of the North Korean offensive, however, and its presumed sponsorship by the Soviet Union persuaded

U.S. leaders that it constituted aggression. With memories of the 1930s and the global bloodletting that followed fresh in mind, surmising after several days of close observation that no other military moves were likely on the Soviet periphery, and possessing the capacity to resist North Korea with American forces nearby, President Truman could hardly shirk the effort.[8]

Still, the road to formal military alliance was far from linear. Assuming that U.S. forces could maintain a foothold in Korea, their commitment at the end of June 1950 probably *did* make their presence there inevitable for a substantial period. Even if the Chinese had failed to intervene in the fall of 1950, the process of pacifying and unifying Korea would have taken many months, perhaps even years, and U.S. troops would have been essential to the task. In the North and South, remnants of the DPRK army would have had to be eliminated. Given the problems in previous years with guerrillas in mountainous areas below the thirty-eighth parallel alone, the task of creating a stable order over the entire peninsula was bound to be difficult. It was likely to be all the more so because former landowners in the North who had migrated to the South after 1945 would probably attempt to reverse the land redistribution carried out under the Soviet occupation. Such attempts could not help but create civil unrest. A final and related problem involved the question of how a truly national government was to be established. Rhee wanted simply to hold legislative elections in the North to fill out the ROK National Assembly, whereas the U.S. State Department, the British Foreign Office, and some of the nations represented on UN commissions prior to June 25 doubted Rhee's capacity to govern the whole country. They were not heartened by ongoing bickering between the president and the National Assembly or reports of heavy-handed activities by Rhee's Youth Corps, which in October followed UN forces into the North.[9] Even granting these problems, had a clear international boundary been established on the Yalu and Tumen Rivers, it is conceivable that American forces would have departed within a decade or remained merely on a token basis without forward deployment and/or a concrete commitment. It was the perpetuation of the country's division, with both sides heavily armed and, even to the present day, the other side refusing to rule out the use of force to achieve unification, that set the stage for alliance and long-term occupation.

Even so, the Americans approached the armistice in 1953 with some hope of avoiding a formal commitment to the ROK. The war had been a long and costly one with which the American people had become increasingly impatient. Indeed, the victory of Eisenhower in 1952, the first instance of a Republican winning the presidency since 1928, was made possible largely by popular discontent over Korea.[10] Furthermore, the expense of the war represented a deep concern to Eisenhower and many others, who feared that U.S. spending abroad would eventually ruin the American economy. In this context Secretary of State Dulles spoke of a new, more flexible strategy in the Cold War in which the United States would intervene at times and places of its own choosing rather than being drawn into peripheral areas on terms essentially dictated by the enemy.[11] In the case of Korea, two additional concerns gave Washington pause. First was the fear that a bilateral treaty would undermine the role of the United Nations, encouraging other contributors to the UNC to withdraw their forces.[12] Second and even more important was fear of getting drawn into a conflict by the volatile Rhee, whose willingness to go along with an armistice without unification remained in doubt. The last thing the Americans wanted was an agreement that would commit U.S. forces to a struggle rooted in Rhee's passionate desire for a united Korea.

Ultimately, the United States agreed to a mutual defense pact because of Rhee's threat to sabotage an armistice. Since the summer of 1950, Rhee had made clear his opposition to any end to the fighting without unification under the ROK. The protracted nature of the negotiations with the Communists had kept this matter in the background, but the move in April 1953 to resume the suspended talks threatened to provoke a crisis in Korean-American relations. At the beginning of the month, Rhee launched a campaign to mobilize support for his position at home. On April 2 the ROK National Assembly unanimously passed a resolution opposing an armistice without unification.[13] Three days later, with U.S. Eighth Army commander Maxwell Taylor sitting on the podium, Rhee lectured a gathering of ROK troops on the necessity of fighting on until the nation was reunited.[14] The

ROK Foreign Ministry and Office of Public of Information spewed propaganda for unification, which South Korean newspapers reproduced and reinforced with editorials. Mass rallies began in Seoul, Pusan, and Inchon.[15]

American observers were not altogether taken in by this display, since draft dodging was widespread among young men in South Korea.[16] Nonetheless, American ambassador Ellis Briggs reminded Washington of Rhee's "general unpredictability."[17] The ambassador recognized an element of bluff in Rhee's "'victory or death' act" but understood that he was a proud and passionate man who could not be taken for granted. Late in the month Briggs advised the State Department that an offer of a mutual security pact might be essential to keep the ROK president in line.[18] With the ROK army now manning over two-thirds of the UN front against North Korean and Chinese troops, Rhee's admonitions had to be considered.

Dulles already had hinted to the ROK ambassador in Washington that a mutual security pact was possible, although he emphasized that the United States would in no way commit itself to anything more than defense of territory below an armistice line. He also stated that it would be best to postpone any security pact until all parties had had an opportunity to discuss unification at a postarmistice political conference.[19]

Progress toward an armistice in May 1953 brought tensions in U.S.-Korean relations to new heights. On May 25 the UN command made a final proposal to the Communists on the POW issue. Fearing Rhee's reaction, the Americans did not inform ROK officials of the move until minutes before it was presented at Panmunjom. Rhee responded so menacingly that Washington finally decided to put a mutual security pact on the table. In a letter delivered to the ROK president on June 7, Eisenhower offered to promptly negotiate such an agreement "after the conclusion and acceptance of an armistice."[20]

Rhee remained dissatisfied. A lifetime of experience had persuaded the octogenarian of U.S. unreliability in pursuing Korean goals of unity and independence. At the moment those goals were more inextricably connected than ever, not only because he perceived the Kim

Il-sung regime as an extension of the great powers to the north and west but also because the United States was determined to rebuild and rearm Japan. A united Korea would be far better able to resist future incursion by the despised former master to the east. Indeed, a united Korea might even enable the United States to place less reliance on a powerful Japan as a bulwark against Asian communism.[21] In addition, at home Rhee had long taken adamant public stands against an armistice without unification and without a withdrawal of Chinese troops from the peninsula. More recently he had spoken out against permitting Communist and Indian officials and troops below the thirty-eighth parallel as members of the Neutral Nations Repatriation Commission and of putting anti-Communist Korean prisoners in their hands. The armistice agreement essentially accepted by the Communists on June 4, 1953, included both these arrangements. Backing down on all these matters would constitute a loss of face that could jeopardize Rhee's survival.[22] On June 18, with all substantive issues now resolved between the UN command and the Communists, Rhee released over twenty-five thousand of the Korean POWs held below the thirty-eighth parallel.[23]

American officials in Seoul and Washington alike were furious. Had Rhee carried out his threat to withdraw ROK troops from the UN command, the United States probably would have removed him from the scene. In the end, the ROK president stepped back from the precipice, as the Americans sent to Korea Assistant Secretary Robertson, a tactful and sympathetic Virginian, to negotiate a deal. Rhee did not receive much of what he wanted, but he did win significant concessions. He got the United States to reopen talks with the Communists so as to exclude Communist or Indian officials, or troops attached to the Neutral Nations Supervisory Commission, from operating in South Korea. He also induced the United States to greatly expedite movement toward a mutual defense treaty. By forcing the Americans to bargain openly with him, he achieved great prestige at home. Perhaps most important of all, he ensured that his ally would never again take him for granted. In a letter to Eisenhower of July 27, he thanked and congratulated his U.S. counterpart "for the statesmanlike vision with which you have brought the relationships of your powerful nation and of our weaker one onto a basis of honest mutuality and two-way cooperation."[24]

Dulles arrived in Korea only days after the signing of the armistice on July 27, and he proceeded rapidly to agreement with Rhee on the terms of a mutual defense treaty.[25] The United States insisted on terms that followed the pattern of its pacts with other Pacific allies, which in contrast to the automatic action in the event of outside attack implied in the North Atlantic Treaty called for a response "in accordance with its [each signatory's] constitutional processes." The treaty also possessed the standard escape clause: that is, either party could terminate it with one year's notice. And Rhee was denied any wording that hinted of American support in the event of a ROK initiation of hostilities against the North. Yet he got a security pact acceptable to the U.S. Senate, which quickly ratified the agreement when it reconvened in January 1954. In a joint public statement signed by Dulles and Rhee, the United States reiterated its commitment to the goal of "a unified, free, and independent Korea" and to negotiate agreements to cover the status of American forces that remained on the peninsula.[26] Finally, Rhee squelched an overture by Dulles to consider proposing to the Communists a neutral, demilitarized Korea under the ROK.[27]

The bilateral relationship still remained an unequal one. For example, American military personnel in Korea continued to be protected by the Taejon agreement of July 12, 1950, which gave the United States full jurisdiction in cases where they committed criminal acts. Although Dulles promised to promptly renegotiate this ageement, the United States, largely because of objections from the Pentagon and Congress, refused to begin comprehensive talks on the matter until 1961. It took until 1965 to reach accord. Meanwhile, crimes by American soldiers against Koreans were common, and their treatment exclusively by U.S. military authorities was an ongoing source of tension in the relationship.[28]

In addition, over time the presence of tens of thousands of U.S. soldiers in South Korea provided a major impetus for the spread of American culture. The radio and television stations established by the U.S. military to inform and entertain its servicemen served as major disseminators to Koreans of the English language as well as American

popular culture. The numerous U.S. military bases and installations
created demands for goods and services that could only be met by
Koreans. Among other things, the resulting interaction led to thousands of marriages between American men and Korean women, which
in turn have provided for several decades a significant source of immi-
gration from the peninsula to the United States.[29] On the other hand,
the South Korean government possessed significantly greater influence
over the United States than it had had prior to the war. General Mark
W. Clark, the commander of UN forces, later recalled with reference
to the crisis provoked by Rhee in June 1953 that the Korean leader
had a "psychological whammy" on the United States, "that no matter
what happened we could not, after three years of war, after all the
blood and treasure we lost, let Korea go to the Reds by default because of a quarrel 'in the family.'"[30] Eisenhower expressed the same
sentiment in a top secret meeting of the National Security Council in
November. In the midst of a discussion of the possibility of threatening to withdraw from Korea if Rhee attacked the North, the president
blurted out that "it was impossible to contemplate walking out of
Korea. To do so would be to cross off three years of terrible sacrifice."[31]
The government that in 1949 had futilely "moved heaven and earth"
in trying to get American troops to stay in Korea now had tens of
thousands of them committed indefinitely to the peninsula and a military security pact to boot. South Korean influence had distinct boundaries, to be sure, as the United States adamantly refused, despite continued urging from Rhee, to endorse the use of military force to
achieve unification. However, the U.S. stake in ROK survival, though
still not critical from a strategic standpoint, had made its abandonment unthinkable, and its leaders would use that fact to bargain not
just on military matters but in the political and economic spheres as
well.

II

The issue to be addressed in the political realm is American influence
on South Korean politics. As early as 1946, Washington defined estab-

lishment of "a democratic government fully representative of the freely expressed will of the Korean people" as one of its three objectives on the peninsula.[32] The objective never disappeared, but the division of the country into two indigenous governments in 1948 led American policy makers to think of that objective as, for the moment, covering the territory below the thirty-eighth parallel alone. For much of the fall of 1950, the larger objective reappeared, only again to be rendered academic by the Chinese intervention. So one question is, How did the war affect the ability and/or willingness of the United States to move the ROK toward a system of democracy recognizable in the West? Another is, How, for the long term, did the American course in this area influence the bilateral relationship?

Prospects for South Korean democratization were uncertain on the eve of war. In a poor and divided country lacking a liberal tradition and led by an aged president with strong authoritarian proclivities, democracy often seemed a faint hope. The Americans recognized Rhee's antidemocratic tendencies, yet in 1948 they moved to create an independent South Korea under conditions that made inevitable Rhee's emergence at the top. Rhee prevented the conservative Korean Democratic Party from imposing a constitution providing for a parliamentary system that would enable it to govern through a strong legislature. The constitution actually adopted in the summer of 1948 provided, on Rhee's insistence, for presidential control of the cabinet. Theoretically, this would enable Rhee, as president, to dominate the government through the bureaucracy and the police. Yet the KDP had other ideas, and Rhee's appointment of only one member of that group, the largest in the National Assembly, to the original cabinet helped to produce a conflict between the executive and legislative branches that often turned violent. Rhee often resorted to arresting members of the legislature and the opposition press, and torture of prisoners by the police and army was commonplace.[33] Despite strong reservations about both the methods and the substance of his rule, the United States continued to provide military and economic aid to the ROK. In September 1949 Ambassador Muccio, never a blind defender of Rhee, put his course in context:

The Government of the Republic of Korea . . . is hardly more than thirty miles . . . from where its soldiers and police are frequently engaged in armed conflict with an aggressive enemy. In various places in South Korea, numerous bands of communist guerrillas . . . raid, murder and plunder the nearby countryside. . . . The Pyongyang radio fills the air with demands for the liquidation of every member of the Government . . . and with appeals to the army and the police to turn their weapons on their leaders on behalf of the communist order. . . . Consequently it has been difficult for me privately to advise the Korean President against certain extreme actions.

The ambassador rebuked those who advocated abandonment of the South Koreans "because they have imperfectly grasped those practices of democratic government which have taken so many centuries to develop in the Occidental world."[34]

By April 1950, however, conditions were such that Washington, with Muccio's support, applied direct pressure on the Rhee government. To be sure, guerrilla activities were on the wane as a result of an ROK army campaign during the previous winter. Economic conditions had improved somewhat after a good fall harvest and substantial increases in the production of coal, electricity, and some finished goods. But American officials were increasingly worried about other trends. Inflation remained a serious problem. Despite repeated U.S. urging for decisive government action, in March the ROK prime minister sent a letter to the head of the American Economic Cooperation Administration in Korea downplaying its significance. Then Rhee expressed a need to postpone until November the legislative elections, which the constitution called for in May, to give the National Assembly an opportunity to pass a budget for the fiscal year beginning in April.[35] The result was an aide-mémoire from Secretary of State Acheson to President Rhee expressing strong disappointment on both these matters and threatening to reconsider U.S. economic and military assistance programs unless immediate action was taken to reverse the trends. Acheson pointedly reminded Rhee that U.S. aid was "predicated upon the existence and growth of democratic institutions within the Republic" and that "free, popular elections, in accordance with the constitution and other basic laws of the Republic, are the foundation of these democratic institutions." To reinforce the point, Acheson called Muccio home for consultations.[36]

The pressure had an immediate impact. Rhee quickly circulated the aide-mémoire in the National Assembly, which by the end of April passed a balanced budget for the fiscal year, as well as taxation and pricing measures to make possible its achievement. He also scheduled elections for the end of May.[37] The campaign and balloting took place under scrutiny of members of the United Nations Commission on Korea and the American mission. Over ten candidates registered per election district, with over two-thirds of them claiming no party affiliation. Of the third who did, slightly over half identified with pro-government groups, but, since there were four of these, some actually contested each other in the same district. Voting was widespread, and the results were generally considered a fair expression of the popular will. Only 31 of 210 incumbents gained reelection; independents emerged as the majority with 126 members. The Korean Nationalist Party, the largest of the pro-Rhee groups, managed to elect only 24 of its 154 candidates. The outcome was considered a sharp defeat for Rhee, a view confirmed by the fact that his first candidate for prime minister, independent O Ha-yong, went down to defeat in the new National Assembly with only 46 positive votes.[38]

Prior to 1960, when, in the aftermath of a rigged election and in the face of massive and overt popular discontent with the outcome, the United States intervened to persuade Rhee to resign from office, there is no more clear-cut illustration of American intervention to foster democracy in Korea.[39] That it came at a time of deep uncertainty in the ROK about the U.S. commitment to its survival suggests the linkage between that uncertainty and American influence. A comparison with the 1952 election crisis adds weight to that linkage.

The ROK constitution called for election of the president by the National Assembly. His term up in 1952, Rhee knew his reelection by the assembly was at best doubtful. The problem was that amending the constitution to provide for popular election of the president required the vote of a two-thirds majority of that body. If Rhee respected constitutional processes, his career as president was likely to be over. This prospect moved from the likely to the definite in January 1952, when the assembly overwhelmingly rejected his call for the proposed amendment. Rhee immediately began a campaign of mobilization and intimidation against the legislature.[40]

The campaign entered its final stage early on May 25, when martial law was declared in Pusan, the temporary capital, and surrounding areas. Over the next two days, several dozen assemblymen were arrested, and many others went into hiding. On the twenty-eighth the National Assembly still managed to put together a quorum, which called for an end to martial law. Under the constitution the president was obligated to comply, but in defense of the "spirit" rather than the "letter" of that document, he refused. He imposed tight censorship and threatened the assembly's dissolution. Youth corps and other groups under his control organized demonstrations against the legislative branch, and his Office of Public Information announced the discovery of "far-reaching Communist connections" among assemblymen.[41]

The crisis came at a most inconvenient time for the Americans. Muccio, who was in the last stage of his ambassadorship, had just left for consultations in the United States. General Clark had only been in Tokyo as UN commander since May 12. The armistice talks were stalemated over the POW issue, and riots among Communist prisoners on Koje-do had forced the reassignment there of some UN troops from the front lines.[42] At home the public standing of President Truman was at an all-time low over his seizure of steel mills to avert a strike, revelations of corruption in his administration, ongoing charges of softness toward subversives in government, and the stalemate in Korea.[43] Whether in Washington, Tokyo, or Pusan, American personnel were not in a strong position to take a decisive stand against Rhee's embarrassing and dangerous campaign to remain in power.

Any possibility for strong U.S. action against Rhee all but disappeared in late May when it became obvious that a division of opinion existed between the American embassy, now led temporarily by chargé E. Allan Lightner, and Generals Clark and Van Fleet. From the start Lightner wanted to stand up to Rhee, even if it meant forcefully removing him from office. His conviction became all the more firm when the ROK army chief of staff, General Lee Chong Chan, stopped by the embassy one evening and offered, with an American green light, to place Rhee and his home minister and martial law commander under house arrest. The jailed legislators would be released and the National Assembly given the opportunity to hold its election for president. The process completed and the new president installed, the army would disappear from the political scene. Lightner later recalled that he was assured that the process would require no direct American action and that "no bloodshed" would occur.[44]

Despite Lightner's enthusiasm for the plan, Clark and Van Fleet demurred. One weakness in the diplomat's case was the absence, among several possibilities, of any clear alternative to Rhee to head the government. Chang Myon, the first ROK ambassador to the United States and later the ROK prime minister, was perhaps the American favorite, but he lacked popular backing or a forceful personality. Legislative powerhouse Shin Ik-hi and Youth Corps leader Yi Pom-suk possessed strong organizational support and personalities, but for a variety of other reasons were, as Muccio put it, "pretty crummy from our point of view."[45] The same could be said of former home minister Chough Byong-ok.

Another problem was that there was no guarantee that the process of removing Rhee could be executed with precision, as he enjoyed strong support from the police and youth corps down to the local level. Short of a clean, quick overthrow of the president, greater turmoil could develop than already existed around Pusan, the major port of entry for UN supplies, in the countryside, or even at the front among ROK units now responsible for holding most of the line against the North Koreans and Chinese. Such developments might force non-Korean units to assume more responsibility on the front line just as some of them had to be pulled southward to ensure stability in the rear.[46]

Divided within its own ranks, Washington agreed only to send a letter from Truman to Rhee expressing shock at recent developments and urging him to "take no irrevocable acts" before Muccio could return to Korea "and convey my further views to you."[47] The message appears to have deterred Rhee from dissolving the assembly, but it also led him to warn Lightner "that the US Govt shld keep out of this internal sitn; that it was not its business and it wld be deplorable if the friendly relations between the two countries shld be impaired." The Korean people, he asserted, "were becoming alarmed and indignant over outside interference," and, if the pressure continued, "we could be sure . . . that through his friends in the U.S. the American people wld get the true story."[48] The contrast with Rhee's reaction to U.S. pressure in the spring of 1950, when he grudgingly accepted legislative elections required by the constitution, could hardly be greater.

Although during June the UN command developed an emergency plan for a coup against Rhee, its implementation never occurred. In early July the U.S. embassy signaled Rhee's opponents that the United States would not support a coup attempt. With that, the overwhelming majority of the cowed assemblymen voted for an amendment for direct election of the president.[49] One British diplomat reported to London that Rhee was "making a monkey out of the United Nations."[50] In early August the monkey fully matured with Rhee's overwhelming victory in the popular vote.[51]

The best U.S. course in the crisis remains unclear, even in retrospect. For one thing, some reasonable and well-informed observers have concluded that Rhee was correct in his claim that he, not the National Assembly, represented the "will of the people."[52] For another, it was by no means certain that removal of Rhee was possible quickly and cleanly and that a viable replacement would have emerged within a short time frame. It is also unclear that encouragement of intervention by the ROK army and its successful execution in this case would have produced a sustainable liberalization of South Korean politics. The best that can be said is that ROK political and economic development between 1952 and 1961 probably would have been no worse off had the coup route been tried and succeeded. Perhaps stronger U.S. pressure short of support for a coup would have led Rhee to accept a compromise, leaving the assembly with a modicum of authority.[53] Yet, unlike in 1950, Rhee was now fighting for his political life, and the National Assembly had taken a strong stand against him. The assertion that limited force by the UN command to protect the National

Assembly would have led to a workable agreement for shared power between the contestants, rather than a chaotic situation threatening the larger military balance, requires a substantial leap of faith regarding the nature of the principals.[54]

What does seem apparent is that the willingness of the United States to apply strong pressure on the ROK president had diminished with the coming of war. Whereas in the spring of 1950 the American military lacked input in the U.S. decision to press Rhee for positive economic and political measures, two years later it played a decisive role in the decision not to take a strong stand. Although the United States continued to lobby for democratic development in Korea, the priority of that objective had declined in relation to that of security, a fact well understood by Rhee and his successors. Only in 1960 and 1987 would the United States act in a determined fashion to promote democracy in the midst of a South Korean political crisis, and in both those cases it was because popular opposition to the incumbent was sufficiently strong to make continued security dependent on movement toward democratization. The shedding of American blood in Korea between 1950 and 1953 and the major U.S. military presence on the peninsula from then on gave ROK leaders a "psychological whammy" over Washington that only a determined and rebellious populace below the thirty-eighth parallel could overcome.[55]

That said, it would be misleading to ignore continuing American efforts and programs designed to promote democracy in Korea over the long term. The United States continued its activities of behind-the-scenes lobbying with Korean leaders, of observing campaigns and the electoral process, and of encouragement of the same by the United Nations commission and foreign newsmen.[56]

In addition, through the United States Information Service (USIS), the Americans developed a series of projects aimed at fostering democratic ideas and institutions in Korea. Contacts between American officials and visiting educators from home on the one hand and Korean educators on the other, between USIS personnel and Korean students and interested adults, and indirectly between Americans and Koreans through media programs all sought to inform the host population about American political culture and its merits.

Such activities, it was recognized, represented a long-term effort. As the "Country Assessment Report" for 1959 remarked,

Democracy is a philosophy alien to the Korean tradition; without the long battles and strong convictions that punctuates the development of democracy in the West, the Republic of Korea was created overnight, largely in the Western image. The danger in this quick transition lies in the possibility that having been made aware of a better life and the advantages of good government, and having enjoyed the benefits of neither, the Koreans might blame the failures on democracy without having actually experienced nor fully understood it, with consequent rejection. The purpose [of USIS] . . . is to promote understanding, to assist Koreans in developing and strengthening their democratic institutions so as to preclude this contingency.[57]

The same report for the following year, compiled between the democratic revolution of the spring of 1960 and the military coup of May 1961, outlined the energetic American response to the former while noting that "USIS found itself in the position of a nurse in an emergency ward, helping by passing bandages and instruments." It concluded that

the question is whether democratic institutions can be made to work adequately to pull this Republic through this time of change. Time alone produces the intuitive, semi-automatic response by the citizenry which is needed for the practical, effective application of the democratic process. Meanwhile, USIS Korea will continue to apply its resources to trying to gain that time.[58]

Time soon ran out. When the coup came, the United States faced a situation of weak leadership in the democratic government under Chang Myon, serious economic problems, and increasing popular discontent with the turmoil created by demonstrations on issues from national unification to inflation.[59] No consensus existed among Koreans against the military takeover. With no immediate threat from the security perspective, the Americans worked mostly quietly toward pressuring Park Chung Hee into reestablishing civilian government and holding free elections.[60] The partial successes of the mid-1960s did not last. After winning an uncomfortably narrow victory for re-election as president in 1971, Park imposed nationwide martial law the following year and put into effect the Yushin (revitalizing reform) constitution, which gave him virtually dictatorial powers. At a time when the United States had announced that Asian allies would increasingly have to bear the manpower burden in protecting their security, had withdrawn most of its troops from Vietnam and reduced by one-third its military personnel in Korea, and had made strong overtures to China, a key North Korean ally, Park justified his actions in terms of external threat. The United States, preoccupied with Vietnam and led by the administration of Richard M. Nixon, which prided itself on its realpolitik, issued no public protest and assured the ROK government privately that it had no intention of interfering in South Korea's internal affairs.[61]

The American emphasis on stability in Korea continued into the 1980s. When in the aftermath of President Park's assassination in October 1979 popular hopes grew for democratic reform, the United States maneuvered behind the scenes in an attempt to bring it about. In the spring and summer of 1980, however, a new military leader, Chun Doo Hwan, seized power, with the Americans standing on the sidelines and accepting the fait accompli.[62] The administration of Jimmy Carter was perhaps the most committed on human rights of any in U.S. history, but in the midst of a variety of crises in other parts of the world and a hotly contested election campaign at home, it, like its predecessors, chose the course that presented the fewest immediate risks on the security front. When Ronald Reagan succeeded Carter as president in 1981, he openly embraced Chun, making him the first Asian head of state to visit the White House in the new administration. Only in 1987, when the Korean middle class followed students into the streets to demand democratic reforms, did the United States move forcefully behind the scenes the ensure change. To have done otherwise would have risked broad civil turmoil, thus worsening the security threat from North Korea.[63]

This time democracy took hold, but anti-Americanism had grown as well. In part this was because of the widespread perception in Korea, following Chun's takeover in 1980, that the United States was hypocritical, that it preached ideals but failed in a pinch to support their implementation. An assumption here was that, because the United States was a great power, maintained troops in the ROK, and on some occasions in the past had intervened in South Korea's domestic affairs, it could determine events as it saw fit. Furthermore, while memories of the Korean War and American sacrifices to prevent a Communist takeover had receded, the continued presence of U.S. military forces, with all the attendant inconveniences and blows to national pride, became a growing source of animus.[64]

The Korean War had brought the security problem to the forefront in U.S.-ROK relations, thus increasing the American presence. While most South Koreans desired that presence, they remained intensely nationalistic. As the ROK's stature grew with the economic successes of the period from the mid-1960s to the late 1980s, so, too, did resentment over continuing dependence on the United States. Fortunately, when democracy finally established strong roots in the ROK, Koreans themselves were in the lead. The painful road to that outcome, however, which was in all likelihood prolonged by the Korean War, had a lasting and not altogether positive effect on the relationship between the United States and Korea.

III

As on the matter of promoting democracy in Korea, the war did not eliminate U.S. desires for ROK economic reforms, but it did reduce American leverage in persuading Rhee to bring them about. We saw earlier that on the eve of war the United States used economic assistance as a whip to gain concessions from Rhee on internal economic policies.[65] The whip proved effective because the American commitment to the ROK was highly uncertain. Ironically, although the State Department possessed many critics of Rhee, and Rhee himself was by no means enamored of Americans in striped pants, the foundation of U.S. support to the ROK rested squarely in that agency. The Economic Cooperation Administration had taken on the task of administering economic aid to Korea only reluctantly, and, with the partial exception of the army, the Pentagon showed little interest in the peninsula. Much the same can be said of Congress, which refused to respond to White House and State Department pleas in June 1949 for the quick approval of $150 million in economic aid to the ROK. In January 1950, irritated by the administration's refusal to propose renewal of assistance to the beleaguered Nationalist Chinese government on Taiwan and pessimistic regarding ROK prospects for survival, a narrow majority in the House of Representatives actually rejected the Korean aid bill. Acheson quickly put together an aid package including funds for the ROK *and* Nationalist China that passed both houses during the next month; however, the amount provided Korea was well below the administration's request, and substantial opposition remained even to the lower figure.[66] The fact was that, before the war, Rhee could not take even limited American aid for granted, and insofar as the ROK had an advocate in Washington, it was the State Department.

The American response to the North Korean attack changed all this. The commitment of U.S. armed forces drastically increased the interest in and influence on Korea among American military leaders. As Donald Macdonald has written, "The brigadier general commanding the Korean Military Advisory Group under the Ambassador was replaced by a galaxy of generals under a five-star United Nations commander."[67] The U.S. embassy soon lost overall control of economic relations, mostly to the UN command, and coordination of economic assistance became more complex. Whatever discipline the Americans had been able to impose on the ROK government largely disappeared, as Korean officials exploited differences among U.S. and UN agencies involved in the process of dispensing aid.[68] Koreans also bridled over the rigidity of U.S. military officials. Of particular moment here was their desire that the ROK either forgive entirely or accept indefinite delays in reimbursement for advances of Korean currency to American soldiers, which by Korean estimates in the spring of 1951 already amounted to $21 million and was a major contributor to inflation.[69]

Rhee had little grasp of complex economic issues, and he resisted U.S. advice on the exercise of fiscal restraint to control inflation with the argument that the problem would be resolved if only the UN command would pay off the advances.[70] When the possibility that

U.S. economic aid would be cut off arose during the political crisis of 1952, Rhee declared to a UN diplomat that the "Korean people are not prepared to sell their birthright for a mess of pottage."[71] The change since the spring of 1950 in Rhee's approach in his dealings with Americans could hardly have been more apparent.

The flow of economic aid never stopped. During his postarmistice visit to Korea, Secretary of State Dulles pledged a $1 billion aid program over three to four years, subject to legislative approval.[72] One-fifth of that amount already had been authorized from savings on military expenditures resulting from the armistice. The huge destruction of property and severe relocation problems created by the war joined the clear U.S. commitment to South Korea's security to put Congress in a generous mood. By the eve of Dulles's visit to the peninsula three years later, over $900 million of the promised aid had been provided.[73] By the end of the decade, the annual amount was under $200 million but still substantially above fiscal year 1950 levels.[74]

Unfortunately, while Rhee remained in power, the bilateral relationship on economic matters failed to resume the hopeful trend established during the spring of 1950. Rhee never forgave the Americans for blocking his hopes for a new military campaign to unify the country, and he resisted long-term economic planning that accepted indefinite division. A U.S. embassy assessment of February 1954 dwelled upon Rhee's weaknesses as a leader—his lack of knowledge of economics, his unwillingness to delegate responsibility, his poor judgment of the character and ability of others, and his priority of personal loyalty above all else—but it also noted his presumption that the United States would never abandon Korea to the Communists.[75] In 1956 the ROK Finance Ministry did develop a five-year economic plan, but, as Macdonald remarks, U.S. officials viewed it as "more of a shopping list [for continued high levels of American aid] than an integrated strategy."[76] Although the United States persuaded the ROK to follow some of its advice on economic issues, Rhee resisted pressure to move toward a cooperative relationship with Japan, a fundamental aspect of the American approach.[77] As before the war, the ROK depended on the United States for its survival, yet the firm American commitment to that objective had undermined U.S. bargaining power.

The United States did not phase out grant aid completely until the mid-1970s. By this time the ROK had derived considerable economic benefits from reforms instituted by Park, the normalization of relations with Japan, and the commitment of two Korean army divisions to back the American cause in Vietnam. By the late 1980s, as Korean prosperity grew, fueled in part by an export-oriented strategy originated by Park, and Washington became increasingly concerned about a foreign trade imbalance, economic issues in the U.S.-ROK relationship had shifted to matters involving the access of American goods and capital to the Korean market. The shift reflected the enormous changes in the economic positions of the ROK and the United States since the Korean War era and the fact that the former's "psychological whammy" on the latter had actually declined as its relative position improved.

THE KOREAN WAR CAUSED A DRAMATIC INCREASE IN THE AMERICAN presence in Korea and in a context that precluded its early reversion to prewar levels. The presence engendered strains between the proud, nationalistic host population and the guest, whose impatience and sense of superiority, both racial and cultural, often grated.[78]

Rhee exacerbated the strains with an obstinacy that frequently created severe problems even among his own people. Passionately committed to Korean unification under his own rule, he constantly pressured the Americans to adopt a course that prioritized his objective above all else in the world. When the Americans demurred in the face of an expanded, possibly global war, he kept pushing, even after grudgingly accepting (but not signing) an armistice. More confident than ever that the United States would never abandon the ROK, he refused to retreat from his public advocacy of unification by force of arms. He permitted, even encouraged, criticism of the United States in the Korean press and often resisted American advice on military, political, and economic matters.[79] Ironically, his failure to develop an efficient and coherent system of economic planning simply magnified ROK dependence on the United States.

There was a more positive side, however, as most Koreans in the

FIG. 20. There were nearly five million refugees during the Korean War, the vast bulk of whom fled from North to South Korea or fled southward within South Korea. Here refugees move southward in the face of the Chinese offensive of January 1951.

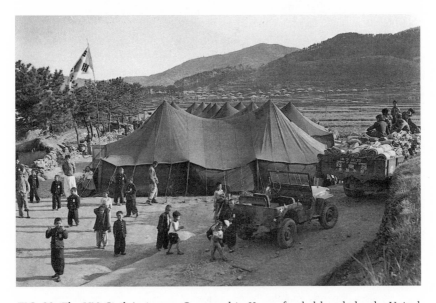

FIG. 21. The UN Civil Assistance Command in Korea, funded largely by the United States, established many refugee camps in the ROK. The view here is of an orphanage on Koje-do, an island off the south coast, which also served as a major location for POW camps.

FIG. 22. Robert E. Neal of the U.S. Air Force holds the hand of "Charlie," his "adopted" son. The Korean orphan was found huddled in sleep under a piece of canvas along the Han River in 1952. After living with Robert at U.S. Air Force quarters for three months, he was placed in a nearby Seoul orphanage.

FIG. 23. In late 1953, members of the Third U.S. Infantry Division assisted in the building of a new primary school for these children of the Pochan Orphanage. The old school was destroyed during the war.

South appreciated the blood and treasure expended by Americans in preventing the fall of all their homeland to Communism. While sometimes resented, the U.S. presence was also accepted as necessary for protection against an aggressive North and a covetous Japan. Despite their sometimes overbearing and insensitive behavior, Americans

FIG. 24. A U.S. airman shows orphans in the Columbia Children's Home some items donated to them by the residents of Fort Worth, Texas, in the aftermath of the war.

treated Koreans far better than did the Japanese and, in general, better than did other foreigners.[80] Accustomed in their own political culture to bargaining rather than dictating, Americans, in particular those outside the military, more often than not possessed the flexibility to work out mutually acceptable accommodations with their Korean partners. As for military personnel, a new sense of the significance of the U.S. presence on the peninsula sparked a variety of community relations programs, such as assistance in rebuilding schools and other public buildings and sponsoring orphanages, which put Americans in a favorable light.

Furthermore, Rhee's intransigence had its limits. Although he frequently tested the boundaries of American tolerance, he understood the ROK's need for a continued U.S. presence, both military and economic. He also knew that, over time, a hostile press in the United

States could erode public and congressional support for the American commitment to the ROK. On the issue of a status-of-forces agreement to define the authority of the ROK and U.S. governments over American soldiers in Korea, for example, he usually behaved with moderation, as he undoubtedly grasped the extreme political sensitivity of the issue in the United States. Even on such issues as unification and political liberalization, he went some distance in accommodating Washington. In the first case, while he never retreated from public advocacy of military action, neither did he actually resort to it. As the Korean War receded into the past, so, too, did Rhee's obsession with pushing the Americans into a new military campaign northward. In internal politics, his use of strong-arm methods to influence elections and the legislative process continued, but he permitted a substantial range of opinion in the press, and his electoral activities did not prevent occasional victories by opponents. The presence of foreign observers, especially journalists from the United States, seemed to engender in him a modicum of restraint.[81] He allowed extensive American cultural programs as well, which for the long term could not help but promote democratic ideas. For their part, the Americans, despite expressions of exasperation in dealing with Rhee, came to understand that patient firmness and the avoidance of public confrontation could induce him to retreat from his most extreme positions.[82]

The relationship that emerged from the war was not altogether healthy, but this also could be said about the prewar period. Nor had ROK dependence on the United States for survival changed. Yet the war increased severalfold the American stake and presence on the peninsula, and, paradoxically, this increased Korean leverage. Rhee exploited that leverage to the fullest, but often in his own, not his people's, interests. Still, the Americans retained enough flexibility in their position to contribute and adapt to his forced departure in 1960.

The "alliance forged in blood" has weathered the many storms on the peninsula since 1953, as well as the transformation of international politics, testimony to both the persistence of common interests and the adaptability of the two parties to new conditions, but also to an emotional attachment greatly deepened if not actually created by the experience of war. Nonetheless, as the emotional attachment has weakened with the passing of generations and the diminishing of the North Korean threat, Americans and Koreans continuously have been challenged to redefine their relationship. With the ROK's democratization and economic development essentially accomplished, the key challenge ahead appears to be to either manage or end an American military presence on the peninsula under circumstances in which it is increasingly harder to defend on traditional grounds and poses a growing affront to Korean pride. The successful completion of negotiations for a new status-of-forces agreement in late 2000 gives hope that the United States will continue to make timely adjustments in the face of new realities; on the other hand, the continued, highly conspicuous presence of American military bases near the centers of Seoul, Pusan, and Taegu leaves much in doubt.[83]

Doubts aside, the centrality of the peninsula's location in northeast Asia has not altered since the Korean War, and the importance of the region's stability to global affairs has if anything increased. Given the risks of an unbridled Sino-Japanese competition over Korea as occurred at the end of the nineteenth century, the continuation in some form of the U.S.-ROK alliance remains a matter of considerable magnitude.

CHAPTER 8

The Korean War as a Challenge

to American Democracy

DURING THE SPRING OF 1951, AS POLITICIANS IN WASHINGTON and much of the American public fumed and bickered over President Truman's firing of General MacArthur, diplomat-soon-to-be-historian George F. Kennan delivered the Charles R. Walgreen Foundation Lectures at the University of Chicago. On leave from the State Department in no small part because of his disillusionment with the thrust of American policy since early 1949, Kennan was not in a generous mood toward the internal system through which the United States conducted its foreign relations. At one point in the lectures he suggested that

> a democracy is . . . uncomfortably similar to one of those prehistoric monsters with a body as long as this room and a brain the size of a pin: he lies there in his comfortable primeval mud and pays little attention to his environment; he is slow to wrath—in fact, you practically have to

whack his tail off to make him aware that his interests are being disturbed, but once he grasps this, he lays about him with such blind determination that he not only destroys his adversary but largely wrecks his native habitat.[1]

Kennan's metaphorical flight centered on two laudable qualities in a foreign policy that he thought democracies had difficulty sustaining, especially in combination: attentiveness and proportionality.

He was not alone in his concern. A year before, the drafters of NSC-68, no friends of Kennan in their emphasis on the military aspects of the Soviet threat, expressed their own reservations about the ability of democratic nations to hold their own with authoritarian competitors. "A free society is vulnerable," the authors wrote, "in that it is easy for people to lapse into excesses—the excesses of a permanently open mind wishfully waiting for evidence that evil design may become noble purpose, the excess of faith becoming prejudice, the excess of tolerance degenerating into indulgence of conspiracy and the excess of resorting to suppression when more moderate measures are not only more appropriate but more effective." The NSC group also saw handicaps in relations among democratic allies. On the one hand, the conduct of relations "on a basis of persuasion and consent rather than compulsion and capitulation" was "a general source of strength." Yet "dissent among us [could] . . . become a vulnerability." In the current situation, for example, the capabilities of "the free world" exceeded those "of the Soviet system," but the former "were far from being effectively mobilized and employed in the struggle against the Kremlin design." "Even the most homogeneous and advanced segment of the free world—Western Europe . . . lacks a sense of unity, confidence, and common purpose," the drafters lamented, and the danger was that "our native impetuosity and a tendency to expect too much from people widely divergent from us" would foster dissent rather than nurture cohesion.[2]

The Kennan and NSC-68 analyses hold considerable value in understanding the Korean War. Inadequate U.S. attentiveness to the volatile situation in Korea contributed substantially to the origins of the conflict. Soviet premier Stalin, we now know, gave the green light for the North Korean attack only because the Americans had withdrawn their troops from the peninsula and signals from the United States indicated that it would not intervene to repulse the move.[3] This situation was partly a result of the stinginess of the president and Congress toward the peacetime U.S. army.[4] In contrast, once the war began, public and partisan pressures helped produce, first, the risky move of U.S. ground troops across the thirty-eighth parallel in the face of a Chinese threat to intervene and, second, MacArthur's headlong march toward the Manchurian border, even after it was clear that China *had* intervened. When the Chinese launched their massive counterattack in late November 1950 and then pushed into South Korea in early 1951 in an attempt to drive UN forces off the peninsula, the domestic climate in the United States added to the Truman administration's difficulties in keeping the war limited, both geographically and in weapons employed.[5] Domestic factors also made difficult a measured approach to German rearmament, an issue that could easily have provoked Soviet preemptive action and/or a compound fracture in the Western alliance.[6] The prehistoric monster had been aroused, and it now threatened action that would not only destroy its enemies but put at risk the native habitat of itself and its allies.

Alas, whether it be regarding an expanded war in Asia or the immediate rearming of West Germany, the United States ultimately chose prudence over adventurism. A reading of the popular press in the United States during the period could easily make one think that, at virtually any moment, American and/or alliance politics would descend into chaos. Yet they never did, and the United States and its NATO allies emerged from the Korean War better armed, better integrated—both militarily and economically—and more secure and prosperous than before. The fears of Kennan and the authors of NSC-68 to the contrary notwithstanding, the early 1950s proved to be a period in which, on balance, Western allies displayed attentiveness and proportionality in their struggle with the Soviet bloc. Tragically, the Korean War took a huge toll in human life and property and left Korea divided. But from a broader perspective the conflict may be seen as a turning point in which, unlike in the 1930s, the political systems of the United States and Western Europe rose to the challenge of authoritarianism in a manner that averted the global bloodbath of the previous decade and positioned the West advantageously in the ongoing Cold War. And this was done without fundamentally altering the nature of those systems.

In this chapter I will analyze conditions in the West on the eve of the war and then move to two key periods of the conflict during which attentiveness and proportionality for the most part prevailed in the Western alliance—those between late June and mid-September 1950 and late November of the same year and June 1951. Admittedly, the period between the two under examination saw a good deal of excessive American behavior, but it was not such as to rule out timely adjustments later on.

In developing this analysis, I will draw upon observations by John Lewis Gaddis on the political culture of democracy, in particular on its "allowance of multiple constituencies to interact at multiple levels" and its predisposition to balance "competing interests in a system."[7] In this sense the United States and its allies functioned more effectively than did the Soviet bloc, and I will demonstrate this point with evidence from the recent literature on the latter.

On the other hand, the performance of democratic institutions was hardly uniformly for the good. Not only was American inattentiveness critical in the coming of the war, but the occasional lack of proportionality during its course, both at home and abroad, helped to create a legacy that contributed to the tragic commitment to a war in Vietnam in the mid-1960s. I will conclude, therefore, with a modest effort to assess the adaptability of American political culture to the challenges of the Korean War era, and I will suggest connections between that period and the nation's fateful course a decade and a half later.

I

A portrait of the Western alliance on the eve of the Korean War bears less resemblance to Kennan's prehistoric monster in his comfortable primeval mud than to a professional football team during its first preseason game. The players have some idea of what they are supposed to do and some fear of the consequences of failing to perform, but they are a bit rusty, and their interests as individuals are sometimes far from identical. Furthermore, the severest of penalties for mediocre efforts are sufficiently distant to ensure their occurrence.

By the spring of 1950, the sizable advantage in conventional forces of the Soviet bloc in Europe, combined with the successful Soviet test of a nuclear device during the previous summer, had created widespread concern in government circles about the developing military balance. To date, a trip wire strategy had sufficed as a deterrent to a Soviet attack on Western Europe. Should Soviet bloc forces attack westward, the reasoning went, the United States would launch atomic attacks on the enemy, secure in the knowledge that it could not harm the American homeland. "Victory," as historian Marc Trachtenberg has written, "would be just a matter of time," and, knowing this, the Soviets would be unlikely to strike in the first place.[8] With the end of the American atomic monopoly, however, the time rapidly approached when this was no longer the case. Once the Soviets could do substantial damage to U.S. war-making potential, the importance of maintaining strong forces, including large conventional units in Europe, would grow dramatically. NSC-68 asserted that by 1954 the Soviet Union would be able to deliver one hundred atomic bombs to the United States. This development would vastly increase the risk of a Soviet attack on the American homeland and on Western Europe, and/or of Soviet bullying everywhere—unless, of course, the United States had built up its own atomic and conventional forces as well.[9]

Still, political problems at home impeded large-scale increases in defense spending. Ernest R. May speculates that, once President Truman discovered how carefully Secretary of State Acheson and his adviser Paul Nitze "had built their base of support for a sharply higher military budget within the administration . . . , he probably recognized that he was trapped," that he could hardly afford "to do nothing." May points out that arguments from the top secret NSC-68 were soon appearing in the press. If Truman rejected its recommendations outright, he could expect the fact to become known and to be used to attack him, especially among right-wing elements in the press and Congress.[10] Yet Truman gave no hint that he was thinking along these lines prior to June 25, 1950. Indeed, his public statements indicated a determination to hold defense expenditures around the $13 billion level he had requested from Congress earlier in the year.[11] As late as June 19, 1950, the Budget Bureau submitted a report to the White House envisioning, *at most*, an increase in military spending of between $1 billion and $5 billion.[12]

Moreover, concrete political reasons existed to believe that a push for higher defense spending would face difficulty in Congress. A congressional election approached in November, and the Republicans, frustrated and embittered by their surprise loss of the presidential and legislative races in 1948, were determined to make inroads. One anticipated area of attack on the Democrats was the federal deficit, which promised to be over $2 billion for the fiscal year ending June 30 and was likely to more than double the following year. Himself a fiscal conservative, Truman strove to hold down the shortfall at the same time that he hoped to push through Congress new appropriations for domestic programs.[13] When in late May Acheson returned from a NATO meeting in London with suggestions that Western Europe needed more help in defending itself, word leaked to the *New York Times* that, "in the more political corners of the Administration," officials believed that funding for such a program could pass only through "an overwhelmingly Democratic Congress."[14] Proceedings on Capitol Hill indicated that legislators were likely to produce a tax bill that would *not* increase revenues, would reduce expenditures on domestic programs, and would provide only a marginal increase in defense spending.[15] Until the November election—and depending on its outcome—major new initiatives on defense were highly problematic.

There was little chance that Great Britain and France would increase their defense efforts without an American initiative. Those two countries already spent larger portions of their gross national products on the military than did the United States, with its far stronger economy.[16] Despite progress over the last two years, neither Great Britain nor France had recovered fully from the economic effects of World War II. Both held large deficits in their dollar accounts.[17] Great Britain had reaped some benefits from its devaluation of the pound during the previous fall, but its Labour government preoccupied itself in the fiscal arena with managing burgeoning health care costs. The British economy possessed little slack with which to ease the way toward increased defense spending.[18] In France, neutralist sentiment was on the rise, fed by sophisticated Soviet propaganda that included both a "peace campaign" and war scare tactics.[19] Led by a shaky coalition government deeply divided over domestic welfare programs, France was an unlikely candidate to take the lead for a defense buildup.[20]

Given the limited resources of Great Britain, France, and their smaller allies, one might think that a West German defense contribution was attractive; on balance, the opposite was the case. The fear of Soviet invasion had not obliterated memories of past German aggression, especially in France, and the fact that West Germany's economic recovery had advanced along with the rest of Western Europe added to the sense of vulnerability. So did the commitment of over a third of France's army to an ongoing war in Indochina. A larger and more permanent Anglo-American military presence on the Continent could reduce fears of a Germany under arms, but in the spring of 1950 that prospect seemed remote.[21] A more hopeful development was French foreign minister Robert Schuman's plan, advanced in May, to integrate French and German coal and steel resources under a supranational authority. If implemented, the plan would greatly reduce the independent war-making capacity of a rearmed Germany.[22] Although Schuman's initiative received widespread applause on the Continent, his plan faced numerous obstacles before it could become an operational reality.

In organization NATO was clearly on a forward track. The North Atlantic Council (NAC) had first met in September 1949, when it established as subsidiary bodies the Defense, Military, and Standing Committees and five Regional Planning Groups. Two months later, the council established a Defense Financial and Economic Committee and a Military Production and Supply Board. By April 1950, the Defense Committee had agreed on a strategic concept for the integrated defense of the North Atlantic area, on ways of developing a program for the production and supply of matériel, and on a four-year defense plan. In its May meeting the NAC, responding to the level of organizational activity already under way, created the Council of Deputies, a constantly functioning London-based civilian body designed to coordinate the others and to execute council directives.[23]

Thus, on the eve of war in Korea, the Western allies showed signs of emerging from hibernation. Nonetheless, absent a sharp jolt—strong evidence, to return to our metaphor, that the regular football season approached—the varied constituencies, in this case both sovereign nations and institutions and groups within them, lacked the cohesion to devote new material resources to the defense enterprise.

This lack of cohesion inside the United States compromised efforts to deter the enemy in Korea. Secretary Acheson believed that the United States, having occupied the southern half of the peninsula in 1945 and subsequently created an anti-Communist regime through the United Nations, possessed a considerable stake in protecting it from attack by the Soviet-sponsored regime in the north. Yet, as noted in chapter 3, he lacked the domestic backing to sustain an effective policy. If higher priorities elsewhere help explain the failure of deterrence in Korea, so, too, do divisions in Congress and between the State Department and the Pentagon.

The North Korean attack of June 1950 united leaders in the West and their domestic constituencies in the view that the Soviet Union, at least through its proxies, stood ready to use military force to achieve its purposes. Even so, "competing interests" remained in the allied system. Building and sustaining cohesion required a constant balancing process that often appeared to be on the verge of breaking down.

II

The North Korean attack had a decisive impact in part because it came during a period of growing fears of Soviet intentions and capabilities in elite circles on both sides of the Atlantic and in part because members of the Western alliance saw in Europe situations having much in common with Korea. There, as in Europe, the United States had permitted enemy forces to develop a superiority over friendly ones. The North Korean move, obviously aided and abetted by the

FIG. 25. A mobilization poster of October 1950.

Soviets, suggested that they might be willing to use their advantage to march their forces westward to the English Channel; or to use the East German "national police," sixty thousand strong, to move into West Berlin or, even worse, West Germany; or to unleash Soviet bloc armies against wayward Yugoslavia. The vigorous U.S. reaction to the North Korean offensive brought sighs of relief in Western European capitals, as it demonstrated that the Americans were willing to use force in the defense of an ally. Still, the rapid retreat of U.S. ground forces on the peninsula throughout July magnified fears of allied weakness in Europe. These fears, in turn, stimulated the collective effort worldwide.[24]

The United States took the lead. On July 24 Truman asked Congress for a $10.5 billion supplement to the military budget for fiscal year 1951, which would cover a manpower increase in U.S. armed forces of 615,000. On August 4 the president asked for $1.6 billion more. Congress provided him with the entire amount less than two months later. Truman also asked for and received an additional $4 billion for foreign military assistance, over 80 percent of which was earmarked for NATO allies.[25] The Europeans had a smaller capacity to increase their efforts, but by the end of August all except Iceland and Portugal had announced plans for substantial increases in their armed forces.[26]

Some of America's formal or potential allies also responded to Washington's call regarding Korea. As Acheson told his Canadian counterpart, Lester B. Pearson, in late July, "if the United States had to do all the fighting in Korea, there was a real danger that public opinion [at home] . . . would favour preparing in isolation for the larger conflict ahead and writing its allies off."[27] An allied contribution to Korea could make the conflict there a turning point in U.S. sentiment on the issue. Although the Pentagon often handled the matter clumsily and the American public was never satisfied with the contribution of others to the UN effort in Korea, by the end of the summer Great Britain, Australia, and the Philippines had sent small combat units to Korea, and Australia, Belgium, Canada, Ethiopia, France, Greece, Luxembourg, the Netherlands, New Zealand, Thailand, and Turkey all had promised to do so.[28] The United States led and made by far the largest non-Korean contribution to the UN effort, but it was far from alone in the endeavor.

Despite the significant strides toward building and/or strengthening anti-Communist coalitions, the United States took some actions that appeared disproportionate in allied circles and risked division. The first was Truman's decision of late June to use the U.S. Seventh Fleet to discourage the Communist regime on mainland China from attacking Taiwan, the last bastion of the Nationalist government. Intended partly to build consensus at home behind American Asian policy, partly to protect the southern flank in impending U.S. military operations in Korea, and partly to discourage further Communist adventurism, the move generated dissent in Great Britain and elsewhere in Western Europe because it threatened to expand the conflict and further alienate Communist China.[29]

Then, early the following month, as U.S. troops stormed into Korea, policy makers in Washington began to consider a march north of the thirty-eighth parallel once the tide of battle shifted in favor of the United Nations. As noted in chapter 4, by the end of August it was generally agreed that such a move should not occur if it would bring the Soviet Union or China into the fray.[30] Nevertheless, congressional elections were on the horizon, and late in the summer Republicans began their campaign with a blistering attack on the Democratic administration's alleged fumbling and timidity in East Asia. Prominent GOP senators cast much of the blame on Secretary Acheson and called for his resignation. In such circumstances Truman and his top foreign policy adviser would find it difficult to exercise restraint in Korea after battlefield conditions changed.[31]

Finally, heightened fears of Soviet military aggression in Europe produced a consensus in the Truman administration on the necessity of West German rearmament. Since NATO could not hope to match Soviet bloc ground forces without a German contribution, the Joint Chiefs of Staff insisted on making its acceptance by allies a prerequisite to the projected four- to six-division American buildup in Europe. The position of the military was difficult to override, as it fed the broadly held sentiment at home that the United States should not make new commitments across the Atlantic unless assured that the Europeans would kick in with their fair share. But the approach was sure to be a hard sell in Europe, where fears of an ultimately uncontrollable Germany remained strong, and where the Soviets hinted at dire consequences if a move was made to rearm the former Nazi nation.[32]

All these trends converged during the fall of 1950; by the end of the year they threatened to tear asunder the Western alliance and perhaps even to provoke a world war. In response to an American march across the thirty-eighth parallel and up to the Yalu boundary with Manchuria, the Chinese had launched a major counteroffensive in Korea, threatening to expel UN forces from the peninsula. Egged on by MacArthur in Tokyo and by the increased number of Republicans in Congress following the November elections, popular pressures grew in the United States to expand the war into China and even to use atomic weapons. Such a move, in turn, would increase the risk of overt Soviet intervention. In Europe resistance grew to German rearmament as events in Korea reinforced the sense of the West's military weakness and undermined confidence in U.S. reliability while the Soviets hinted at preemptive action. West German chancellor Konrad Adenauer, who previously had appeared most receptive to rearmament, suddenly expressed qualms. Faced with substantial domestic opposition, fearful of the Soviet response, and anxious to expand his government's sovereign prerogatives, he now proposed to move slowly.[33] As if this were not enough to confound the plans of the Truman administration, vocal opposition to the dispatch of new U.S. divisions to Europe mounted in Congress and among such prominent Americans in the private sector as Herbert Hoover and Joseph Kennedy.[34]

Yet since mid-1947 the United States had pursued a multilateral approach to the European and Korean situations, in the first case through the Marshall Plan and NATO, in the second through the United Nations. As the crisis intensified, American leaders turned reflexively to multinational institutions. In December the United States took the lead in forming the NATO military command, appointing General Eisenhower as its first head. It also continued to work through the United Nations on the Korean issue, despite widespread dissent there over recent American conduct of the war. In the face of British opposition, Washington already had vetoed General MacArthur's call for the hot pursuit of enemy planes back to their Manchurian bases. Now America's allies and neutrals led by India joined forces at the United Nations to delay any move toward escalation, hoping that military conditions would eventually improve and restore a sense of priorities in Washington.[35]

The tactics of delay worked. It was not until early February 1951 that the Americans had cobbled together a broad coalition to condemn Beijing and prepare the way for additional measures against the new enemy in Korea. By this time UN forces had ended their retreat on the peninsula and executed a limited probe northward. And the General Assembly resolution condemning China set no timetable for implementing new action—military, political, or economic—against the adversary. Meanwhile, the Truman administration had retreated from its insistence on early German rearmament while holding firm on proceeding rapidly with the dispatch of new American troops to Europe, despite a "great debate" on the issue in Congress.

Still, we can imagine that leaders of the Communist powers derived a good deal of comfort from watching the ongoing squabbling within and among the Western democracies. Think of autocrats Stalin and Mao reading reports of the partisan cat-fighting in Washington following MacArthur's April 1951 dismissal from all his commands or of the charges and countercharges in the national presses and legislative bodies that flew back and forth across the Atlantic among the NATO allies. To be sure, battlefield events in Korea did not go well for the Communists after mid-January; steeped in the Marxist-Leninist belief in the contradictions among the capitalist powers, however, Communist leaders surely reasoned that time was on their side if only they persisted in their effort and played their diplomatic cards properly.[36]

In fact, internal conflicts in the West, whether within or between nations, produced a good deal more smoke than fire. MacArthur's removal received an extraordinarily favorable response in Western Europe, and it came after the U.S. Senate passed a resolution endorsing Truman's plan to send four more divisions across the Atlantic. With new U.S. divisions in the works for continental Europe, with Western European countries increasing their defense budgets, and with Greece and Turkey moving toward admission into NATO, a coordinated military buildup of anti-Soviet forces in the key theater of the Cold War was on the horizon.[37]

Important progress also occurred in the area of economic coordination. By sparking Western rearmament, the Korean War greatly stimulated demand for strategic raw materials, especially metals, which were also needed for consumer durables in the private sector. This demand created shortages, fueled inflation, and threatened Western Europe's economic recovery, thus fostering resentment over America's advantage in competing for scarce resources. Early in 1951 the United States, Great Britain, and France initiated the International Materials Conference to recommend methods of rationalizing the distribution of key commodities. Although the conference had authority only to advise, the U.S. government helped matters along by reducing its purchases of certain items, especially rubber, tin, and wool, the prices of which dropped sharply beginning in March. Other items responded more slowly, and in late April the Labour Left in Great Britain included the raw materials situation prominently in its indictment of U.S. leadership. Yet a spring tour of Europe by Charles E. Wilson, the director of defense mobilization in the United States, proved reassuring on the issue. Most observers anticipated further improvement after July 1 with implementation of the Controlled Materials Plan, designed to curb prices of aluminum, copper, and steel.[38] Recent agreement between West Germany and the occupying powers on a framework for the European Coal and Steel Community reinforced perceptions that the raw materials problem was manageable.

Finally, through a series of intense negotiations with individual nations outside the Soviet bloc, the United States constructed broad if sometimes grudging agreement among its allies on a lenient peace treaty with Japan and a postponement of discussion on the Taiwan issue until the end of the war in Korea. American military agreements regarding Japan, Australia, New Zealand, and the Philippines were in the works, thus raising prospects for an anti-Communist security system in the Pacific.[39]

By the late spring of 1951, therefore, not only was the worst over in Korea but strong momentum existed toward consolidation in the West. The Western democracies had not necessarily functioned efficiently in producing this result, and the turmoil in interallied relations was not about to disappear, but the trend of international developments had turned positive and would largely continue in that direction.

The question remains, Did the political culture of democracy contribute positively to this outcome, or was it merely incidental or secondary? A comparison of Western diplomacy during the Korean War with that of the Soviet bloc suggests some tentative conclusions.

III

The Soviet bloc emerged from the Korean War in a shaky condition compared with that of the Western alliance. In June 1953, demonstrations and riots erupted in Czechoslovakia, sparked by a currency reform that virtually wiped out the savings of a substantial portion of the population. Czech authorities suppressed the disorders, but the economic conditions that provoked them remained. In the same month demonstrations broke out in East Berlin and quickly spread to 250 towns throughout East Germany. Again authorities quickly restored order, yet only broad reforms could get to the root of the trouble. Although overt unrest did not break out in Hungary or Poland, it seethed just below the surface. As in the other cases, the economic measures behind much of the discontent had been initiated in the late 1940s but had not reached their brutal extreme until Korean War rearmament took a firm hold.[40] The prosperity and political stability of the United States and Western Europe stood out in bold contrast.

The Sino-Soviet alliance, on the other hand, appeared solid at the end of the war. Early in 1953 the Soviets resumed funding for a series of projects in China that had begun in 1950 but were suspended as a result of the Korean War. Shortly after Stalin's death in March, Moscow agreed to expand funding to cover dozens of new projects.[41] Public statements emanating from Moscow and Beijing showed no cracks in the alliance.

Still, within seven years an open split had occurred, and we now know that its roots extended well back in time. The Korean War hardly provided the seeds of the split, but it certainly created circumstances in which they were sowed. For one thing, Mao would have preferred to complete the unification of his own country through the conquest of Taiwan before the North Korean attack. Despite his interest in the matter, it is not clear that he was brought in on the plan to attack until mid-May 1950, and even then the approach from Kim Il-sung, who claimed he had Stalin's approval, was such as to make it nearly impossible for Mao to object.[42] When the war broke out, of course, the United States immediately took action to protect Taiwan. As for Korea itself, Stalin gave Mao the impression that, if it became necessary for China to intervene directly, it would have Soviet air support for its troops. When in October 1950 the point came for such intervention, however, Stalin first withdrew the offer while pressing Mao to push forward with intervention. Then the Soviet air force did provide support, but only in areas close to the Korean border with Manchuria. Stalin provided a good deal of matériel support as well, yet it was slow in coming, was often in poor condition, and was to be paid for at a later date. Given the risks and sacrifices China endured in Korea, Stalin's support was far from satisfying. In dealing with the Soviets, Mao never felt he was being treated as an equal, and he resented the fact.

This inequality came through clearly at various levels. One had to do with Soviet advisers in China, the numbers of whom increased substantially after late 1950. China wanted advisers, to be sure, but Stalin insisted that they be given special privileges, including immunity from Chinese jurisdiction if they violated local rules.[43] Apparently Mao accepted Stalin's demands, but the movements of Soviet citizens in China still were sharply restricted during the war.[44]

The question remains as to how much the problems within the Soviet bloc resulted from the prevailing authoritarian political culture. Difficulties in Eastern Europe clearly grew out of economic conditions, and Soviet aid to the Chinese surely was restricted in part by the Soviet Union's limited capacity to produce modern arms and the competing priority of building up military strength in the West. One could argue that the greater stability and prosperity of the Western alliance at the end of the Korean War derived from the fundamentally stronger national economies among its members going in. While Western Europe and Japan in 1950 were yet to fully recover from World War II, they received backing from the United States, the economy of which was greatly strengthened by the war; in contrast, the Soviet Union entered that event in a relatively backward state and was devastated by it. Moscow possessed a far more limited capacity to assist its allies than did Washington.

These facts constitute an important part of the equation, but they omit some critical points. First, the high degree of central control that Stalin imposed on the Eastern European regimes derived to a considerable extent from political rather than economic concerns. Traditional patterns of trade among Eastern European nations leaned heavily toward the west rather than the east, yet from 1948 onward Stalin forced an unnatural and decisive shift eastward. He also destroyed early post–World War II efforts at integration among Eastern European nations.[45] One might think that creation in 1949 of the Council for Mutual Economic Assistance (CMEA) represented a move toward broad economic integration of the Soviet bloc. In fact, CMEA was a largely nonfunctioning organization for the remainder of Stalin's life. As a means of political control, the despot preferred bilateral relations between the Soviet Union and individual satellites over multilateral institutions.[46]

Admittedly, the Americans often pressed allies to adapt their trade relationships to political and strategic realities as perceived in Washington. The pressure occurred within a multilateral, largely cooperative context, however, wherein due consideration was given to internal economic consequences. On the eve of war in Korea, for example, the United States, Canada, and their European allies organized an international body to determine restrictions on exports to Soviet bloc countries and established oversight and decision-making groups to meet quarterly in Paris. Members did not always move in lockstep, as the United States imposed a total embargo on exports to China in December 1950, while the others never went to that extreme. By 1952, nonetheless, American pressure had led the others to accept tight restrictions. When the Korean War ended, sentiment grew to loosen up, and in 1957, despite continued U.S. adherence to a total embargo, others began to increase trade with China on a limited basis. The bargaining process among the allies was not always pretty, as debate frequently spilled into the public arena.[47] Still, accustomed to a democratic system at home in which political leaders had to take the public welfare into account, U.S. statesmen naturally were sensitive to the similar concerns of their allied partners.

Japan represented perhaps the classic illustration of this point. The Korean War sparked an economic surge in Japan, as demand skyrocketed for items ranging from jeeps and barbed wire to textiles and foodstuffs. The war also pushed U.S. hostility toward China, traditionally Japan's largest market, to new extremes, however, thus eliminating it as a major player in reintegrating the recently defeated island nation into international trade. Japan's long-term economic well-being became even more uncertain in the face of general hostility in Europe, Great Britain in particular, toward permitting Japan to develop markets in Southeast Asia. In a complex series of bilateral and multilateral negotiations during 1952, Washington moved decisively toward establishing a structure that at once kept Japan in line regarding trade with China by integrating it into the Paris group while setting the stage for Japan's long-term prosperity and development by holding open new markets in the United States and nudging the British toward permitting Japan's penetration of Southeast Asia.[48] Of course it might be claimed that Stalin's imposition of the extreme austerity on Eastern Europe that produced the unrest of 1953 was dictated by a combination of the threat from abroad and the relative economic weakness of the Soviet bloc. However, the movement toward austerity and rearmament began prior to the outbreak of war in Korea and the commencement of the Western military buildup.[49] Moreover, Stalin had numerous chances to end the Korean War, with the likelihood of reducing thereby the level of international tension and slowing or perhaps even eliminating the enemy's armaments campaign. Before the war began and immediately after Stalin's death—indeed, probably even during Stalin's last year in power—there existed a strain of thought in the Soviet leadership that argued for a soft rather than a hard foreign policy as the best means of dividing and weakening the West.[50] Yet in the face of continuing Western consolidation and military growth, Stalin insisted in October 1952, in what turned out to be his last will and testament, that war was inevitable *within* the capitalist camp![51]

The fact that Soviet policy shifted so clearly and quickly after Stalin's death raises the question of whether the patterns in the East-West balance that emerged most prominently during the Korean War reflect the superior adaptability of democratic as opposed to authoritarian political culture or whether those patterns reflect merely the inferiority of the particular system created by one man. One could argue that the subsequent failures of the successors of Stalin resulted from the difficulties of reforming the system he had created rather than the inherent deficiencies of authoritarianism itself.[52] The argument has merit, but in the specific case of the Soviet Union the combination of authoritarianism and a universalistic ideology, both of which preceded Stalin, appears to have produced problems that, while exacerbated by, were still deeper than the pathology of a single individual. One of these was what Gaddis refers to as a tendency toward "authoritarian romanticism," an inclination to overreach oneself as a result of an ideologically grounded misreading of external conditions.[53]

Since the Korean War provides striking examples of overreaching on both sides, one wonders if any of them can be explained in systemic terms. I suggested earlier that the U.S. decisions to cross the thirty-eighth parallel and then *not* to halt well below the Yalu River, even after Chinese intervention, were at least in part explicable in terms of domestic political pressures on the Truman administration. On the other hand, China overreached itself later on when it moved southward across the thirty-eighth parallel, and it would be difficult to claim that Mao's decision in this case derived from domestic political pressures, even though he may have regarded a continuing fight in Korea as serving positive purposes at home.[54] The difference, though, is that Mao overreached in the face of contrary advice from his military commander in the field and opposition from much of his Politburo over whether China should have intervened in the first place. In addition, it took several months and several costly setbacks before he changed his mind, whereas Truman initially acted in a manner consistent with the advice of his field commander only to alter his objective rather quickly once the magnitude of China's intervention became apparent. Truman restrained the "military romanticism" of MacArthur and ultimately fired him; Mao persisted for some time in a military romanticism of his own grounded in an ideology that emphasized the power of the masses to overcome modern technology.[55] Truman was pressured by his democratic allies to exercise restraint, while Mao was pressured by his authoritarian partners to continue pursuit of total victory.

Explaining the difference requires not just reference to the illusions of grandeur promoted by a revolutionary ideology, as proponents of the same ideology often advance different prescriptions in the same circumstances. In addition to individual differences, we must also consider the different patterns of authority and information flow between democratic and authoritarian regimes. In Moscow, Beijing, and Pyongyang, the pattern of authority was far more centralized than in Washington and other capitals of the Western alliance, and the price paid for dissenting from established policy was far more steep. As a result, the flow of information among and within the Communist powers was far less free. A key consequence was that Truman and his top advisers constantly received a heavy flow of information and opinion from below within their own system and horizontally from their foreign allies, and their limited authority and flexible habits of mind forced upon them frequent reality checks; leaders of the Communist powers, in contrast, were prone to dig in their heels and persist in courses in which the ends sought exceeded the means available for their achievement.[56] For the short term the costs were bearable, as the Korean War ended without clear winners and losers among the great powers. For the long term, however, certain trends were exacerbated that redounded distinctly to the disadvantage of the Soviet Union in its Cold War competition with the United States. And we can reasonably conclude that the decisions that produced those trends were in part a result of the authoritarian and ideological nature of the Soviet regime.

IV

It would hardly be appropriate to close with an unqualified celebration of American democracy, since much that happened in the United States during the Korean War represented both a substantial departure from the ideals of freedom and tolerance and a disproportionate response to the threat at hand. The most egregious example is the second Red Scare, which although under way by June 1950 sharply escalated in the months that followed.

Only days before the outbreak of war in Korea, George Kennan penned an emotional letter to journalist William Henry Chamberlin, tearing into the politicians and members of the press who were questioning the loyalty of many of the foreign policy professionals engaged over the last decade in shaping U.S. China policy. Senator Joseph R. McCarthy had leapt onto the national political stage the previous February with charges, backed by not a scintilla of credible evidence, that the State Department housed dozens, if not hundreds, of Communists. Although his wild charges faced substantial criticism in the press and Congress, many conservative commentators and the Republican leadership on Capitol Hill appeared willing to take them seriously, or even to promote them. "What we are witnessing," a worried Kennan wrote,

> is not really an attack on subversion in our Government: it is an attack on the self-confidence of the American people themselves as a body politic. . . . Do you really believe that the formulation of policy in this Government proceeds on so shallow and erratic a basis that great decisions are taken because some communist whispers something in some credulous person's ear? To seek the explanation of our current situation in such fantasies is a form of political necromancy.

The diplomat concluded with a warning that

> the attitudes and methods of which we have been the witnesses in past weeks and months [possess] . . . all the seeds of an American totalitarianism. Does the danger of penetration from *international* totalitarianism really seem so great that you are prepared to accept a sort of *national* totalitarianism to combat it? That, in may opinion, is what these things are tending to.[57]

Conditions soon worsened. The North Korean attack heightened emotions, emboldening the scaremongers. In September, with off-year elections only two months away, Congress passed the McCarran Act over Truman's veto. This legislation required members of the Communist Party and front organizations to register with the attorney general, provided for their internment in national emergencies, and barred them from employment in government and defense industries and from securing passports. Fearful of the consequences to their careers of a negative vote, many Democratic liberals supported the measure.[58] By the next April, with the Chinese intervention in Korea magnifying fears still further, the president was sufficiently caught up in the climate to issue an executive order altering the criterion for dismissal from federal employment from "reasonable grounds for belief in an employee's disloyalty" to "reasonable doubt as to loyalty."[59] The Employee Loyalty Program established in 1947 without judicial oversight became still more threatening to federal workers who in the past had expressed now-unpopular views or associated with Communists or "fellow travelers." In June 1951 the Supreme Court joined the anti-Communist crusade when it upheld the conviction of the American Communist Party under the Smith Act of 1940, which outlawed teaching or advocating—even indirectly—the overthrow of the government or the joining of any organization that did so.[60] These are merely prominent examples of a campaign that extended far beyond the federal government and sought to root *alleged* subversives out of the entertainment industry, the public school systems, and the universities, frequently with minimal concern for the rights of the accused.

The domestic climate exacerbated by the Korean War did more than harm the careers of a few thousand individuals. It also narrowed the range of what was considered to be legitimate political debate.[61] Among other things, this development helped to produce an Asian policy that was far from uniformly positive. Prior to June 1950, East Asia represented a secondary theater to the United States, one in which expenditures and commitments were kept well in check. With the creation of the Sino-Soviet alliance in February 1950, to be sure, concerns about the region increased, and in May the United States began providing assistance to the French in Indochina. Reconsideration of the January decision *not* to provide new aid to the Nationalist regime on Taiwan also gained momentum, and the State Department stepped up pressure for a peace treaty with Japan that, in all likelihood, would exclude the Communist powers. Republican attacks on U.S. Asian policy under the Democratic Truman administration added pressure on decision makers to consider new initiatives. Once the North Korean attack occurred, the domestic climate encouraged the president to act boldly, both in Korea and elsewhere in the region, to prevent the further advance of Communism. Prior to the attack, nonetheless, a good chance remained for a cautious American course in Asia, one based primarily on protecting an offshore defense perimeter that would not include Taiwan and on the presumption that the new China was not an irreconcilable enemy.[62] Indeed, fears of overcommitment contributed mightily to a course in Korea that failed to deter the Communists from initiating overt military action.

This changed quickly after June 25. The United States joined the fray in Korea, moved to protect Taiwan, and increased aid to the French in Indochina. Any remote chance of turning back disappeared with Chinese intervention in Korea in the fall. American defense pacts in East Asia proliferated, culminating with one with South Korea and Taiwan and creation of the multilateral Southeast Asia Treaty Organization. Although the Republican Eisenhower administration that came to power in 1953 strove to develop a strategy to avert limited wars such as the one in Korea and resisted the temptation to intervene militarily in Indochina in 1954, it made commitments, including ones to the Ngo Dinh Diem regime in South Vietnam, that risked future embroilment in Asian conflicts. Ironically, in 1965 a retired Eisenhower backed President Lyndon Johnson's escalation in Vietnam, quibbling only with its gradual nature.[63] The combination of bitterness toward and fear of China, both legacies of Korea, left most American leaders determined to prevent its expansion through Southeast Asia even after the Sino-Soviet split at the beginning of the decade.

The Korean War, of course, gave fuel to Republican attacks on the Democrats for permitting a Communist victory on mainland China, to McCarthyite witch-hunts against State Department China experts, and to the GOP campaign to defeat the Democrats in the presidential and congressional elections of 1952. The Democratic administrations of the 1960s never lost sight of the domestic political cost of the fall of an Asian country into the Soviet orbit. Scholarly judgments nowadays often incline to the view that the continuation of John F. Kennedy in the White House would have led to an outcome far different from Johnson's subsequent escalation, but there remains little question that the increase of U.S. involvement in South Vietnam from 1961 to 1963 was in part a result of the president's fear of the domestic political consequences of that country's fall to Communism.[64] The same can be said of Johnson during 1964 and 1965.[65] In the latter case, fear of the negative consequences on domestic programs of either withdrawal or a rapid, well-publicized escalation encouraged a middle course that, for the long term, compromised any possibility of military victory and seriously undermined popular support at home.

Ironically, the domestic scene had changed a good deal since the early 1950s. A younger generation had emerged that had not faced the harsh challenges of depression and world war, that had grown up in affluence and with educational opportunities undreamed of by its predecessors. It also had grown up with the ever-present danger of nuclear war. This combination of privilege and potential nightmare produced a generation a substantial portion of which was unwilling to accept uncritically a decision for war by the nation's leaders. Often encouraged by an inquisitive press and an academic elite no longer cowed by anti-Communist crusaders, American youth mounted a serious challenge to U.S. intervention in Vietnam. As historian Alonzo Hamby has observed, whereas protest against Korea was

> spearheaded by a political Right outraged by what it considered administration bungling and a no-win policy . . . , protest against Vietnam found its center of gravity in the political Left outraged by the alleged moral depravity of American foreign policy. Korean War protesters waved the American flag; Vietnam protesters frequently burned it. Disapproval of Korea was encased in a lifestyle characterized by patriotism and conventional moral behavior; disapproval of Vietnam was inextricably tied to a counter-cultural revolution that defiantly challenged traditional morality.[66]

To American leaders, memories of the past masked the significance of critical changes in domestic conditions until the country was already committed in Vietnam.

A similar point may be made regarding the assessment of pertinent conditions abroad. By the mid-1960s, American policy makers looked back on Korea as a successful exercise in limited war, one in which U.S. aims were achieved through an employment of military power restrained in both scope and scale. This perception encouraged them to believe they could achieve a repeat performance. Yuen Foong Khong has shown that, of all the historical analogies used by government officials leading up to the escalation of 1965, Korea appeared the most often. While dictating restraint in taking military action in North Vietnam, it also encouraged the belief that victory was possible, that South Vietnam was a viable political entity in the same way that South Korea had been. Not everyone bought into this analogy, but the extensive debate that occurred both within and outside the government proved no guarantee that wisdom would prevail.[67]

THE BAGGAGE ACCUMULATED DURING AND CARRIED FORWARD from Korea reminds us that much can go wrong through and even because of the democratic process. Yet this qualification should not blind us to the fact that during the Korean War American institutions provided a framework within which attentiveness and proportionality usually prevailed. Rearmament of the West did occur on a scale sufficient for a generation to discourage the Soviet Union from launching or supporting military moves such as that by North Korea. If in retrospect that rearmament appears excessive, it remains true that by fiscal year 1953 a backlash had occurred against Pentagon requests. While the armed services asked for $73 billion for that year, not including foreign military assistance programs, concerns about rising federal deficits and other dangers to the economy led to cuts down to $47.2 billion in the final budget, a substantial reduction from the previous year. With the Korean War at an end, the fiscal year 1954 budget fell below $40 billion, despite ongoing complaints from the armed services.[68] This was still three times the expenditure for the pre–Korean War period, but it was a far cry from the "garrison state" levels that some critics had feared. And the key figure in containing defense expenditures from 1953 onward was President Dwight Eisenhower, a military hero who had risen to the White House largely as a result of public discontent with the war. The American system had produced a level of military preparedness that proved effective and sustainable without undermining the economic health of the country. If taxes were higher and a military draft required many young men to do time in the armed forces, the basic freedoms of the citizenry were not fundamentally compromised over the long term.

The Korean War also strengthened the power of the presidency and the executive branch, perhaps to an unhealthy degree. When Truman deployed American forces to Korea during the summer of 1950, he referred to the move as a "police action" and decided that his authority as commander in chief was adequate to cover it. Congress was never asked to formally approve the military action, despite the fact that it soon grew into what by any reasonable standard constituted a major war. The conflict had not created the "imperial presidency," but it certainly raised it nearly to its peak.

Even so, there were limits to the president's power. When Truman seized the steel industry in April 1952 to prevent a strike that might compromise the war effort, he claimed the same authority he had used to send forces into Korea. Now, though, he was challenged by the steel companies, and in June a divided Supreme Court ruled in their favor.[69] Although other efforts by the Truman administration to centralize management of the economy for national security purposes, such as wage and price controls, did not generate the legal counteraction provoked by the steel seizure, they did produce criticism from Congress and the business community that encouraged moderation.[70] The American system of checks and balances, in other words, remained a vital constraint on the concentration of power.

Even in the areas of cultural and political expression, the United States of the Korean War era generated activity that distanced it substantially from its "totalitarian" opponents abroad. Despite the attacks on left-wing sentiments, the Communist newspaper the *New York Daily Worker* never ceased publication. In 1952, while the war in Korea still raged on, I. F. Stone was able to publish an account of the origins and early stages of the conflict sharply at odds with the official version.[71] Despite the growing politicalization of culture, important works of fiction and social thought continued to appear, including seminal novels by J. D. Salinger and Ralph Ellison and pathbreaking works in the social sciences by Erik Erikson and David Riesman.[72] Although Hollywood sought to capitalize on the domestic climate by producing dozens of films on anti-Communist themes and the Korean War, the American public generally refused to make them box office hits.[73] Cultural historian Stephen J. Whitfield is correct in concluding that repression at home in the Korean War era rightly undermined the ability of the United States "to be seen as an attractive and just society"; but he is also correct in the assertions, first, that American culture in the 1950s was by no means devoid of independent thinking, a fact that distinguishes "a relatively free society from a political system with totalitarian tendencies," and, second, that the relatively "conformist public culture" of the period shifted within a decade to a condition in which widespread dissent flourished.[74]

In the midst of another crisis growing in part out of past inattentiveness and presenting immense challenges to our sense of proportionality, it is worth observing that, whether individually or collectively, the examples of imperfection in U.S. domestic and foreign policy during the Korean war do not negate Gaddis's point: democratic habits of mind and action show up well in comparison to their authoritarian counterparts. Whether it be in cobbling together and sustaining alliances abroad or maintaining balance between capabilities and objectives (or correcting imbalances when they occur), American democracy more than matched Soviet authoritarianism. In juggling the sometimes conflicting values of freedom and order inside the United States, Americans and their system sometimes leaned dangerously toward the latter, but ultimately they resisted whatever temptation that existed to adopt a form of "totalitarianism" at home in order to resist it abroad. That the process was messy and advanced certain trends that would be costly in the future should merely remind us of Winston Churchill's refrain of the period that "democracy is the worst form of government except all those others that have been tried from time to time."[75]

Abbreviations

America's	Michael C. Sandusky. *America's Parallel.* Alexandria, Va.: Old Dominion Press, 1983.
CRKW	Chen Jian. *China's Road to the Korean War.* New York: Columbia University Press, 1995.
CWIHPB	*Cold War International History Project Bulletin.* Washington, D.C.: Woodrow Wilson International Center for Scholars, 1993–.
DSB	U.S. Department of State. *Department of State Bulletin.*
FRUS	U.S. Department of State. *Foreign Relations of the United States.* Washington, D.C.: Government Printing Office, 1955–85.
HJCS	James F. Schnabel and Robert J. Watson. *The History of the Joint Chiefs of Staff.* 4 vols. Wilmington, Del.: Michael Glazier, 1979.
HST	Harry S. Truman Papers, HSTL.
HSTL	Harry S. Truman Library, Independence, Missouri.
HUSAFIK	"History of United States Armed Forces in Korea." 3 vols. Unpublished manuscript available in Historical Office, U.S. Army Military Headquarters, Yongsan, Seoul, Republic of Korea.
"Korean"	Evgeniy P. Bajanov and Natalia Bajanov. "The Korean Conflict, 1950–1953: The Most Mysterious War of the 20th Century—Based on Secret Soviet Archives." English translation of unpublished manuscript based on the Presidential Archives of the former Soviet Union. I wish to thank Professor Ohn Chang-il of the Korean Mili-

tary Academy, Seoul, Republic of Korea, for providing me a copy of this work.

KW	William Stueck. *The Korean War: An International History*. Princeton, N.J.: Princeton University Press, 1995.
LC	Library of Congress, Manuscript Division, James Madison Building, Washington, D.C.
Mao's China	Chen Jian. *Mao's China and the Cold War*. Chapel Hill: University of North Carolina Press, 2001.
MMR	Shu Guang Zhang. *Mao's Military Romanticism: China and the Korean War, 1950–1953*. Lawrence: University Press of Kansas, 1995.
MSFE	U.S. Congress, Senate, Armed Services and Foreign Relations Committees. *Military Situation in the Far East*. 82d Cong., lst sess., 1951.
MZM	Jianguo Yilai Mao Zedong Wengao. *Mao Zedong's Manuscripts since the Founding of the PRC*. Vols. 1–3. Beijing: Central Document Publishing House, 1987.
NAII	National Archives II, College Park, Maryland.
NWF	Charles Turner Joy. *Negotiating While Fighting: The Diary of Admiral C. Turner Joy at the Korean Armistice Conference*. Edited and with an introduction by Allan E. Goodman. Stanford, Calif.: Hoover Institution Press, 1978.
NYT	*New York Times.*
Origins	Bruce Cumings. *The Origins of the Korean War*. 2 vols. Princeton, N.J.: Princeton University Press, 1981, 1990.
PPPUS	U.S. Presidents. *Public Papers of the Presidents of the United States*. Washington, D.C.: Government Printing Office, 1965–.
Present	Dean G. Acheson. *Present at the Creation: My Years in the State Department*. New York: Norton, 1969.
PRO	Public Records Office. Kew, England.
"Red"	Xiaoming Zhang. "Red Wings over the Yalu River: China, the Soviet Union, and the Air War in Korea, 1950–1953." Unpublished ms. in my possession. I wish to thank the author for permitting me to see this work.
Reluctant	James Irving Matray. *The Reluctant Crusade: American Foreign Policy in Korea, 1941–1950*. Honolulu: University of Hawaii Press, 1984.
RG	Record Group (NAII).
Rhee	Robert T. Oliver. *Syngman Rhee and American Involvement in Korea, 1942–1960: A Personal Narrative*. Seoul: Panmun Book Co., 1978.
Road	William Stueck. *The Road to Confrontation: American Policy toward China and Korea, 1947–1950*. Chapel Hill: University of North Carolina Press, 1981.
SDR	Records of the Department of State Relating to Internal Affairs of

Korea, 1940–44. Microfilm edition, 3 rolls. Wilmington, Del.: Scholarly Resources, 1986.

Socialism   Eric van Ree. *Socialism in One Zone: Stalin's Policy in Korea, 1945– 1947*. Oxford: Berg, 1989.

Truman   Paul G. Pierpaoli Jr. *Truman and Korea: The Political Culture of the Early Cold War*. Columbia: University of Missouri Press, 1999.

Uncertain   Sergei Goncharov, John W. Lewis, and Xue Litai. *Uncertain Partners: Stalin, Mao, and the Korean War*. Stanford, Calif.: Stanford University Press, 1993.

USAKW   U.S. Department of the Army. *United States Army in the Korean War*. 4 vols. Washington, D.C.: Government Printing Office, 1961–72.

U.S.-Korean   Donald S. Macdonald. *U.S.-Korean Relations from Liberation to Self-Reliance: The Twenty-Year Record*. Boulder, Colo.: Westview Press, 1992.

Notes

INTRODUCTION

1. John Mueller, *Retreat from Doomsday: The Obsolescence of Modern War* (New York: Basic Books, 1989), 118.

2. *KW*, 3.

3. B. C. Koh, "The War's Impact on the Korean Peninsula," in *A Revolutionary War: Korea and the Transformation of the Postwar World*, ed. William J. Williams (Chicago: Imprint Publications, 1993), 246.

4. For my earlier book, see *KW*.

5. David Rees, *Korea: The Limited War* (New York: St. Martin's Press, 1964). For an appreciative assessment of this book, see my "The Korean War as History: David Rees' *Korea: The Limited War* in Retrospect," http://www.nara.gov/research/coldwar/program.html.

6. Nikita Khrushchev, *Khrushchev Remembers*, introduction, commentary, and notes by Edward Crankshaw; translated and edited by Strobe Talbott (Boston: Little, Brown, 1970); Khrushchev, *Khrushchev Remembers: The Last Testament*, translated and edited by Strobe Talbott (Boston: Little, Brown, 1974).

7. Key monographic works include *Reluctant*; *Road*; Bruce Cumings, ed., *Child of Conflict: The Korean-American Relationship, 1943–1953* (Seattle: University of Washington Press, 1983); and Charles M. Dobbs, *The Unwanted Symbol: American Foreign Policy, the Cold War, and Korea, 1945–1950* (Kent, Ohio: Kent State University Press,

1981). More synthetic efforts drawing upon new documentation include Burton I. Kaufman, *The Korean War: Challenges in Crisis, Credibility, and Command* (New York: Knopf, 1986); Clay Blair, *The Forgotten War: America in Korea, 1950–1953* (New York: Times Books, 1987); Max Hastings, *The Korean War* (New York: Simon and Schuster, 1987); and Joseph Goulden, *Korea: The Untold Story of the War* (New York: Times Books, 1982).

8. *Origins*, vol. 1.

9. I. F. Stone, *The Hidden History of the Korean War* (New York: Monthly Review Books, 1952). For major revisionist works of the 1970s, see Joyce Kolko and Gabriel Kolko, *The Limits of Power: The World and United States Foreign Policy, 1945–1954* (New York: Harper and Row, 1972), chaps. 10, 21–22; and Robert R. Simmons, *The Strained Alliance: Peking, P'yongyang, Moscow, and the Politics of the Korean Civil War* (New York: Free Press, 1975).

10. Bruce Cumings and Jon Halliday, *Korea: The Unknown War* (London: Viking, 1988); *Origins*, vol. 2.

11. *Socialism*.

12. *Uncertain*.

13. Major works include *CRKW*; *MMR*; "Korean"; Alexander Y. Mansourov, "Communist War Coalition Formation and the Origins of the Korean War" (Ph.D. diss., Columbia University, 1997); Kathryn Weathersby, "Soviet Aims in Korea and the Origins of the Korean War, 1945–1950: New Evidence from Russian Archives," Working Paper No. 8, Cold War International History Project, Woodrow Wilson International Center for Scholars, 1993; Weathersby, "Korea, 1949–50: To Attack, or Not to Attack? Stalin, Kim Il Sung, and the Prelude to War," *CWIHP* 5 (spring 1995): 1–4; Shen Zhihua, "Sino-Soviet Relations and the Origins of the Korean War: Stalin's Strategic Goals in the Far East," *Journal of Cold War Studies* 2 (spring 2000): 44–68; Richard C. Thornton, *Odd Man Out: Truman, Stalin, Mao, and the Origins of the Korean War* (Washington, D.C.: Brassey's, 2000).

14. An early work that emphasized the Korean origins of the war without denying an important international dimension is John Merrill, *Korea: The Peninsular Origins of the War* (Newark: University of Delaware Press, 1989).

15. For revisionist coverage of the war itself, see *Origins*, 2:625–756; Simmons, *Strained Alliance*, 137–270; Cumings and Halliday, *Korea*, 95–219.

16. Rees, *Korea*, 446–48.

17. See John Lewis Gaddis, *We Now Know: Rethinking Cold War History* (New York: Oxford University Press, 1997); Aaron L. Friedberg, *In the Shadow of the Garrison State: America's Anti-Statism and Its Cold War Strategy* (Princeton, N.J.: Princeton University Press, 2000); *Truman*; Michael J. Hogan, *A Cross of Iron: Harry S. Truman and the Origins of the National Security State* (New York: Cambridge University Press, 1998); and Stephen J. Whitfield, *The Culture of the Cold War*, 2nd ed. (Baltimore: Johns Hopkins University Press, 1996).

Chapter 1
THE COMING OF THE COLD WAR TO KOREA

1. This and the next two paragraphs are based on *America's*, 226–28, and my interview with Dean Rusk on July 24, 1972, in Athens, Ga.

2. *USAKW*, 3:11.

3. *FRUS, 1945*, 6:657–60, 1039.

4. *America's*, chap. 9.

5. *FRUS, 1945*, 2:643.

6. U.S. Department of State, *The Record on Korean Unification, 1943–1960: Narrative Summary with Principal Documents* (Washington, D.C.: Government Printing Office, 1960), 47–48.

7. See *HUSAFIK*, 92–136.

8. Ibid., 136–221; *Socialism*, chap. 14.

9. "Possible Soviet Attitudes toward Far Eastern Questions," October 2, 1943, Box 119, Records of Harley A. Notter, 1939–45, RG59, NAII.

10. On general concern about Russian expansion, see Akira Iriye, *Pacific Estrangement: Japanese and American Expansion, 1897–1911* (Cambridge, Mass.: Harvard University Press, 1972), 70–73. For examples of Roosevelt's thinking, see Roosevelt to Herman Speck von Sternberg, August 28, 1900, in *The Letters of Theodore Roosevelt*, ed. Elting Morison, vol. 2 (Cambridge, Mass.: Harvard University Press, 1951), 1394; and Roosevelt to G. F. Becker, July 8, 1901, as quoted in Howard K. Beale, *Theodore Roosevelt and America's Rise to World Power* (Baltimore: Johns Hopkins University Press, 1956), 263.

11. For a detailed analysis, see William George Morris, "The Korean Trusteeship, 1941–1947: The United States, Russia, and the Cold War" (Ph.D. diss., University of Texas at Austin, 1975), 13–38. For specific documentation on Roosevelt's views, see *FRUS, 1943*, 3:37, and memorandum by Rear Admiral Wilson Brown on the 30th Meeting of the Pacific War Council in the White House, March 31, 1943, Box 168, Map File, Franklin D. Roosevelt Papers, Roosevelt Library, Hyde Park, N.Y.

12. These included "Korea: Internal Political Structure," April 1943; "Korea: Economic Developments and Prospects," May 25, 1943; "Korea: Territorial and Frontier Problems," May 25, 1943; and "Korea: Internal Political Structure," May 26, 1943, all in Box 63, Notter File, RG59, NAII. Unless otherwise noted, all quotations and information in this and the next three paragraphs are, unless otherwise noted, taken from these documents.

13. For copious documentation of divisions among Koreans in China and the United States, see Rolls 1–3, SDR.

14. Clarence Gauss (U.S. ambassador to China) to Secretary of State Cordell Hull, January 15, 1943, Roll 2, SDR.

15. See Wayne Patterson, *The Ilse: First-Generation Korean Immigrants in Hawai'i 1903–1973* (Honolulu: University of Hawai'i Press, 2000), 186–89, 204.

16. For Haan's reports to American officials in the State Department and the White House, see Rolls 1–2, SDR; and Official File 1143, Roosevelt Papers, Roosevelt Library.

17. *FRUS, The Conferences at Malta and Yalta, 1945,* 770. See also *Socialism,* 39.

18. *Socialism,* 34–44.

19. *America's,* 172.

20. For reports on Hopkins's talks with Stalin, see Robert E. Sherwood, *Roosevelt and Hopkins,* rev. ed. (New York: Grosset and Dunlap, 1950), 887–912; and *FRUS, 1945, Conference of Berlin,* 1:24–59.

21. *FRUS, The Conference of Berlin, 1945,* 2:252–53; *Socialism,* 46–47.

22. *FRUS, The Conference of Berlin, 1945,* 2: 351, 415.

23. *Reluctant,* 39–46.

24. See Michael Schaller, *The U.S. Crusade in China, 1938–1945* (New York: Columbia University Press, 1979), 252–53, 258–60.

25. Although Stalin saw advantages in avoiding an early break with the Americans, he had never regarded the alliance with the United States as more than temporary. By the Yalta conference, he clearly regarded the time as approaching when the alliance would likely end. In mid-January 1945 he told Georgi Dimitrov, the head of the Bulgarian Communist Party, that "the crisis of capitalism led to the division of the capitalists into two factions—the one fascist, the other democratic. . . . We are today with one faction against the other, but in the future we shall also be against that faction of capitalists." As quoted in Eduard Mark, "'Popular Democracy' in Romania: An Instance of Stalin's Plan for Postwar Europe," (paper presented at a conference at Yale University on the international history of the cold war, September 1999). I wish to thank Dr. Mark for providing me with a copy of this paper.

26. *Socialism,* 60–61.

27. *FRUS, 1945,* 6:657–60; *America's,* chap. 8.

28. *FRUS, 1945,* 6:665–66. For Stalin's earlier suspicions of American collusion with Germans on the European front, see Vojtech Mastny, *Russia's Road to the Cold War: Diplomacy, Warfare, and the Politics of Communism, 1941–1945* (New York: Columbia University Press, 1979), 258–59.

29. For a detailed treatment of Soviet operations in the war against Japan, see *Socialism,* chap. 3. For the argument, with which Van Ree concurs, that the Americans had the capacity to move units to Korea quickly, see *America's,* 252.

30. For correspondence regarding American pressure on the Soviet Union to retreat from demands on the Nationalist government regarding Dairen and other issues involving the Soviet position in Manchuria and Stalin's ultimate concessions, see *FRUS, 1945,* 7:957–73.

31. Ibid., 6:667–68.

32. *America's,* chap. 8.

33. See Weathersby, "Soviet Aims in Korea," 6–7. The quotations are from Weathersby's translation of the document from the Russian.

34. See William Stueck, "The United States, the Soviet Union, and the Division of Korea: A Comparative Approach," *Journal of American–East Asian Relations* 4 (spring 1995): 9–15.

35. For relevant correspondence, see Roll 1, SDR.

36. *Origins*, 1:34–38.

37. On the Austrian communists, see Radomir V. Luza, *The Resistance in Austria, 1938–1945* (Minneapolis: University of Minnesota Press, 1984), 101. On the Koreans, see Robert Scalapino and Chong-sik Lee, *Communism in Korea* (Los Angeles: University of California Press, 1972), vol. 1, chap. 2; and *Socialism*, chap. 1.

38. The best analysis is *Socialism*, 85–186.

39. Stueck, "The United States, the Soviet Union, and the Division of Korea," 6–7.

40. For Kim's early advocacy of a separate organization in the North, see his report of October 10, 1945, in Kim Il-sung, *Works* (Pyongyang: Foreign Languages Publishing House, 1981), 1:272–92. On Soviet moves in the North, see *Socialism*, chap. 5.

41. Weathersby, "Soviet Aims," 9.

42. *Origins*, 1:122–29; *America's*, 24–25, 265–71.

43. The story in this and the next paragraph is well known. See, among others, *Origins*, vol. 1, chaps. 3, 5–6.

44. *HUSAFIK*, vol. 2, chap. 1, 56–57.

45. As quoted in Weathersby, "Soviet Aims in Korea," 13.

46. As quoted in ibid., 13–14.

47. *Socialism*, 114–18.

48. Ibid., 137.

49. Vladislav Zubok and Constantine Pleshakov, *Inside the Kremlin's Cold War: From Stalin to Khrushchev* (Cambridge, Mass.: Harvard University Press, 1996), 48.

50. Jonathan Haslam, "Russian Archival Revelations and Our Understanding of the Cold War," *Diplomatic History* 21 (spring 1997): 224; see also Vladislav Zubok, "Stalin's Plans and Russian Archives," *Diplomatic History* 21 (spring 1997): 301.

51. For expressions of concern about the demobilization process, see *NYT*, November 14, 17, 21, and 28, 1945.

52. *Socialism*, 139–40.

53. Scalapino and Lee, *Communism in Korea*, 1:280.

54. *FRUS, 1945*, 6:1130–33, 1146; *Origins*, 1:219–21.

55. As quoted in *Socialism*, 145.

56. *FRUS, 1946*, 8:622.

57. For an excellent discussion of the various sources on Kim's background, see *Socialism*, 24–32.

58. Ibid., 149–52.

59. *Origins*, 1:231–37.

60. *Socialism*, 146–47.

61. *Origins*, 1:225–30.

62. *FRUS, 1946*, 8:653.

63. *Socialism*, 198–200.

64. *HUSAFIK*, vol. 2, chap. 4, 212–13.

65. *FRUS, 1946*, 8:677, 682–83.

66. *America's*, 259–65.

67. For a favorable treatment of Stilwell, see Barbara Tuchman, *Stilwell and the American Experience in China, 1911–1945* (New York: Macmillan, 1970).

68. *Origins*, 1:188–93.

69. *Reluctant*, 59.

70. As quoted in Harry S. Truman, *Memoirs*, vol. 2 (Garden City, N.Y.: Doubleday, 1955), 318.

71. *FRUS, 1946*, 8:667–74; *Reluctant*, 88–90.

72. *FRUS, 1946*, 8:697.

73. Ibid., 706.

74. Ibid., 713.

75. George M. McCune, *Korea Today* (Cambridge, Mass.: Harvard University Press, 1950), 129–30.

76. *Reluctant*, 85–89.

Chapter 2
SYNGMAN RHEE, THE TRUMAN DOCTRINE, AND AMERICAN POLICY TOWARD KOREA, 1947–1948

1. John Edward Wiltz, "Did the United States Betray Korea in 1905?" *Pacific Historical Review* 44 (August 1985): 251.

2. *Reluctant*, 84–96. For a rich account of the process of alienation between Rhee and the Americans during 1945–46 by a Rhee partisan, see *Rhee*, 16–45.

3. *FRUS, 1946*, 8:774–82.

4. Ibid.

5. *FRUS, 1947*, 6:604–5.

6. *PPPUS, Harry S. Truman, 1947*, 176–80.

7. *NYT*, March 13, 1947.

8. *NYT*, March 19, 1947.

9. *NYT*, March 21, 1947.

10. These events are covered in greater depth in *Road*, 84–105.

11. *FRUS, 1947*, 6:605–6.

12. Hodge to M. Preston Goodfellow, January 28, 1947, M. Preston Goodfellow Papers, Hoover Institution Library, Stanford, Calif.

13. See, for example, XXIV Corps, G-2, Historical Section, "G-2 Summary, Period January 19 to 26, 1947," RG332, NAII.

14. The principal primary source on these activities is SDR.

15. Headquarters, United States Armed Forces in Korea, Office of the Assistant Chief of Staff, G-2, "Dr. Rhee's Lobby in America and Its Recent Activities," Box 7129, RG59, NAII; John Carter Vincent (director of the Office of Far Eastern Affairs) to Secretary of State George Marshall, January 31, 1947, Box 3825, and Memorandum of Conversation, by John Z. Williams, January 20, 1947, RG59, NAII.

16. *NYT*, January 24 and 29, 1947.

17. General Dwight D. Eisenhower (Army Chief of Staff) to General Douglas Mac-Arthur (Commander, U.S. Forces, Far East), February 9, 1947, 091 Korea (TS), RG319, NAII; *FRUS, 1947*, 6:605–6.

18. E. S. Larsen, "Korea: Potential Leadership of Koreans Outside Korea," May 28, 1945, Box 12, Records of the Office of Assistant Secretary and Under Secretary of State Dean Acheson, 1941–1948, RG59, NAII.

19. See *Rhee*, 95–98.

20. Hilldring to Hodge, n.d. (clearly July 1947), Box 3, Records of the Office of the Assistant Secretary of State for Occupied Areas, 1946–1949, RG59, NAII.

21. On the relationship between Oliver and Hilldring, see *Rhee*, 95–98.

22. For a listing of his articles during 1947, see *Rhee*, 494.

23. Vincent to Marshall, January 31, 1947, Box 3825, RG59, NAII; and Memorandum of Conversation between John Z. Williams and Robert T. Oliver, January 20, 1947, ibid.

24. *FRUS, 1947*, 6:609. Fiscal year 1948 would begin on July 1, 1947.

25. Ibid., 608–18.

26. See, for example, Dean Acheson's account in *Present*, 217–19.

27. Petersen to Patterson, March 1, 1947, 092, RG319, NAII.

28. Summary of Conclusions of Staff Meeting in the State Department, April 8, 1947, and Edwin M. Martin to Wood, March 31, 1947, Box C-213, RG59, NAII; Vincent to Acheson, April 8, 1947, Vincent to Hilldring, March 27, 1947, and Hilldring to Vincent, March 25, 1947, Box 3827, ibid.

29. *DSB* 16 (March 23, 1947): 544–47.

30. U.S. Congress, Senate, Committee on Foreign Relations, *Legislative Origins of the Truman Doctrine, Hearings before the Committee on Foreign Relations in Executive Session on S. 938*, 80th Cong., 1st sess., 1973), 21–22.

31. *NYT*, March 19, 1947.

32. *NYT*, March 25, 1947.

33. On press support for aid to Korea, see "Daily Summary of Opinion Development," March 26, April 3, April 10, 1947, Box 3, Records of the Office of Public Opinion Studies, Department of State, RG59, NAII. On Marshall's overture in Moscow, see U.S. Department of State, *Korea's Independence* (Washington, D.C.: Government Printing Office, 1947), 35–37.

34. *Congressional Record* 93 (April 16 and 25, 1947): 3482, 3774.

35. *Present*, 227–30.

36. See, for example, General Arthur Lerch to Hodge, June 27 and July 18, 1947, Box 67, RG338, NAII; Acheson to Marshall, June 27, 1947, 740.00119 (Control Korea), RG59, NAII; Hilldring to E. A. Jamison, July 30, 1947, Box 3, Records of the Office of the Assistant Secretary of State for Occupied Areas, RG59, NAII.

37. Lerch to Hodge, July 7, 1947, Box 67, RG338, NAII. On Marshall's Harvard speech, see *Present*, 232–34.

38. See the analysis in my *Wedemeyer Mission: American Politics and Foreign Policy during the Cold War* (Athens: University of Georgia Press, 1984), chap. 1.

39. Edward A. Kolodjiez, *The Uncommon Defense and Congress, 1945–1963* (Colombus: Ohio State University Press, 1966), 60–65.

40. Minutes of meeting of Secretaries of State, War, and Navy, January 29, 1947, 337 SANACC, RG319, NAII.

41. *FRUS, 1947,* 6:817–18.

42. See, for example, Major General Lauris Norstad to Patterson, January 4, 1947, and Major General S. J. Chamberlin to Norstad, February 11, 1947, 091 Korea (TS), RG319, NAII.

43. For correspondence regarding complaints from Americans in Korea, see Box 67, RG338, NAII. In an interview with the author on October 21, 1973, General William O. Reeder, an army supply officer stationed in Washington in 1947, emphasized complaints from soldiers in the field as a factor in the momentum for withdrawal.

44. See *Road*, 87.

45. On Rhee's strength as a political leader, the U.S. political adviser to the occupation, Joseph E. Jacobs, wrote to Secretary of State Marshall the following perceptive analysis on February 9, 1948: "[Rhee is] the outstanding leader in a confused, ill-informed society lacking in leadership—no doubt a bad, self-seeking and unwise leader, but nevertheless a dominating, shrewd, positive, feared character. His large following has nothing to do with love or veneration for the man. . . . It is . . . the result of a wide belief that Rhee is the source of all present and future political power in South Korea, the supreme protector of vested interests and the existing order of things, and that he is the man on whom to stake all one's fortunes. Although treatment of him by the United States and events at times should have created doubts on this score, his unfailing success, through a variety of circumstances in stealing every important and historical public show in South Korea confirms and reconfirms this belief." See Box 7125, RG59, NAII.

46. U.S. Congress, House, Committee on Foreign Affairs, *Korean Aid, Hearings on S. 938*, 81st Cong., 1st sess., June 8–23, 1949, 37, 57, 105.

47. McCune, *Korea Today*, 131–33.

48. See Merrill, *Korea*, chaps. 3–4.

49. Ibid., 90–92.

50. On the Soviet decision to withdraw, see Mansourov, "Communist War Coalition Formation," 84–97.

51. *Rhee*, 98.

52. Ibid.

53. For example, whereas Korea appeared four times in the reports of the State Department's "Daily Summary of Opinion Development" between March 12 and April 10, it was absent from those of July and August. See Box 3 in the Records of the Office of Public Opinion Studies, Department of State, RG59, NAII.

54. *Rhee*, 61–62.

55. Acheson to U.S. embassy in China, March 28, 1947, Box 3829, RG59, NAII.

56. *FRUS, 1947*, 6:645.

57. Ibid., 647–48; *Rhee*, 64–65.

58. Lerch to Hodge, July 15, 1947, Box 67, RG338, NAII.

59. See Joungwon Alexander Kim, *Divided Korea: The Politics of Development, 1945–1972* (Cambridge, Mass.: Harvard University Press, 1975), 76–78.

60. The most detailed account of the negotiations within the Joint Commission is in *Socialism*, chaps. 7–8.

61. See XXIV Corps, G-2, "Periodic Reports," July 17 and August 1, 1947, Box 18, RG332, NAII.

62. Ibid., August 19, 1947, and "G-2 Summary," August 31–September 7, 1947, Box 10, RG332, NAII.

63. Kim, *Divided Korea*, 78.

64. For more on conditions in South Korea in September 1947, see *Road*, 87–91.

65. *Socialism*, 264.

66. The likely issue would have been representation of the two zones in a provisional government. The United States previously had demanded representation in proportion to population, which would give the South a one-third greater representation than the North, while the Soviet Union had demanded equal representation.

67. John Lewis Gaddis accentuates this point in his "Korea in American Politics, Strategy, and Diplomacy, 1945–50," in *The Origins of the Cold War in Asia*, ed. Yonosuke Nagai and Akira Iriye (New York: Columbia University Press, 1977), 280–83. However, he largely ignores the domestic political side of the equation, which only became manifest in the summer of 1947 with the demise of new aid for Korea and the reduction of the defense budget.

Chapter 3
WHY THE KOREAN WAR, NOT THE KOREAN CIVIL WAR?

1. For a detailed account of the North Korean attack and the early days of fighting, see *USAKW*, vol. 1, chap. 3. For a detailed rebuttal to the argument that South Korean action began the fighting on the Ongjin Peninsula, see Kwang-Soo Kim, "The North Korean War Plan and the Opening Phase of the Korean War: A Documentary Study," *International Journal of Korean Studies* 5 (spring/summer 2001): 11–33.

2. Estimates of the size of North Korea's army vary. My figures are taken from ibid., 10–11, 18. For an estimate, based on a study of the Korea Institute of Military History, that gives the North Koreans an even greater advantage, see John K. C. Oh, "The Forgotten ROK Soldiers of the Korean War" (paper presented at "The Korean War Forgotten No More: A 50th Anniversary Commemorative Conference," Georgetown University, June 2000, 5–6). Estimates also vary on the number of Koreans in the attacking forces who had fought in the Chinese civil war. The figure may be as high as forty-two thousand. See *Mao's China*, 44–45; and Shen Zhihua, "Sino-Soviet Relations and the Origins of the Korean War: Stalin's Strategic Goals in the Far East," *Journal of Cold War Studies* 2 (spring 2000): 65.

3. *USAKW*, 1:17–18.

4. The most detailed treatment of U.S. decision making in the crisis is Glenn D. Paige, *The Korean Decision, June 24–30, 1950* (New York: Free Press, 1968). Paige wrote before most official U.S. documents had become available, but he compensated for this fact with intensive interviews with most of the key actors. For my own writings on the intervention, see *Road*, chap. 6; *KW*, 10–13, 41–44.

5. U.N. Document S/1946, June 25, 1950.

6. U.N. Document S/1508, Rev. 1, June 27, 1950.

7. The most succinct statement of this view is by Robert R. Simmons in *The Strained Alliance:* "The proper study of the Korean war should, while recognizing that both Moscow and Peking were intimately involved, emphasize its civil nature. The causes of the war must be sought on the Korean peninsula itself, an intensely nationalistic land whose people had been arbitrarily divided at the end of World War II. The opposing nature of the ideologies resident in the two halves of the nation served only to reinforce the passionate desire for reunification. In short, the proper appellation for the conflict is the Korean Civil War" (xv). The best-known and most sophisticated proponent of the view is the two-volume *Origins*.

8. *Origins*, 1:60.

9. The classic treatment of these groups is Chong-sik Lee, *The Politics of Korean Nationalism* (Los Angeles: University of California Press, 1963).

10. *Origins*, vol. 1: chap. 10; 2:237–50.

11. *Origins*, 2:250–90, 398–407; Merrill, *Korea*, 181.

12. *Origins*, 2:283.

13. Ibid., 399; see also 289, 398–407.

14. *CWIHPB* 6–7 (winter 1995–96): 92; Mansourov, "Communist War Coalition Formation," 70–71. I wish to thank Dr. Mansourov for providing me with a copy of this work.

15. "Korean," 17–18.

16. Ibid., 18.

17. *CWIHPB* 5 (spring 1995): 4.

18. Ibid., 2.

19. *Origins*, 388–98.

20. "Korean," 7–11.

21. "Korean," 17.

22. Ibid., 18–19; *CWIHPB* 5 (spring 1995): 6.

23. *CWIHPB*, 5, 7:8; "Korean," 29–33.

24. Shen, "Sino-Soviet Relations," 65.

25. *CWIHPB*, 5 (spring 1995): 8.

26. On the guerrilla war in the South during the summer and fall of 1949, which was aided by the infiltration from the North of over thirteen hundred men, see Merrill, *Korea*, 143–51. On the winter of 1949–50, see pp. 154–65.

27. *CWIHPB* 5 (spring 1995): 9.

28. "Korean," 38.

29. On the last point, see Kathryn Weathersby, "'Should We Fear This?': Stalin and the Korean War," (paper presented at conference "Stalin and the Cold War," Yale University. September 1999), 13–14. For NSC-48, see Thomas Etzold and John Lewis Gaddis, *Containment: Documents on American Policy and Strategy, 1946–1950* (New York: Columbia University Press, 1978), 252–76; for Acheson's speech, see *DSB* 22 (January 23, 1950): 114–16. For an English-language text of the Sino-Soviet treaty, see *Uncertain*, 260–61.

30. "Korean," 40–42.

31. Shen, "Sino-Soviet Relations," 51–62.

32. For an English-language text of the public agreement, see *Uncertain*, 261–63. On the secret protocol, see pp. 126–27.

33. Shen, "Sino-Soviet Relations," 60.

34. Ibid., 48; see *CRKW*, 87–88, for evidence of earlier Mao-Stalin discussions on Korea.

35. He Di, "'The Last Campaign to Unify China': The CCP's Unmaterialized Plan to Liberate Taiwan, 1949–1950," *Chinese Historians* 5 (spring 1992): 4–12.

36. Mansourov, "Communist War Coalition Formation," 320–21.

37. For an insightful discussion of the Stalin-Mao relationship, see *Uncertain*, chap. 1. On the secret protocols, see pp. 121–22, 125–26.

38. On Japan, see Robert Swearingen and Paul Langer, *Red Flag in Japan: International Communism in Action, 1919–1951* (Cambridge, Mass.: Harvard University Press, 1952), chaps. 18–20. On Indochina, see Qiang Zhai, *China and the Vietnam Wars, 1950–1975* (Chapel Hill: University of North Carolina Press, 2000), chap. 1.

39. See my analysis in *Road*, 102–6.

40. For material in this and the next three paragraphs, see my *Road*, 153–59.

41. Ibid., 164–70. The border clashes of 1949 were quite disturbing to the Americans, who recognized *at least* partial South Korean responsibility.

42. Harold Joyce Noble, *Embassy at War*, edited and annotated with an introduction by Frank Baldwin (Seattle: University of Washington Press, 1975), 229.

43. Ibid., 140–43, 146, 158, 161–62.

44. *DSB* 22 (January 23, 1950): 116.

45. Acheson to Ambassador Alan Kirk in Moscow, June 28, 1950, RG84, NAII. Although Acheson wrote this message on the twenty-eighth, the logic behind it obviously applies to the decisions regarding American troops over the next two days. The only thing missing on the twenty-eighth was a recommendation from the field commander that American ground units were necessary and could do the job.

46. *FRUS, 1949,* 7:1047, 1054–55. The preceding analysis is presented in greater depth in *Road,* 185–90.

47. *Road,* 187.

48. On Truman's use of historical analogy in this case, see Harry S. Truman, *Memoirs,* vol. 2 (Garden City, N.Y.: Doubleday, 1956), 334.

49. *Origins,* 2:618.

50. Kaufman, *The Korean War,* 1.

Chapter 4
THE ROAD TO CHINESE INTERVENTION, JULY–NOVEMBER 1950

1. *DSB* 23 (July 10, 1950): 46.

2. *USAKW,* 3:77–78.

3. Ibid., 139–40.

4. *Road,* 203–4.

5. The most detailed account of the summer fighting is *USAKW,* 1:59–487; see also Blair, *The Forgotten War,* 119–325.

6. *FRUS, 1950,* 7:716.

7. *Road,* 227–28, 235–36.

8. *FRUS, 1950,* 7:852.

9. *Road,* 231. For an English translation of the Chinese minutes of the Zhou-Panikkar conversation, see Shuguang Zhang and Jian Chen, *Chinese Communist Foreign Policy: New Documentary Evidence, 1944–1950* (Chicago: Imprint, 1996), 163–64.

10. *CRKW,* chaps. 6–7; Thornton, *Odd Man Out,* chap. 12. The order of October 8 is published in English translation in Zhang and Chen, *Chinese Communist Foreign Policy,* 164–65.

11. *Road,* 239.

12. On the early skirmishes, see *USAKW,* 1:673–88.

13. *FRUS, 1950,* 7:1058 n.

14. *Road,* 243–46.

15. Douglas MacArthur, *Reminiscences* (New York: McGraw-Hill, 1964), 373.

16. *MSFE,* 3491–92.

17. Ibid., 3295.

18. The resolution is reprinted in *FRUS, 1950,* 7:211.

19. Ibid., 393–95.

20. Ibid., 460–61.

21. *NYT*, June 28, 1950.

22. *NYT*, July 2, 1950.

23. *Time*, September 4, 1950, 12; *NYT*, September 1, 1950; "Scrapbooks," vol. 16, Richard B. Russell Papers, Russell Library, University of Georgia, Athens, Ga.

24. *FRUS, 1950*, 7:506, 508.

25. Ibid., 235–92.

26. See Marc Trachtenberg, "'A Wasting Asset'? American Strategy and the Shifting Nuclear Balance, 1949–1954," *International Security* 13 (winter 1988–89): 5–49. On the U.S. war plan and strategic missile capability, see *HJCS*, 4:161–77. On Allison's shift, see *FRUS, 1950*, 7:571–72.

27. *DSB* 23 (August 28 and September 11, 1950): 330–31, 407.

28. *FRUS, 1950*, 7:656, 679–83, 776–79.

29. Ibid., 655–56.

30. *KW*, 85–86; D. Clayton James, *The Years of MacArthur* (Boston: Houghton Mifflin, 1985), 3:464–85.

31. On Republican politics and the rise of McCarthy, see Robert Griffith, *The Politics of Fear: Joseph R. McCarthy and the Senate* (Lexington: University Press of Kentucky, 1970), 54–122. On the political climate in the United States during the summer and fall from Truman's perspective, see Alonzo L. Hamby, *Man of the People: A Life of Harry S. Truman* (New York: Oxford University Press, 1995), 546–51.

32. James, *Years of MacArthur*, 3:452–64.

33. *KW*, 71–74.

34. Ernest Bevin, "Review of the International Situation in Asia in the Light of the Korean Conflict," August 30, 1950, CP (50) 200, Public Records Office, Kew, England.

35. *KW*, 92.

36. Ibid., 91–93.

37. Ibid., 94–96.

38. *Road*, 133.

39. *KW*, 105–6, 97.

40. *DSB* 23 (September 18, 1950): 460–64.

41. *FRUS, 1950*, 7:868–69.

42. Ibid., 717–18.

43. *CWIHPB* 6–7 (winter 1995–96): 95–97.

44. *CRKW*, 111–13, 134–35, 156.

45. Alexandre Y. Mansourov, "Stalin, Mao, Kim, and China's Decision to Enter the Korean War," *CWIHPB* 6–7 (winter 1995–96): 95–97.

46. Ibid., 98–99, 111–14; Zhang Xi, "Peng Dehuai and China's Entry into the Korean War," *Chinese Historians* 6 (spring 1993): 5–6.

47. *CRKW*, 156.

48. Ibid., 136–37, 140.

49. As quoted in ibid., 142–43.

50. *MZM*, 1:454–55, 469, 485.

51. Quoted in Whiting, *China Crosses the Yalu*, 79.
52. Quoted in ibid., 84–85.
53. *CWIHPB* 6–7 (winter 1995–96): 43.
54. Ibid., 44.
55. "Red," 77.
56. *CWIHPB* 6–7 (winter 1995–96): 45.
57. "Red," 78–82.
58. Goncharov, Lewis, and Xue, *Uncertain Partners*, 180.
59. Zhang and Chen, *Chinese Communist Foreign Policy*, 164–65.
60. *CWIHPB* 6–7 (winter 1995–96): 114–15.
61. *CRKW*, 174–75, 181–84. On the Mao-Peng relationship, both before and after 1950, see Philip Short, *Mao: A Life* (New York: Henry Holt, 1999), 232–33, 323, 493–500.
62. *CWIHPB* 6–7 (winter 1995–96): 116.
63. The best of the many accounts on this series of events is "Red," 94–99.
64. Quoted in *CRKW*, 143.
65. Zhang and Chen, *Chinese Communist Foreign Policy*, 164.
66. *MMR*, 81.
67. *CRKW*, 128–29.
68. *KW*, 105–6; *Origins*, 2:738–39.
69. *CRKW*, 17–21.
70. *MMR*, 17.
71. On Mao's relationship with his father, see Short, *Mao*, 28–30.
72. On Mao's 1917 article, see ibid., 58–60; *MMR*, 25.
73. Short, *Mao*, 411.
74. *MMR*, 18–25.
75. Ibid., 76.
76. Mao Tse-tung, *Selected Works of Mao Tse-tung* (Peking: Foreign Languages Press, 1961), 4:21–22, 97–101; Mark Ryan, *Chinese Attitudes toward Nuclear Weapons: China and the United States during the Korean War* (Armonk, N.Y.: M. E. Sharpe, 1989), 14–17.
77. Ryan, *Chinese Attitudes*, 28–29.
78. *MZM*, 1:539–41, 558–59.
79. *FRUS, 1950*, 7:948–60.
80. Actually, MacArthur's response in this case was not without foundation, although a more traditional general probably would have wired home asking for permission before actually giving the orders. For a more detailed discussion of the issue, see *Road*, 239–41.
81. See Blair, *Forgotten War*, 377–79.
82. *FRUS, 1950*, 7:1107–10.
83. This interpretation cannot be proven, but the evidence regarding MacArthur's later reaction to the Chinese counteroffensive indicates that he did, indeed, believe

that Washington would expand the war to China. When this did not occur imme-diately, he tried to create what his leading biographer calls "a false dilemma," namely, that the United States must either expand the war or withdraw entirely from Korea, to get his way. See James, *Years of MacArthur*, 3:547–59.

84. *FRUS, 1950*, 7:1102–3.

85. Ibid., 1117–21, 1204–8.

86. *Road*, 248–50.

87. *FRUS, 1950*, 7:1181–83.

88. Edward Barrett to F. H. Russell, November 13, 1950, Box 92, George Elsey Papers, HSTL.

89. *Present*, 467–68.

90. "Red," 105, 115–16.

91. Transcript of the Princeton Seminars, February 13, 1954, HSTL. This is a rec-ord of intensive discussions of the experiences of several State Department officials of the Truman era shortly after they had left office.

92. On the limited Soviet air intervention in Korea, see "Red," 114–26.

93. *NYT*, December 1, 1950, 1.

Chapter 5
WHY THE WAR DID NOT EXPAND BEYOND KOREA, NOVEMBER 1950–JULY 1951

1. *CWIHPB* 8–9 (winter 1996–97): 237–38.

2. *MMR*, 118.

3. Ibid., 121–22.

4. "Korean," 109–10.

5. *MMR*, 123. Mao's source is unknown. In fact, Collins's report on his return contained a good deal of ambiguity, as would be expected in circumstances of consid-erable fluidity. See *FRUS, 1950*, 7:1469–70; J. Lawton Collins, *War in Peacetime* (Bos-ton: Houghton Mifflin), 232–33; Schnabel and Watson, *HJCS*, 3:368–69.

6. *MMR*, 127.

7. Collins, *War in Peacetime*, 231–32.

8. *FRUS, 1950*, 7:1630–33.

9. Sherman to JCS, January 3, 1951, 452 China, RG218, NAII.

10. *FRUS, 1951*, 7:70–72.

11. Ibid., 78.

12. *KW*, 204–8.

13. *NYT*, June 24, 1951, 4.

14. *Truman*, 49–81.

15. *FRUS, 1950*, 7:1242, 1263–65, 1279, 1308, 1312–13, 1327–28.

16. Ibid., 1144, 1156–62.

17. Trachtenberg, "'A Wasting Asset'?" 5–49.

18. *NYT*, December 1, 1950.

19. *Nation*, December 9, 1950, 520–21.

20. *Present*, 484.

21. *FR, 1950*, 7:1462–65, 1476–79.

22. UN General Assembly, *Official Records*, sess. 5, comm. 102, 1950, 435.

23. *FRUS, 1950*, 7:1549–50.

24. Ibid., 1440, 1541, 1576–77, 1590, 1600, 1605.

25. *KW*, 139–42.

26. *MMR*, 131–32.

27. Blair, *Forgotten War*, 640–47.

28. Ibid., 669–82; *MMR*, 134–42.

29. The ensuing account of UN activities represents a condensation of the analysis in *KW*, 148–57.

30. *FRUS, 1951*, 7:27–28.

31. For public opinion polls regarding Korea, see George H. Gallup, *The Gallup Poll: Public Opinion 1935–1971*, vol. 2 (New York: Random House, 1972), 960–61; on Hoover's speech, see *KW*, 146; for the debate on more troops to Europe, see *Present*, 488–96.

32. *Present*, 513.

33. *FRUS, 1951*, 7:115–16.

34. Ibid., 135.

35. See Blair, *Forgotten War*, 715–800; Roy E. Appleman, *Ridgway Duels for Korea* (College Station: Texas A&M University Press, 1990), 376–429.

36. James, *Years of MacArthur*, 3:581–84; Dennis D. Wainstock, *Truman, MacArthur, and the Korean War* (Westport, Conn.: Greenwood Press, 1999), 116–18.

37. *NYT*, March 24, 1951.

38. *Present*, 519.

39. *KW*, 178–79.

40. "Red," 172.

41. Ibid., 180–81.

42. Memo for the Record, by Bradley, April 24, 1951, RG218, NAII.

43. Roger Dingman, "Atomic Diplomacy during the Korean War," *International Security* 13 (winter 1988/89): 69.

44. Morrison to Sir Oliver Franks (British ambassador to the United States), April 6, 1951, FO371/92757, PRO.

45. *KW*, 182–84, 188.

46. *NYT*, April 8, 1951; *FRUS, 1951*, 7:316–17.

47. *NYT*, April 26, 1951.

48. *FRUS, 1951*, 7:386–87.

49. *KW*, 188–89.

50. *MSFE*, 42, 51–52, 104, 110, 121–22.

51. *NYT*, May 7, 1951.

52. *Congressional Record*, 97 (May 9, 1951): 5101–02.

53. *KW*, 190–92. The Soviet bloc refused to participate in the voting, and Arab-Asian neutrals, plus Sweden, abstained.

54. *NYT*, April 22 and May 6, 1951.

55. For Chiang's statement, see *NYT*, May 17, 1951. For Rusk's speech, see *DSB* 24 (May 28, 1951): 846–48.

56. *MSFE*, 731–33, 756, 898, 937–38.

57. Ibid., 1379, 1385, 1393, 1398–99.

58. "Korean," 125.

59. *MMR*, 148; "Red," 148.

60. "Korean," 109–10; *KW*, 145–46; *FRUS, 1951*, 4:1522–23. The drafter of the State Department memorandum remarked that "the source mentioned is one who has proven accurate in every previous conversation."

61. *FRUS, 1951*, 4:1522– 23.

62. *KW*, 160–62.

63. Appleman, *Ridgway Duels for Korea*, 553–80.

64. *KW*, 146, 164, 199–200, 201–2.

65. Ibid., 200–201.

66. *MMR*, 133, 160, 177, 222–23; Zhang Shuguang, "Sino-Soviet Economic Co-operation," in *Brothers in Arms: The Rise and Fall of the Sino-Soviet Alliance, 1945–1953*, ed. Odd Arne Westad (Washington, D.C., and Stanford, Calif.: Woodrow Wilson Center Press and Stanford University Press, 1998), 199.

67. "Korean," 136–37.

68. Ibid., 132–33, 135–36.

69. *MMR*, 132.

70. Kathryn Weathersby, "The Soviet Role in the Early Phase of the Korean War: New Documentary Evidence," *Journal of American–East Asian Relations* 3 (winter 1994): 15–16.

71. *MMR*, 205–9.

72. Ibid., 156–57; *Mao's China*, 97–98. On the internal situation in China, see British chargé in Beijing Leo Lamb's dispatches to the Foreign Office of June 22 and July 14, 1951 (FO371/92191 and FO371/92201, respectively, PRO); and U.S. State Department, Office of Intelligence Research, "Current Public Opinion in Communist China," OIR Report No. 5532, May 14, 1951, Box 303, Averell Harriman Papers, Library of Congress, Washington, D.C.

73. "Korean," 126–33.

74. *KW*, 202, 205–7.

75. "Korean," 134–35.

76. *FRUS, 1950*, 7:1549–50.

77. "Korean," 134; also *MMR*, 156–57.

78. *FRUS, 1950*, 7:1242, 1263–65, 1279, 1308, 1312–13, 1327–28.

79. See Frank Holober, *Raiders of the China Coast: CIA Covert Operations during the Korean War* (Annapolis, Md.: Naval Institute Press, 1999).

80. Pusan 213 to Department of State, June 16, 1951, and Pusan 8 to Department

of State, July 6, 1951, Box 4273, 795.00, RG59, NAII; Muccio to Acheson, June 6, 1951, Box 9, Selected Records Related to the Korean War, HSTL; *NYT*, July 2, 1951.

81. *NYT*, July 1, 1951; *FRUS, 1951*, 7:601–4.

82. *FRUS, 1951*, 7:645.

83. *USAKW*, 3:405.

Chapter 6
NEGOTIATING AN ARMISTICE, JULY 1951–JULY 1953:
WHY DID IT TAKE SO LONG?

1. *KW*, 210, 221.

2. *Mao's China*, 100.

3. Weyland to Ridgway, July 3, 1951, Ridgway Papers, U.S. Army War College Library, Carlisle Barracks, Pa.

4. Ridgway to the Joint Chiefs, July 4, 1951, Selected Records Related to the Korean War, HST, HSTL.

5. "Notes on Cabinet Meeting, July 6, 1951," Box 1, Connelly Papers, HSTL. On political pressures threatening rearmament, see *Truman*, 122–27.

6. *USAKW*, 2:19.

7. *FRUS, 1951*, 7:787–89.

8. Charles Turner Joy, "My Battle inside the Korean Truce Tent," *Collier's*, 130 August 16, 1952, 40.

9. Ibid.; see also *NWF*, 13–14.

10. Charles Turner Joy, *How Communists Negotiate* (New York: Macmillan, 1955), 4–5.

11. *FRUS, 1951*, 7:651.

12. *KW*, 221.

13. Ibid., 225.

14. For Acheson's statement, see *NYT*, June 27, 1951.

15. *FRUS, 1951*, 7:599.

16. Ibid., 748–52.

17. Ibid., 751–52.

18. Ibid., 762.

19. Ibid., 781.

20. *Mao's China*, 102.

21. *KW*, 232.

22. *Mao's China*, 103; "Korean," 176–77; *MMR*, 159–165.

23. *FRUS, 1951*, 7:847–48.

24. *NWF*, 33–34; *FRUS, 1951*, 7:848–49; *USAKW*, 2:42–44.

25. As quoted in *Mao's China*, 104, from a telegram from Beijing to the CPV command of August 23, 1951.

26. *MZM*, 2:433.

27. "Korean," 136–40.

28. In developing this interpretation, I benefited from conversations in June 2000 with Tibor Meray, a Hungarian journalist who arrived in Kaesong in August 1951 to report on the negotiations. On the Chinese belief that the Americans were unwilling, either politically or psychologically, to continue the war in Korea indefinitely, see *MMR*, 220–21.

29. "Korean," 153.

30. Ibid., 157–58.

31. *Time*, July 23, 1951, 14.

32. *NYT*, August 4, 1951.

33. *USAKW*, 2:40–43.

34. See "Korean," 164–65, which quotes a telegram from Mao to Stalin of August 27, 1951.

35. *KW*, 416 n. 142.

36. *NYT*, August 19, 1951, sec. 4, pp. 1, 3; Acheson to certain diplomatic and consular officers, August 24, 1951, Moscow Embassy Files, RG84, NAII.

37. See the analysis in a U.S. State Department study, "Estimate No. 27," attached to W. Park Armstrong, Jr., to Acheson, August 22, 1951, Box 4275, 795.00, RG59, NAII.

38. *USAKW*, 2:44–51; *KW*, 234–37.

39. Ibid., 119.

40. *KW*, 240–41.

41. Ibid., 239–40.

42. *CWIHPB* 6–7 (winter 1995–96): 72.

43. Ibid., 71; *KW*, 247–48.

44. Mao, *Selected Works*, 4:61–62.

45. Blair, *Forgotten War*, 802.

46. *KW*, 242–43.

47. *FRUS, 1951*, 7:735.

48. Ibid., 727–28.

49. Ibid., 599–600, 1149, 1175.

50. Ibid., 754–56.

51. Quoted in *USAKW*, 2:235.

52. *FRUS, 1951*, 7:666–67; General Headquarters, FEC, Joint Strategic Plans and Operations Group, "Location of and Authority 1 to Visit Prisoner of War Camps," July 8, 1951, Box 8, RG338, NAII.

53. See, for example, Ridgway to Collins, November 16 and 19, 1951, Ridgway Papers. The estimates were over six thousand against Americans prisoners alone, but fewer than 400 of them could be proven.

54. *FRUS, 1951*, 7:626–27.

55. Ibid., 622.

56. Headquarters, Eighth Army (Korea), Staff Study, "Arrangements Pertaining to Prisoners of War," n.d. but clearly summer 1951, Box 8, RG338, NAII.

57. *USAKW*, 2:136–37.

58. *FRUS, 1951*, 7:792–93. This argument was made in the Pentagon during the summer but later was countered by Ridgway's claim that the UNC had scrupulously avoided any promise of asylum.

59. On the trend toward an all-for-all exchange in November, see ibid., 1167–70.

60. Ibid., 1073.

61. For the Joy statement, see ibid., 1382.

62. Ibid., 1374; *USAKW*, 2:141.

63. *FRUS, 1951*, 7:1373–74; *USAKW*, 2:141–43.

64. *FRUS, 1951*, 7:1244 n, 1290–96. On the sound basis of Truman's fear, see *Truman*, 119–59; Frieberg, *In the Shadow of the Garrison State*, 122–23.

65. *NWF*, 184; *NYT*, January 3, 1952.

66. *NWF*, 199.

67. See Mark R. Elliott, *Pawns of Yalta: Soviet Refugees and America's Role in Their Repatriation* (Urbana: University of Illinois Press, 1982).

68. I refer here to the $100 million appropriated by Congress during October 1951 for use by exiles from the Soviet bloc or dissidents within it as part of a U.S. plan to take the offensive in the Cold War. See John Joseph Yurchenko, "From Containment to Counteroffensive: Soviet Vulnerabilities and American Policy Planning, 1946–1953" (Ph.D. diss., University of California, Berkeley, 1980), chap. 2.

69. *NWF*, 190; *FRUS, 1952–1954*, 15:13–14; *USAKW*, 2:146, 154–55.

70. "Memorandum of Conversation at Dinner at British Embassy, Sunday, January 6, 1952," January 7, 1952, Dean Acheson Papers, HSTL.

71. *KW*, 259–61.

72. Edward W. Barrett to H. Freeman Matthews, February 5, 1952, Box 2, Records of the Bureau of Far Eastern Affairs, Lot 55D128, RG59, NAII.

73. *KW*, 260, 262–63.

74. Truman's journal is in Box 333, President's Secretary's Files, HSTL.

75. *FRUS, 1952–1954*, 15:44.

76. *KW*, 264–67.

77. *NWF*, 367–68.

78. *USAKW*, 2:868–74.

79. *NWF*, 401.

80. Ibid., 355.

81. *USAKW*, 2:170–71.

82. For the most balanced treatment of the bacteriological warfare campaign, see Ryan, *Chinese Attitudes toward Nuclear Weapons*, chap. 4.

83. *KW*, 271–72.

84. *FRUS, 1952–1954*, 15:192, 204, 207, 248–49.

85. William M. Leary, *Perilous Missions: Civil Air Transport and CIA Covert Operations in Asia* (Tuscaloosa: University of Alabama Press, 1984), 132–42.

86. *USAKW*, 2:199–200.

87. Ibid., 180; *MMR*, 160–65.

88. *MMR*, 184–85.

89. *USAKW*, 2:239.

90. "Briefing of Ambassadors on Korea, by Hickerson," March 18, 1952, Box 3, Selected Records Relating to the Korean War, Truman Papers, HSTL.

91. *USAKW*, 2:175–205.

92. Ibid., 243–55.

93. *KW*, 276–78; for more on the ROK political crisis and the United States, see chapter 7.

94. Robert Frank Futrell, *The United States Air Force in Korea* (New York: Duell, Sloan, and Pearce, 1961), 475–521.

95. *Mao's China*, 109.

96. *KW*, 283–92.

97. Ibid., 292–98.

98. For more detail on events described in this and the next paragraph, see *KW*, 298–306.

99. *Mao's China*, 111.

100. For the records of the Stalin-Zhou conversations, see *CWIHPB* 6–7 (winter 1995–96): 10–19.

101. *MMR*, 233; *MZM*, 632, 638, 656–58, 667–68.

102. On Eisenhower's activities, see Stephen Ambrose, *Eisenhower* (New York: Simon and Schuster, 1984), 2:30–35; *NYT*, December 7 and 8, 1952. On naval maneuvers, see James Field Jr., *History of United States Naval Operations: Korea* (Washington, D.C.: Government Printing Office, 1962), 442.

103. *MMR*, 233–36; *MZM*, 3:632, 638, 656–58.

104. *NYT*, February 3, 4, 8, 1953; *USAKW*, 2:357–61.

105. As quoted in *MMR*, 239.

106. *Mao's China*, 114–15.

107. *FRUS, 1952–1954*, 15:716–17, 785–86, 788–90.

108. Dimitri Volkogonov, *Stalin: Triumph and Tragedy* (New York: Grove Weidenfeld, 1988), 570.

109. See Weathersby, "Soviet Role in the Early Phase of the Korean War," 17.

110. *CWIHPB* 6–7 (winter 1995–96): 80–82.

111. *KW*, 313–26.

112. *FRUS, 1952–1954*, 15:1053, 1059–63, 1064–68. On Communist airpower, see Futrell, *U.S. Air Force in Korea*, 374–80.

113. *KW*, 326–30.

114. For more background on the action, see chapter 7.

115. *DSB* 28 (June 29, 1953): 906–7.

116. *USAKW*, 2:451; *FRUS, 1952–1954*, 15:1210–11, 1223–24.

117. Mark Clark, *From the Danube to the Yalu* (New York: Harper and Brothers, 1954), 284.

118. Memorandum of Conversation, Soviet Communication Concerning Truce Negotiations (plus attachment), June 29, 1953, 795.00/6-2953, RG59, NAII.

119. For a recent account of the incident, see Amy Knight, *Beria* (Princeton, N.J.: Princeton University Press, 1994), 194–200.

120. *KW*, 341.

121. *DSB* 29 (July 20, 1953): 73–74.

122. *USAKW*, 2:474–76.

123. *FRUS, 1952–1954*, 15:1357–60, 1368–69.

124. *Times* (London), July 28, 1953.

125. *USAKW*, 2:488–91.

126. *NYT*, July 27, 1953.

127. For more on the mutual defense pact, see chapter 7.

Chapter 7
THE KOREAN WAR AND THE AMERICAN RELATIONSHIP WITH KOREA

1. I wish to thank Tom Ganschow, my colleague at the University of Georgia, for providing this connection.

2. Muccio to W. Walton Butterworth (assistant secretary of state for the Far East), August 27, 1949, RG59, NAII. For an excellent secondary source detailing ROK resistance to the withdrawal, see *Reluctant*, 189–99.

3. Everett Drumright (U.S. chargé to the ROK) to Secretary of State Dean Acheson, June 13, 1949, RG59, NAII.

4. *DSB* 22 (January 23, 1950): 116.

5. For Connally's statement, see *U.S. News and World Report*, May 6, 1950, 4; for Acheson's response, see *FRUS, 1950*, 7:67 n.

6. See Muccio's complaint on this matter in *FRUS, 1950*, 7:88–89.

7. See my analysis in *Road*, 164–70.

8. See ibid., 185–90.

9. *KW*, 108–11.

10. Robert A. Divine, *Foreign Policy and U.S. Presidential Elections*, vol. 2 (New York: New Viewpoints, 1974), 50–70.

11. See John Lewis Gaddis, *Strategies of Containment: A Critical Appraisal of Postwar American National Security Policy* (New York: Oxford University Press, 1982), chap. 5.

12. *USAKW*, 2:446.

13. Graham to the British Foreign Office, April 4, 1953, FO371/105484, PRO.

14. Headquarters, U.S. Far Eastern Command, Military History Section, "History of the Korean Conflict: Korean Armistice Negotiations (July 1951–May 1952)," unpublished manuscript available at the Military Records Branch, NAII, pt. 4, vol. 1, 67–71.

15. Ibid., 70–74, 88–89; FRUS, 1952–1954, 15:906.

16. See note 14.

17. *FRUS, 1952–1954,* 15:907.

18. Ibid., 910–14, 917–19, 938–40, 947–50.

19. Ibid., 897–900.

20. *PPPUS, Dwight D. Eisenhower, 1953,* 377–80.

21. *FRUS, 1952–1954,* 15:1368–69.

22. Ibid., 1159–60; Briggs to Dulles, June 6 and 11, 1953, RG59, NAII; *USAKW,* 2:449.

23. For a more detailed account of the crisis that followed, see *KW,* 332–39.

24. *FRUS, 1952–1954,* 15:1444.

25. For the American record of the talks, see ibid., 1466–90.

26. For the texts of the treaty and the joint statement, see *DSB* 29 (August 17, 1953): 203–4. For the ROK draft treaty, see *FRUS, 1952–1954,* 15:1359–61.

27. *FRUS, 1952–1954,* 15:1474–75, 1481.

28. *U.S.-Korean,* 85–90.

29. See Eui Hang Shin, "Effects of the Korean War on Social Structures of the Republic of Korea," *International Journal of Korean Studies* 5 (spring/summer 2001): 145–47, 150– 51.

30. Clark, *From the Danube to the Yalu,* 272.

31. *FRUS, 1952–1954,* 15:1597.

32. *U.S.-Korean,* 3.

33. Donald Stone Macdonald, "Korea and the Ballot: The International Dimension in Korean Political Development as Seen in Elections" (Ph.D. diss., George Washington University, 1978), 225–54, 260–62; Kim, *Divided Korea,* 116–32.

34. Muccio to Niles Bond (assistant to the director of the Office of Northeast Asian Affairs in the State Department), September 12, 1949, RG59, NAII.

35. For American correspondence on these matters, see *FRUS, 1950,* 7:35–40.

36. Ibid., 43–44.

37. Drumright to Acheson, April 28, 1950, in ibid., 52–58.

38. For a description of the electoral process and an analysis of the results, see Macdonald, "Korea and the Ballot," 265–86. Macdonald, an American diplomat stationed in Korea in 1950, observed the procedures.

39. On the U.S. role in 1960, see Macdonald, "Korea and the Ballot," 481–82; Kim, *Divided Korea,* 163.

40. For background on the 1952 crisis covered in this and the next paragraph, see Kim, *Divided Korea,* 328–38; W. D. Reeve, *The Republic of Korea: A Political and Economic Study* (London: Oxford University Press, 1963), 43–45; John Kie-chiang Oh, *Korea: Democracy on Trial* (Ithaca, N.Y.: Cornell University Press, 1968), 39–43; and Edward C. Keefer, "The Truman Administration and the South Korean Political Crisis of 1952: Democracy's Failure?" *Pacific Historical Review,* 60 (May 1991): 152–56.

41. Oh, *Democracy on Trial,* 43.

42. Robert O'Neill, *Australia in the Korean War 1950–53,* vol. 1, *Strategy and Diplomacy* (Canberra: Australian Government Printing Service, 1981), 294–96.

43. Robert J. Donovan, *The Presidency of Harry S. Truman, 1949–1953,* vol. 2, *Tumultuous Years* (New York: Norton, 1982), 365–91; Truman, chap. 5.

44. E. Allan Lightner Oral History, October 26, 1973, by Richard D. McKinzie, transcript on file at the HSTL, 114.

45. *FRUS, 1952–1954*, 15:50.

46. For documentation on the split between the embassy and the military, see ibid., 117–20; *FRUS, 1952*, 15:254–56, 264, 274–77. On Rhee's organizational support at the local level, see Kim, *Divided Korea*, 136. For a detailed analysis of the 1952 election crisis, see Macdonald, "Korea and the Ballot," 328–65.

47. Macdonald, "Korea and the Ballot," 285–86.

48. Ibid., 290.

49. Lightner oral history, 120–21; John J. Muccio oral history, October 26, 1973, by Richard D. McKinzie, transcript on file at the HSTL, 33.

50. Alec Adams (British chargé in Pusan) to the Foreign Office, July 10, 1952, FO 371/99551, PRO.

51. Macdonald, "Korea and the Ballot," 343–50.

52. Ibid., 349. Macdonald himself believes this. Even Lightner conceded that "no doubt Rhee has large popular following including inarticulate masses." He believed, however, that most educated people "wld welcome change govt." *FRUS, 1952–1954*, 15:255.

53. See Keefer, "Democracy's Failure?" 167–68.

54. In fairness to Keefer, during the crisis between Rhee and the United States during the summer of 1953, Clark employed subtle pressures on Rhee that probably helped persuade him not to attempt to prevent an armistice (see *KW*, 336–37). It is not clear, however, that anything short of forcing Rhee's departure in 1952 would have led to a significant change in ROK politics.

55. On the 1960 case, see Oh, *Democracy on Trial*, 60–71. On 1987, see William Stueck, "Democratization in Korea: The United States Role in 1980 and 1987," *International Journal of Korean Studies* 2 (fall/winter 1998): 1–26. It should be pointed out that the war strengthened authoritarian trends in Korean political culture as well. See Kongdan Oh, "The Korean War and South Korean Politics," in *War and Democracy*, ed. David McCann and Barry S. Strauss (Armonk, N.Y.: M. E. Sharpe, 2001), 184–86.

56. For a summary ranging from the election of 1948 through that of 1960, see *U.S.-Korean*, 61–70.

57. USIS Seoul to USIA Washington, January 25, 1960, RG306, Despatches 1954–65, Box 2, NAII.

58. USIS Seoul to USIA Washington, January 30, 1961, ibid.

59. For a description of the period from the ousting of Rhee to the military coup by Park Chung Hee, see Oh, *Democracy on Trial*, 82–93.

60. For a discussion of U.S. policy from the Park coup through the restoration of civilian government and presidential and assembly elections in 1963, see *U.S.-Korean*, 208–26.

61. For the domestic context of Park's actions, see John Kie-chiang Oh, *Korean Politics: The Quest for Democratization and Economic Development* (Ithaca, N.Y.: Cornell

University Press, 1999), 58–60; for the context of U.S.-Korean relations, see Don Oberdorfer, *The Two Koreas: A Contemporary History* (Reading, Mass.: Addison-Wesley, 1997), 37–41.

62. For the recollections of American participants in Korea, often based on consultation of key documents from the period, see William H. Gleysteen Jr., *Massive Entanglement, Minimum Influence: Carter and Korea in Crisis* (Washington, D.C.: Brookings Institution Press, 1999); John A. Wickham Jr., *Korea on the Brink: A Memoir of Political Intrigue and Military Crisis* (Washington, D.C.: Brassey's, 2000); and James V. Young, "Memoirs of a Korea Specialist," unpublished manuscript in possession of the author.

63. See my analysis in "Democratization in Korea."

64. For an analysis of anti-Americanism in Korea, see Oh, *Korean Politics*, 87–89.

65. See above, 315–16.

66. Soon Sung Cho, *Korea in World Politics, 1940–1950* (Los Angeles: University of California Press, 1967), 241–43.

67. *U.S.-Korean*, 249.

68. Ibid., 250.

69. Ibid., 82–85, 265–66. The ROK did not receive even partial U.S. reimbursement until September 1951. A broad settlement was reached in February 1953, but the issue remained a controversial one for the remainder of Rhee's stay in the presidency of the ROK.

70. Ibid., 262.

71. James Plimsoll (Australian representative on United Nations Commission for the Unification and Rehabilitation of Korea) to Department of External Affairs, Canberra, June 6, 1952, as quoted in O'Neill, *Australia in the Korean War*, 1:305.

72. *DSB* 29 (August 17, 1953): 203.

73. "Briefing Summary for the Secretary of State, Mr. John Foster Dulles: Economic Aid to the Republic of Korea," n.d., Box 2, Bureau of Far Eastern Affairs, Misc Subj Files, 1956, Lot 58D3, RG59, NAII.

74. See "President's Far Eastern Trip June 1960: United States Economic Aid to the Republic of Korea," June 10, 1960, Ann Whitman File, Papers of Dwight D. Eisenhower, Eisenhower Library, Abilene, Kans.

75. *U.S.-Korean*, 255–56.

76. Ibid., 270–71.

77. See Jong Won Lee, "The Impact of the Korean War on the Korean Economy," *International Journal of Korean Studies* 5 (spring/summer 2001): 108–10.

78. For a powerful indictment of American racism in Korea during the summer of 1950, see *Origins*, 2:690–702.

79. The documents on Korea in the *FRUS, 1955–57* (vol. 23) and *1958–1960* (vol. 18) are rich in illustrations of these points.

80. One of the striking things to me in comparing American and British records related to Korea for the period is how much less impatience and condescension shows up in the former than in the latter.

81. For a revealing if somewhat optimistic analysis of American influence on Rhee regarding internal politics, see Walter S. Dowling (U.S. ambassador to the ROK) to Walter Robertson, January 23, 1959, *FRUS, 1958–60*, 18:534–40.

82. See, for example, Dulles's telegram 206 to the U.S. embassy in Korea of September 29, 1953, RG84, NAII.

83. On the new status-of-forces agreement, see the *Korea Times*, December 29 and 30, 2000, and the *Los Angeles Times*, December 29, 2000. The biggest problem in reaching agreement on moving military bases, of course, is cost—that is, who will pay for the move? Far from all of the problems relating to American bases derive from ones located in major cities. For example, one current lawsuit seeks compensation for villagers living fifty miles southwest of Seoul near a U.S. Air Force base. A key complaint of the villagers is noise pollution created by American planes (see *Environmental News Service*, May 15, 2001). Still, the Yongsan base in Seoul, located in the midst of South Korea's most densely populated area (over 20 percent of the country's population lives in Seoul), cannot help but create the most widespread resentment.

Chapter 8
THE KOREAN WAR AS A CHALLENGE TO AMERICAN DEMOCRACY

1. George F. Kennan, *American Diplomacy, 1900–1950* (Chicago: University of Chicago Press, 1951), 59. For Kennan's story of the setting of the lectures and his state of mind at the time, see his *Memoirs, 1950–1963* (Boston: Little, Brown, 1972), 70–77.

2. Ernest R. May, ed., *American Cold War Strategy: Interpreting NSC 68* (New York: Bedford Books, 1993), 43–44. This volume includes the text of NSC-68 in its entirety.

3. See chapter 3.

4. *Road*, chaps. 3 and 5.

5. *KW*, chaps. 2–4.

6. See, for example, *Present*, 437–40, 488–93.

7. Gaddis, *We Now Know*, 201.

8. Marc Trachtenberg, *A Constructed Peace: The Making of the European Settlement, 1945–1963* (Princeton, N.J.: Princeton University Press, 1999), 96.

9. May, *American Cold War Strategy*, 52–56.

10. Ibid., 14.

11. See *PPPUS, Harry S. Truman, 1950*, 286, 477.

12. Hogan, *Cross of Iron*, 304. Hogan concludes that "it took the Korean War to break the logjam in the administration on defense spending." In his *Truman*, Paul G. Pierpaoli Jr. draws essentially the same conclusion (27).

13. On Truman's domestic program, see Alonzo Hamby, *Beyond the New Deal: Harry S. Truman and American Liberalism* (New York: Columbia University Press, 1973), chap. 15.

14. *NYT*, May 28, 1950.

15. Friedberg, *In the Shadow of the Garrison State*, 112–14; Hogan, *Cross of Iron*, 134–35.

16. France was spending about 6.5 percent of its GNP on the military, Great Britain about 7.2 percent. The United States was devoting merely 5.4 percent to defense. See *NATO Facts and Figures* (Brussels: NATO Information Service, 1971), 256.

17. *NYT*, May 21, 1950. For a balanced assessment of the economic situation in Western Europe during the spring of 1950, see Richard P. Stebbins, *The United States in World Affairs, 1950* (New York: Harper and Brothers, 1951), 134–35.

18. Kenneth O. Morgan, *Labour in Power, 1945–1951* (Oxford: Oxford University Press, 1984), 409–15.

19. On the Soviet Union's use of propaganda as an instrument of foreign policy during this period, see Marshall D. Schulman, *Stalin's Foreign Policy Reappraised* (Cambridge, Mass.: Harvard University Press, 1963), chaps. 4–5.

20. On political and economic conditions in France during late 1949 and early 1950 and their relationship to diplomatic issues, see Irwin M. Wall, *The United States and the Making of Postwar France, 1945–1954* (New York: Cambridge University Press, 1987), 172–94; and Jean-Pierre Rioux, *The Fourth Republic, 1944–1958* (New York: Cambridge University Press, 1987), chaps. 10–11.

21. See Timothy P. Ireland, *Creating the Entangling Alliance* (Westport, Conn.: Greenwood Press, 1981), chap. 5. During hearings on the ratification of the NATO treaty before the U.S. Senate of the previous year, Acheson had been asked if the United States "would be expected to send substantial numbers of troops over there as a more or less permanent contribution to the development of these countries' capacity to resist." The secretary of state's response was a "clear and absolute, 'No.'" Quoted in Phil Williams, *The Senate and U.S. Troops in Europe* (New York: St. Martin's Press, 1985), 23.

22. For important secondary accounts of the Schuman plan's presentation, see John Gillingham, *Coal, Steel, and the Rebirth of Europe, 1945–1955* (New York: Cambridge University Press, 1991), 148–77; Alan Bullock, *Ernest Bevin, Foreign Secretary* (New York: Norton, 1983), 768–90; and Michael J. Hogan, *The Marshall Plan: America, Britain, and the Reconstruction of Western Europe, 1947–1952* (New York: Cambridge University Press, 1987), 364–72. For a retrospective account by the originator of the idea, see Jean Monnet, *Memoirs* (Garden City, N.Y.: Doubleday, 1978), chaps. 12–13. See also *Present*, chap. 42.

23. *NATO Facts and Figures*, 27–28.

24. See, for example, *NYT*, July 2, 1950; *Present*, 436; Konrad Adenauer, *Memoirs 1945–1953*, translated by Priscilla Johnson MacMillan (New York: Harper and Row, 1967), 271–74; Alexander Werth, *France, 1940–1955* (New York: Henry Holt, 1956), 470–73; and David Bruce (U.S. ambassador to France) to Acheson, July 14, 1950, Box 4299, RG59, NAII.

25. Doris M. Condit, *History of the Office of the Secretary of Defense*, vol. 2, *The Test*

of War, 1950–1953 (Washington, D.C.: Government Printing Office, 1988), 224–27; Stebbins, *United States in World Affairs, 1950*, 253.

26. Stebbins, *United States in World Affairs, 1950*, 262–63; *NYT*, August 20 and 31, September 3 and 6, 1950.

27. Lester B. Pearson, "Discussions with Mr. Acheson and Officials in Washington Saturday and Sunday, July 29th and 30th, 1950," vol. 15, Pearson Papers, Public Archives of Canada, Ottawa.

28. *KW*, 56–58, 71–75.

29. *Road*, 196–98.

30. On the Taiwan and thirty-eighth parallel issues, see *Road*, chap. 6.

31. On the GOP campaign, see Ronald J. Caridi, *The Korean War and American Politics: The Republican Party as a Case Study* (Philadelphia: University of Pennsylvania Press, 1968), 58–64.

32. Trachtenberg, *Constructed Peace*, 107–10.

33. Ibid., 112–13.

34. *KW*, 146.

35. For details on interpretations in this and the next paragraph, see *KW*, chap. 4.

36. For recent accounts emphasizing Soviet beliefs regarding contradictions in the capitalist camp, see Odd Arne Westad, "Secrets of the Second World: The Russian Archives and the Reinterpretation of Cold War History," *Diplomatic History* 21 (spring 1997): 265; Vladislav Zubok, "Stalin's Plans and the Russian Archives," *Diplomatic History* 21 (spring 1997): 301; Kathryn Weathersby, "Deceiving the Deceivers: Moscow, Beijing, Pyongyang, and the Allegations of Bacteriological Weapons Use in Korea," *Bulletin of the Cold War International History Project* 11 (winter 1998): 179; Vojtech Mastny, *The Cold War and Soviet Insecurity: The Stalin Years* (New York: Oxford University Press, 1996); and *KW*.

37. For a balanced contemporary account, see Richard P. Stebbins et al., *The United States in World Affairs, 1951* (New York: Harper and Row, 1952), 222–25; for an excellent later analysis, see Thomas Alan Schwartz, *America's Germany: John J. McCloy and the Federal Republic of Germany* (Cambridge, Mass.: Harvard University Press, 1991), chap. 7.

38. Stebbins, *The United States in World Affairs, 1951*, 222–25; *NYT*, May 9 and 13, June 9 and 17, and July 9, 1951.

39. *KW*, 200–201.

40. On the East German uprisings, see "'This Is Not a Politburo, but a Madhouse': The Post-Stalin Succession Struggle, Soviet *Deutschlandpolitik* and the SED: New Evidence from Russian, German, and Hungarian Archives," introduced and annotated by Christian F. Osterman, *Bulletin of the Cold War International History Project* 10 (March 1998): 61–110; Arnulf Baring, *Uprising in East Germany: June 17, 1953* (Ithaca, N.Y.: Cornell University Press, 1972). For the impact on Hungary and the unrest elsewhere in Eastern Europe, see Imre Nagy, *On Communism* (New York: Praeger, 1957), xii, 38–39, 66–74.

41. Shu Guang Zhang, "Sino-Soviet Economic Cooperation," in *Brothers in Arms: The Rise and Fall of the Sino-Soviet Alliance 1945–1963*, ed. Odd Arne Westad (Stanford, Calif.: Stanford University Press, 1999), 197, 201.

42. *CRKW*, 88–90, 106–13; also Chen Jian and Yang Kuisong, "Chinese Politics and the Collapse of the Sino-Soviet Alliance," in Westad, *Brothers in Arms*, 250–51.

43. Zhang, "Sino-Soviet Economic Cooperation," 199.

44. For a revealing incident on this matter, see Lionel Lamb (British chargé in Beijing), "Record of Conversation with Indian Ambassador, Sardor Panikkar, on 14 July 1951," FO371/92201, PRO.

45. Zbigniew M. Fallenbuchl, "Eastern European Integration: COMECON," in U.S. Congress, Joint Economic Committee, *Reorientation and Commercial Relations of the Economies of Eastern Europe* (Washington, D.C.: Government Printing Office, 1974), 79–81.

46. Thomas W. Simons Jr., *Eastern Europe in the Postwar World* (New York: St. Martin's Press, 1991), 107.

47. See, for example, Yoko Yasuhara, "Japan, Communist China, and Export Controls in Asia, 1948–1952," *Diplomatic History* 10 (winter 1986): 75–89; and Rosemary Foot, *The Practice of Power: U.S. Relations with China since 1949* (Oxford: Clarendon Press, 1995), chap. 3.

48. See the citations in note 47; also Roger Dingman, "The Dagger and the Gift: The Impact of the Korean War on Japan," in *A Revolutionary War: Korea and the Transformation of the Postwar World*, ed. William J. Williams (Chicago: Imprint Publications, 1993), 208–12; and Sayuri Shimizu, *Creating People of Plenty: The United States and Japan's Economic Alternatives, 1950–1960* (Kent, Ohio: Kent State University Press, 2001), chaps. 1–3.

49. David Holloway, *Stalin and the Bomb* (New Haven, Conn.: Yale University Press, 1994).

50. On pre–Korean War internal debates on Soviet strategy, see Ronald Lee Leteney, "Foreign Policy Factionalism under Stalin, 1949–1950" (Ph.D. diss., Johns Hopkins University, 1971). For a recent briefer account of internal debates, see S. J. Ball, *The Cold War: An International History* (London: Arnold, 1998), chap. 2.

51. J. Stalin, *Economic Problems of Socialism in the USSR* (Moscow: Foreign Languages Publishing House, 1952), 37–39.

52. For an interesting example shortly after Stalin's death of Soviet tactics toward an ally, China, that could easily be interpreted as an outgrowth of authoritarian culture, see Weathersby, "Deceiving the Deceivers," 178–80.

53. Gaddis, *We Now Know*, 289–91.

54. See *CRKW*.

55. See *MMR*.

56. The release of some Soviet records has stimulated debate regarding the *degree* to which bad news was prevented from reaching Stalin for fear of the consequences to its conveyer. No one denies, however, that the circulation of information and the

range of internal debate were severely restricted. For opposing views on the matter, see Ball, *Cold War*, chap. 2, and Robert C. Tucker, "The Cold War in Stalin's Time: What the New Sources Reveal," *Diplomatic History* 21 (spring 1997): 273–81, who follow an essentially totalitarian model; and Jonathan Haslam, "Russian Archival Revelations and Our Understanding of the Cold War," *Diplomatic History* 21 (spring 1997): 217–28, who sees Stalin as permitting some dissent from his views in private.

57. Kennan to Chamberlin, June 21, 1950, Kennan Papers, Seeley Mudd Library, Princeton University, Princeton, N.J.

58. Robert Griffith, *The Politics of Fear: Joseph R. McCarthy and the Senate* (Lexington: University of Kentucky Press, 1970), 118–22.

59. Robert J. Donovan, *Tumultuous Years: The Presidency of Harry S. Truman, 1949–1953* (New York: Norton, 1982), 306–7.

60. Ellen Shrecker, *The Age of McCarthyism: A Brief History with Documents* (New York: Bedford Books, 1994), 45.

61. For more on the implications of this development on domestic issues, see Ellen Shrecker, "McCarthyism and the Korean War," in *War and Democracy: A Comparative Study of the Korean War and the Peloponnesian War*, ed. David McCann and Barry S. Strauss (Armonk, N.Y.: M. E. Sharpe, 2001), 191– 215.

62. For the best account of the state of the Taiwan issue in U.S. policy on the eve of the war, see Robert Accinelli, *Crisis and Commitment: United States Policy toward Taiwan, 1950–1955* (Chapel Hill: University of North Carolina Press, 1996), chap. 1.

63. David Anderson, *Trapped by Success: The Eisenhower Administration and Vietnam, 1953–1961* (New York: Columbia University Press, 1991), 205.

64. See, for example, John W. Newman, *JFK and Vietnam* (New York: Warner Books, 1992).

65. For one of the more recent accounts emphasizing memories of the 1949–53 period in Johnson's decisions of 1964 and 1965, see Brian VanDeMark, *Into the Quagmire: Lyndon Johnson and the Escalation of the Vietnam War* (New York: Oxford University Press, 1991). For an older account, see David Halberstam, *The Best and the Brightest* (New York: Random House, 1972).

66. Hamby comment in Francis H. Heller, ed., *The Korean War: A 25-Year Perspective* (Lawrence: Regents Press of Kansas, 1977), 170.

67. Yuen Foong Khong, *Analogies at War: Korea, Munich, Dien Bien Phu, and the Vietnam Decisions of 1965* (Princeton, N.J.: Princeton University Press, 1992), chap. 5.

68. Kolodziej, *Uncommon Defense and Congress*, 152–79.

69. Donovan, *Tumultuous Years*, 382–91.

70. *Truman*, 79–80, 187, 201–3.

71. I. F. Stone, *The Hidden History of the Korean War* (New York: Monthly Review Press, 1952).

72. J. D. Salinger, *The Catcher in the Rye* (Boston: Little, Brown, 1951); and Erik Erikson, *Childhood and Society* (New York: Norton, 1950); David Riesman, *The Lonely*

Crowd (New Haven, Conn.: Yale University Press, 1950); Ralph Ellison, *The Invisible Man* (New York: Random House, 1952).

73. James T. Patterson, *Grand Expectations: The United States, 1945–1974* (New York: Oxford University Press, 1996), 236–39; Whitfield, *Culture of the Cold War*, 12–13; Lary May, "Reluctant Crusaders: Korean War Films and the Lost Audience," in *Remembering the "Forgotten War,"* ed. Philip West and Suh Ji-moon (Armonk, N.Y.: M. E. Sharpe, 2001), 110–36.

74. Whitfield, *Culture of the Cold War*, 11–12; Whitfield, "Korea, the Cold War, and American Democracy," in *War and Democracy*, 228.

75. Lewis D. Ergin and Jonathan P. Siegel, *The Macmillan Dictionary of Political Quotations* (New York: Macmillan, 1993), 109.

Index

Boldface numbers indicate maps and photographs.